ANDRÉ GREEN REVISITED

International Psychoanalytic Association's Psychoanalytic Classics Revisited Series

Series Editor: Gabriela Legorreta

Other titles in the Series

ANDRÉ GREEN REVISITED

Representation and the Work of the Negative

edited by

*Gail S. Reed and
Howard B. Levine*

Routledge
Taylor & Francis Group

LONDON AND NEW YORK

First published 2018
by Routledge
2 Park Square, Milton Park, Abingdon, Oxon OX14 4RN

and by Routledge
711 Third Avenue, New York, NY 10017

Routledge is an imprint of the Taylor & Francis Group, an informa business

British Library Cataloguing-in-Publication Data
A catalogue record for this book is available from the British Library

Library of Congress Cataloging-in-Publication Data
A catalog record has been requested for this book

ISBN: 9-781-78220-630-9 (pbk)

Typeset in Palatino
by The Studio Publishing Services Ltd
email: studio@publishingservicesuk.co.uk

CONTENTS

The Classic Revisited Series, launched by Gennaro Saragnano in 2015, comes after the four successful series previously published under the auspices of the International Psychoanalytic Association. Its aim is to make available to psychoanalysts, and other scholars in related fields, a reinterpretation of the classics of psychoanalysis by authoritative colleagues from various countries and different theoretical approaches, in the light of the most recent developments in contemporary psychoanalysis.

In a historical period characterised by the increased internationalisation of psychoanalysis, and its fast spread in Eastern Europe and Asia, we believe that there is an increased demand for psychoanalytical culture and for further investigating the great classics of this discipline. These classics could be either books, single papers, or the individual contribution of a specific thinker, whose outstanding contribution have marked the history of the theoretical and clinical development of psychoanalysis. We think that the word "Classics" include all those contributions that, far from being comprehensible only if viewed against a specific historical and cultural backdrop, are capable of continuously revealing to us their capacity of stimulating psychoanalytic thought in a creative and anti-dogmatic manner, and therefore remain as inalienable theoretical and clinical landmarks, regardless of the personal opinions and approach of each psychoanalyst.

The Publications Committee is pleased to launch the third volume of this series with the book *André Green Revisited: Representation and the Work of the Negative.* Besides being a prominent voice for French psychoanalysis, André Green was and continues to be exceptionally influential within the international psychoanalytic community. His insightful understanding of the psyche led to the formulation of a theory of mind from which he developed a new model of the understanding and treatment of patients whose difficulties reside beyond the neurotic spectrum. His creative ideas have contributed enormously to the understanding of border line personalities. Green preferred to replace this diagnostic category with that of the livelier term "private madness".

A true disciple of Freud, he understood that his legacy was a rich breeding ground, from which old concepts such as representation, symbolisation, and the drives could be revitalised and expanded and from which new concepts such as negative hallucination, the work of the negative, and many others emerged. These new conceptualisations also led to advances in technique and variation of the analytic setting.

This volume is an acknowledgement to André Green's prodigious contribution and to his great scientific creativity. It is also a testimony to the way in which he influenced the theory and practice of psycho-analysis around the world, and the way in which he inspired other psychoanalysts to continue expanding, complementing, and debating his ideas. In this volume, we have the privilege of contributions from psychoanalysts who knew André Green closely, as a friend and colleague for many years. We learn from them not only about the rich-ness of his legacy and the exchanges and debates they had with him, but also about André Green as a man, as a colleague, and as a friend.

We are thankful to Gail S. Reed and Howard B. Levine for having gathered excellent contributions from the three regions of the IPA to reflect on the ways in which André Green has contributed to their analytic identity as well as to reflect on how his contributions have developed, changed, and advanced.

The variety, richness, and originality of the contributions makes this book an invaluable addition to all psychoanalysts and other scholars interested in the work of André Green.

I have no doubt that this new book in the Classics Revisited Series will be of great value to those who want to become more acquainted with this work as well as those who want to deepen their knowledge of his legacy and be inspired to continue the development of his ideas.

Gabriela Legorreta
Series Editor
Chair, IPA Publications Committee

The editors

Howard B. Levine is a member of the Psychoanalytic Institute of New England, East (PINE), the Contemporary Freudian Society, the Newport (California) Psychoanalytic Institute, the Group for the Study of Psychoanalytic Process, and the Boston Group for Psychoanalytic Studies, Inc. He is a former member of the Board of Directors of the IPA, on the editorial Boards of the *International Journal of Psychoanalysis* and *Psychoanalytic Inquiry*, and in private practice in Brookline, Massachusetts. He has authored many articles, book chapters, and reviews on psychoanalytic process and technique, intersubjectivity, the treatment of primitive personality disorders, and the consequences and treatment of early trauma and childhood sexual abuse. His most recent co-edited books include: *Growth and Turbulence in the Container/Contained* (Routledge, 2013); *Unrepresented States and the Construction of Meaning* (Karnac, 2013); *On Freud's Screen Memories Paper* (Karnac, 2014); *The W. R. Bion Tradition* (Karnac, 2015); *Bion in Brazil* (Karnac, 2017); *Engaging Primitive Anxieties of the Emerging Self* (Karnac, 2017).

Gail S. Reed is the co-editor of *Unrepresented States and the Construction of Meaning* (Karnac, 2013) and *On Freud's Screen Memories* (Karnac, 2014). She is also the author of *Transference Neurosis and Psychoanalytic Experience: Perspectives on Contemporary Clinical Practice* (Yale University Press, 1994). She is the founder and a member of the Group for the Study of the Psychoanalytic Process, a member of, and training analyst in, the Contemporary Freudian Society and the Berkshire Psychoanalytic Institute and a member of NPAP. She is also Associate Book Review Editor for foreign books of the *Journal of the American Psychoanalytic Association*, an Editorial Board Member of *Psychoanalytic Inquiry*, a former Editorial Board Member of *Psychoanalytic Quarterly*, and a former member of the Publications Committee of the IPA. She practises psychoanalysis and psychoanalytic psychotherapy in New York City.

The contributors

Francis Baudry is a training and supervising analyst at the New York Psychoanalytic Institute, on the psychotherapy faculty at Mount Sinai Hospital in New York and author of papers on character, supervision, subjectivity in the analytic situation, contemporary Kleinian thought, and applied analysis. He has taught courses on Kleinian and French psychoanalysis and on object relations theory.

Rachel Boué-Widawsky, PhD is a psychoanalyst in training at the Institute for Psychoanalytic Education at NYU School of Medicine. She has written articles on French psychoanalysis for the Journal of the American Psychoanalytic Association and regularly contributes to its foreign Book Reviews. She is also a literary scholar and the author of books and articles on literary criticism. She has taught literature at Wesleyan University, Connecticut College and at the University of Denis Diderot in Paris, where she earned her Doctorate under the direction of Julia Kristeva.

Marie France Brunet is a full member of the Chilean Psychoanalytic Association (APCh), and Professor and Director of the APCh's Training Institute. She directs study groups on the work of Bion and André Green, has participated in and led several Encounters and Colloquia about their work in Chile, Argentina, and FEPAL and has published several articles about thought and the theory of thinking. She has also translated several of Green's books into Spanish for college Editorials and Amorrortu Ed.

Talya S. Candi is a Doctor of Clinical Psychology, a member of the Brazilian Psychoanalytical Society and the IPA and practises psycho-analysis and analytic psychotherapy in São Paulo in both Portuguese and French. She is the author of *O duplo limite: O aparelho psiquico de André Green* (Ed Escuta São Paulo, 2010) and editor of *Dialogos Psicanaliticos contemporaneos .o representavel e o irrepresentavel em André Green e Thomas Ogden* (Escuta, 2015).

Cláudio Laks Eizirik is a psychoanalyst, full member and training and supervising analyst at the Porto Alegre Psychoanalytic Society, Professor Emeritus of Psychiatry at the Federal University of Rio Grande do Sul, former IPA President (2005–2009), recipient of the 2011 Sigourney Award, and author of papers, research, book chapters, and books on the psychoanalytic relationship (countertransference, the analyst's mind, and the analytic field), analytic training, an analytic perspective on the process of aging, and the relation of psychoanalysis to culture.

Luciane Falcão is a full member and training analyst of the Porto Alegre Psychoanalytical Society and a professor at its Institute of Psychoanalysis. She is the author of several articles and book chapters on psychoanalysis, addressing such topics as the death drive in the analytic scene and the constitution of the psyche, child sexuality, narcissism and hate, the hallucinatory in the analytic session, and what she calls "acted representability and the body flash". She has represented the Porto Alegre Psychoanalytical Society at the Congrès des Psychanalystes de Langue Française.

Zelig Libermann is a full member and training analyst of the Porto Alegre Psychoanalytical Society (SPPA) and a professor at its Institute of Psychoanalysis, as well as President of SPPA between 2018–2019. He is the author of several articles and book chapters on psychoanalysis, addressing such topics as memory, resignification, *après-coup*, narcis-sism, death drive, and self-object differentiation.

Anna Migliozzi is a full member of the Italian Psychoanalytical Society and supervisor in the analysis of children and adolescents. She has studied and trained with Frances Tustin, Donald Meltzer, Eric Brenman, Antonino Ferro, and Franco De Masi and is committed to the use of Bionian theory in the treatment of children. She has a private practice in Milan, where she works with children and adults who suffer from severe psychotic and borderline disorders. In the past, she has worked in the Italian psychiatric hospital criminal justice system with adolescents and young adults who have committed violent acts and are being reintroduced into the community. Her recent publications include "Passion", in *The W. R. Bion Tradition* (edited by H. B. Levine & G. Civitarese, Karnac, 2015); "The attraction of evil" (in *International Journal of Psychoanalysis*, 2015); "Castration and conformity", in *Psychoanalytic Inquiry*, 2018).

Rosine Jozef Perelberg is a training analyst of the British Psychoanalytic Society, Visiting Professor in the Psychoanalysis Unit at University College London and Corresponding Member of the Paris Psychoanalytical Society. Her books include *Dreaming and Thinking; Freud: A Modern Reader, and The Greening of Psychoanalysis* (2017, with Gregorio Kohon*).* She is the author of *Time, Space and Phantasy* (2008) and *Murdered Father, Dead Father: Revisiting the Oedipus Complex* (2015). *Psychic Bisexuality: A British–French Dialogue* will be published in the New Library of Psychoanalysis in 2018. In 1991, she won the Cesare Sacerdoti Prize at the IPA Congress in Buenos Aires. In 2007, she was named one of the ten women of the year by the Brazilian National Council of Women.

Elias Mallet da Rocha Barros is a training and supervising analyst at the Brazilian Psychoanalytical Society of São Paulo, Fellow of the British Psychoanalytical Society and of the British Institute of Psychoanalysis, He is a Past Editor for Latin America of the *International Journal of Psychoanalysis*, Latin American Chair of the Task Force for the International Encyclopedia of Psychoanalysis (IPA), and recipient of the 1999 Sigourney award.

Jean-Claude Rolland is a full member and former president of the Association Psychanalytique de France (APF), co-director (from 2000–2014) of the biannual review of psychoanalysis entitled *les Libres*

Cahiers pour la Psychanalyse (Inpress, Paris), author of four volumes published by Éditions Gallimard, Paris: *Guérir du mal d'aimer* (1998); *Avant d'être celui qui parle* (2006); *Les yeux de l'âme* (2010); *Quatre essais sur la vie de l'âme* (2015).

Rene Roussillon is a full member of the Paris Psychoanalytic Society, a professor of clinical psychology at Lyon University and the former Director of that department from 1989–2013. He also led a research team between 1989–2014 that studied symbolisation, borderline states, and subjectivity, and is a member and former president of the Lyon/ Rhone Alps Psychoanalytic Group. He has written seventeen books and manuals translated into a dozen languages, nearly 250 articles, forty-five of which have been translated into English, German, Spanish, Italian, Portuguese, Russian, Turkish, Romanian, Polish, Swedish, etc. He received the Prix Groove and Prix Bouvet in 1991 and the Sigourney Award in 2016.

Fernando Urribarri is an associate member of the Argentine Psycho-analytic Association, where he has co-ordinated the André Green Seminar since 2001. He is a lecturer at Buenos Aires University, and Visiting Professor at Paris VII and Paris X universities and at Columbia University in New York. He collaborated with Green in the preparation of several of his books, from *Key Ideas in Contemporary Psychoanalysis* (2001) to Green's final, posthumously published volume, *La Clinique psychanalytique contemporaine* (2012). Their many years of collaboration are reflected in the book, *Dialoguer avec André Green* (2013), in which six interviews that took place between 1991 and 2011 are published.

Introduction:
André Green, a personal appreciation*

Howard B. Levine

The death of André Green marked an enormous loss for psycho-analysis. He was a brilliant thinker and innovative contributor to our field. The fire of his ideas ignited a passion for discovery in so many colleagues who knew him personally as analyst, supervisor, and teacher, or had heard his lectures or read his texts. He will be sorely missed, but his thoughts will continue to instruct and inspire.

Green was a leading voice in French psychoanalysis, one whose contributions sit at a crossroads, where the challenges posed and the opportunities presented by the work of Lacan, Klein, Winnicott, and Bion meet the still generative insights of Freud, many of which, Green reminds us, have yet to be fully appreciated or developed. This volume of essays is a response to, and appreciation of, Green's contributions and struggles to expand the reach of our theory and practice to patients whose difficulties lie beyond the spectrum of neurotic

---

* Various portions of this chapter originally appeared in "Representations and their vicissitudes: the legacy of André Green", by H. B. Levine © *The Psychoanalytic Quarterly*, 2009, LXXVIII(1); and "André Green. Une appreciation personnelle" by H. B. Levine © *Revue Belge de Psychanalyse*, 60: 29–31. We are indebted to these journals for permission to reprint elements of the original articles here.

disturbances for which classical psychoanalysis was originally intended. We invite our readers to join with us as we continue Green's attempts to understand and explore the tension between presence and absence, loss and remainder, the creative, dialectical arc between them and their role in psychic development and the analytic process.

No one writing today has been as masterful as Green in investigating and explicating the dynamics of presence and absence and their centrality to the emergence of the psyche. He revitalised metapsychology, making it come alive as a clinical theory by reinvigorating Freud's theory of psychic representations. If Freud provided us with the scaffolding, Green, through his synthesis and masterful extension of the ideas of not only Freud, but those of Winnicott, Bion, as well as his French predecessors, including Lacan, with whom Green often sharply disagreed, but who never seemed to be far from his thoughts as counterpart or foil, and through his own extraordinary capacity for theory building and clinical intervention, has helped us to scale new and greater heights of understanding..

Green embodied that very French rallying cry: "Back to Freud!" His classic London Congress paper (Green, 1975) on symbolisation and absence rests heavily on a foundation in Freud and, what might be especially important for many contemporary North American Anglophone analysts, makes a powerful case for the essential role of the drives, which Green sees as central to the construction of meaning, the development of the capacity to experience vitality and meaningfulness in life, and the formation, strengthening, and emergence of psychic processes.

Green's formulation and explication of negative hallucination, the work of the negative, negative narcissism, disobjectalisation, psychic voids, and their relation to, and reflection of, the death instinct offer us seminal contributions to the understanding and treatment of borderline patients and other "limit cases" (*états limites*), whose psychic functioning lies "beyond the pleasure principle". In addition to his formidable contributions to psychoanalytic theory and practice, there is a poetry in Green's prose style. Even in translation from the French, it has a unique flavour marked by erudition and grace. The combination continues to remind us of the wisdom of Freud's felicitous choice of the word "psyche" for the seat of our mental life, because, in Greek, the word psyche means soul.

Once one has become accustomed to the terminology used and the literary style of Green's writing, we believe that readers will discover that Green's work is accessible, thought-provoking, original, and deeply rooted in the complex challenges of day-to-day clinical practice. He insists upon the centrality of the drives, while restoring a vital human dimension to analytic theory that is breathtaking and liberating. His work is deeply engaged with the role of drive, perception, representation, language, and words in the structure and functioning of the psyche. Unlike Lacan, however, who turned away from the drives and affect and asserted that the unconscious is structured like a language, Green views the drives as a foundational concept and believes, as did Freud, that the id consists of unbound and unrepresented impulsion and action that cannot be captured by, or associated with, words and their "presentations".

"What Freud is trying to tell us . . . is that the unconscious can only be constituted *by a psyche which eludes the structuring of language*, it is constituted essentially of thing-presentations [i.e., impulses and affects]" (Green, 2005a, p. 99, original italics).

Thus, for Green, "the separation between preconscious and unconscious is not open to discussion. There exists a real break, a change of regime separating the two agencies . . ." (Green, 2005a, p. 98).

This position is reflected in Green's clinical theory, in which the transference is the locus of a primordial struggle between discourse and action: that which can be bound by and put into words *vs.* "the elements of the psyche that cannot justifiably be connected with language" (Green, 2005a, p. 50).

Green's *oeuvre* offers a compelling development of the implications of representation (which Freud believed was intimately connected to the role of words in the psyche) and non-representation for psychoanalytic theory. His discussions of time and timelessness, affect and idea, perception and negative hallucination, Eros, and the work of the negative constitute major clinical and theoretical contributions, all of which are consistent with, and evolve from, fundamental tenets in the work of Freud.

At the heart of Green's work is the distinction between neurotic and non-neurotic (borderline) structures. In this sense, Green is working out the implications of "the epistemological break"—"the turning point of 1920" (Green, 2005a, p. 97)—that marked Freud's (1920g, 1923b) shift from the topographic to the structural theory. In Green's view, the challenge that psychoanalysis faces is how to take account of the "growing number of non-neurotic structures in analytic practice" and "recognize the commonly acknowledged insufficiency of the [topographic] Freudian theory to account for the non-neurotic structures" (Green, 2005a, p. 16).

As Green convincingly describes it, the major development in Freud's theory was the change from

> one model, at the centre of which one finds a form of thinking (desire, hope, wish), to another model based on the act (impulse as internal action, automatism, acting) . . . the analyst now not only has to deal with unconscious desire but with the drive itself, whose force (constant pressure) is undoubtedly its principle characteristic, capable of subverting both desire and thinking. (Green, 2005a, p. 47)

Green further argues that the clinical realities—unconscious guilt, masochism, various forms of the negative therapeutic reaction—that necessitated this change in models have had a wide-ranging theoretical impact on our field.

> . . . the dispersion, or even fragmentation of psychoanalytic thought into many opposing theories (ego psychology, Kleinism, Lacanism, Bionian, Winnicottian and Kohutian, etc) could all be interpreted as attempts to propose a solution to the limitations of the results of classical treatment. (Green, 2005a, p. 47)

This reading of Freud's theoretical shift is significantly different from that of the ego psychologists. While Green concurs with the latter that the ego "registers, observes, judges, decides, while remaining under the triple influence of the id, the superego and reality" (Green, 2005a, p. 103), he believes that the recognition that portions of the ego remain unconscious, coupled with the discovery of various forms of unconscious guilt and self-destructive tendencies, splitting of the ego, and disavowal (Freud, 1927e), led Freud to lose confidence in the ego as a reliable ally in the treatment.

> It seems undeniable that, from 1923 on, both with regard to masochism and to splitting, it was the ego's responsibility to which Freud wanted to draw attention, as if he wanted to warn analysts that they not only had to deal with a terrible adversary that was unknown to

them, the death drive, but, in addition to that, the agency which they
thought was on their side in the cure, was nothing but a double agent.
(Green, 2005a, p. 111)

For Green, the significance of portions of the ego remaining unconscious goes far beyond the phenomena of unconscious defensive
activity.

> . . . it implies taking into consideration the awakening of instinctual
> life, the acceptance of it, the recognition of its manifestations, the
> conservation and introduction of what is attached to it, the sorting out
> according to their qualities, among the erotic and destructive aspects,
> of those which respect the major prohibitions and conserve the ego's
> vitality, without the risk of disorganization and without the contrary
> danger of sterilization. (Green, 2005a, p. 104)

The primary task of the ego, then, is not predominantly that of
defence, but how best to maintain aliveness while navigating "*between
chaos and sclerosis*" (Green, 2005a, p. 104, original italics).

In close agreement with Freud, Green remains keenly aware that
while the topographic theory was extremely successful when applied
to patients with a neurotic organisation, it is insufficient as a theory of
therapy when faced with the clinical problems increasingly encountered in contemporary analytic practice. The crucial distinction is
between that which can be represented and that which cannot yet be
connected to language. The latter, which can only manifest itself as
drive pressure, impulse, and action (*Agieren*) will first require transformation, often through the intervention of intersubjective, dialogic
work, and linkage to language ("word presentations") in order to be
contained by, and made accessible to, psychological processes.

Thus, in describing clinical work, Green places the dialogical
couple at the heart of the "active matrix" of the treatment and emphasises that the transformational processes of the session are intersubjective as well as intrapsychic. For the patient, these processes reflect
two aspects of the transference: transference on to speech and transference on to the object. The former is "the result of the conversion of
all the psychic elements into discourse" (Green, 2005a, p. 50). The
capacity to effect a transference on to speech is the consequence of
good enough attunement, availability, and responsiveness on the part
of the object. This capacity will develop as a result of the binding of

drive impulses by words in the process of representation of satisfaction that follows from repeated experiences of drive satisfaction provided by a sufficiently invested libidinal object.

'Transference on to the object' implies that there are dimensions of the analytic relationship (e.g., impulse, action, enactment, raw feelings, somatic reactions) that cannot be contained or mediated by discourse alone. These reflect unbound areas of drive pressure, which can be made more peremptory and disorganising by repeated and/or traumatic experiences of failed drive satisfaction. When disorganisation leads to failure of representation, object attachment and associational links can be weakened or severed and the fabric of the psyche might be torn, so that self-continuity, object constancy, and meaning itself might be severely disrupted. In the context of a progressive analytic experience, however, the two components of the transference, taken together, imply that, for the patient, transference will include not only the *repetition* of the past, but the dialogical, intersubjective *creation* of what has not yet been fully experienced—that is, that which has not yet, or only weakly, been represented or symbolised.

For the analyst, it is crucial to remain receptive and emotionally available towards his or her own associations and responses, as well as those of the patient. This requires tolerance, as well as understanding, with a special concern for maintaining a sense of aliveness in both members of the dyad.

> Sometimes, paradoxically, it will be less damaging to the process to allow a lively countertransference reaction to be expressed, even if negative, in order to gain access to the internal movements animating the analyst. These are all evidence of ... spontaneity ... having more value for the patient than a conventional pseudo-tolerant discourse which will be experienced by the patient as artificial and governed by technical manuals. (Green, 2005a, p. 35)

For Green, as for Winnicott, vitality and aliveness are essential considerations for the analyst to bear in mind; and like Freud, Green believes that the affects that sustain these qualities are closely related to the movement and expression of libidinal drive energy. Thus, in his formulations, sexuality and desire play a central and organizing role in the psyche, especially the organised, represented, and symbolically invested psyche of the neurotic.

But what of the non-neurotic patients, whose problems lie 'beyond the pleasure principle"? These patients, who are perhaps the most numerous in contemporary caseloads, are the subjects of some of Green's most powerful and persuasive contributions. As already noted, however, "the necessity of taking into account states that are situated beyond neurosis does not do away with the cardinal role of sexuality . . ." (Green, 2005a, p. 63).

This implies that psychoanalysis must retain an interest in, and recognition of, "the importance of the body as an erotogenic body" (Green, 2005a, p. 61) and the centrality of sexuality–pleasure—gratification, frustration, and desire—in the structuring and functioning of the psyche. What animates the latter is "the search for an object capable of procuring the satisfaction of the [drive] pleasure that is not immediately accessible" (Green, 2005a, p. 62).

Thus, Green emphasises that one cannot choose between theories that valorise the intrapsychic, the relational, the ego/self, or the object. Instead, for Green, drive and object each imply the existence of the other and form an indissoluble pair that must be central to any comprehensive psychoanalytic theory. The "fundamental cell of the theory" is "the drive–object couple" (Green, 2005a, p.113), seen to be "two currents, at once independent of each other and richly interconnected, in which subjective formations and object formations are linked together" (Green, 2005a, p. 113).

The object, then, elicits and excites the drive, just as the drive searches out and helps internally constitute the object. "The construction of the object leads retroactively to the construction of the drive, which constructs the object" (Green, 2005b, p. 48, original italics).

A key element in this process is the stimulus of unsatisfied drive tensions produced by the absence or failure of the object: "If the object was not lacking, we would not know that the drive existed, for it is precisely then that it manifests itself with urgency" (Green, 2005b, p. 41).

Green's theory is very much cognisant of the fact that the way that the object responds to the demands of the instinct "contributes to the primitive, organizing structuration" (Green, 2005b, p. 43) of the mind. The experience, perception, and, hence, internalisation and representation of drive, self, and object are all dependent upon the quality of the interaction—frustration, satisfaction—between the self and its objects. As a stark illustration, Green reminds us of the Schreber case

(Freud, 1911c) and the essential question raised by Winnicott: "What is the effect of having a mother who is psychotic or mad, or a father who is mad?" (Green, 2005b, p. 43)

Thus, Green believes that the drive and the object are inextricably and dialectically linked and together contribute to the matrix of the self. Any theory that fails to recognise the role of the drives in this process does so at its own peril, because "a subject with its instinctual dimension amputated, is an inanimate, mechanical, operative, and if you wish, cognitive entity" (Green, 2005a, p. 114).

The work of the drive "drives" the psyche to invest in objects and seek satisfaction in order to reduce the somatic tensions at the bodily source of the drive. This work not only includes searching for realisation in the external world, but internal movements towards psychic representation and the creation of meaning—symbolisation, "signification", and the creation of links (Green, 2005b, p. 45).

From this perspective, the reality that is most crucial to the structuring and development of the mind is the internal reality of the demands of the drives, the internal constraints "pushing the mind to search for solutions in order to obtain the satisfaction that it is lacking" (Green, 2005a, p. 114). But since satisfaction usually requires an object and the veridical nature of the object and its response are often, if not always, decisive to the quality and degree of satisfaction, then the object (and its "shadow") as well as the drive must be taken into account in any comprehensive theory of psychic functioning. In some formulations, this has led to a valorisation of the object at the expense of the drive and/or the self. Herein, Green tells us, lies the source of the confusion and debate about whether humans are to be seen as fundamentally pleasure seeking or object seeking.

For the neurotic patient,

> ... the essence of psychoanalytic experience, in so far as the classical treatment is concerned, depends on the very fact of the analyst's presence–absence (that is, his invisibility), on psychic activity inducing representation and exciting the patient's earlier memory traces which are here put to the test in the transference. (Green, 2005a, p. 128)

In contrast, the non-neurotic patient, whose emotional balance is apt to swing wildly between devitalisation on the one hand and affective flooding and fragmentation on the other, often cannot respond to the absence or loss of the analyst with phantasy and wish, even a repressed or disguised phantasy or wish. Instead, separation or absence provokes disorganisation, devitalisation, affective flooding, impulsive action, or somatic illness. In these circumstances, the tactical aim of the analytic encounter must be altered from uncovering or discerning what is disguised or hidden to strengthening the processes involved in the formation, associational linkage, and symbol signification of enlivened—and enlivening—psychic representations.

What is lacking for the non-neurotic is the capacity of the mind to link primary and secondary processes, which is needed to imbue words and images with libidinal investment and symbolic significance and link them to other symbol-laden elements to form true associational chains. Without this work which Green (2005a) called the tertiary processes, interpretation of hidden meanings cannot effectively take place, because the patient's speech, upon which these interpretations must be based, is apt to be flat, empty, and devoid of depth and greater meaning. For non-neurotic patients,

> The representative network, including the world of things and of words, is severed at the level of thought—the thought circulating between things and words. These patients complain that their thought is empty; thus, there is nothing to say. (Green, 2005b, p. 49)

At times, this emptiness of discourse might become extreme.

> In certain analyses, and I am thinking particularly of borderline cases, patients say that they are unable to speak. This does not mean censorship is at work, as with neurotics who hold back what they are thinking because it is bad to say it or to think it. No, it is not so much prohibition that is involved here as impossibility. (Green, 2005b, p. 49)

When this is the case, that is, in those parts of the psyche or in those patients in whom non-neurotic structures predominate, where representation and symbolisation do not play a dominant role, then raw, peremptory affect and action assume prominence. However, it is important to note that these are not ordinary "feelings" or acts as action in the external world intended to remove to remove frustrations and obtain satisfaction of drives and wishes. Rather, they are more matters of unmodulated feelings and primitive acts that have been internalised and then discharged, often internally into the body (Green, 2005a, p. 101).

While it is common to refer to such discharges as the consequence of "desire", Green cautions us that it may be misleading to do so. We often

> speak of desire . . . [when] it is legitimate to ask . . . if this category is really present . . . [the] raw, and barely nuanced forms [of action], expressions of imperious instinctual demands, throw a doubt over the relevance of this qualification. (Green, 2005a, p.102)

To put it succinctly, while sexuality is common to all patients and is essential in the structuring of the mind, "desire" is the provenance of neurotic patients, and differs in both quality and quantity from the blind, instinctual, action-orientated discharge and demands of the non-neurotic.

Green's understanding of borderline conditions and non-neurotic states is closely allied to his reformulation of Freud's final drive theory (Eros *vs.* death instinct). Following Freud, he describes Eros as generating linking, investing processes and movements that connect the ego and psychic representations with life, pleasure, objects, words, symbols, and meaning. In contrast, the death instinct moves towards stasis, withdrawal of investment, disconnection from internal and external objects and representations, disconnection from psychic processes and functions, and abandonment of the search for satisfaction.

These descriptions of non-neurotic states of mind have tremendous implications for analytic technique and the meaning of the transference. Rather than the disguised repetition of repressed conflicted complexes, in these conditions we are in the realm of the not yet or only weakly represented, of inchoate sensations and not yet actualised feelings achieving psychological form, perhaps for the first time. What is required is an intersubjective work akin to Bion's (1970) description of alpha function and containment. This is a work of what Botella and Botella (2005) call "figurability" (i.e., the "co-making" of the unrepresented and not yet psychologically usable accessible to adaptive psychological operations), rather than an intrapsychic work of the patient's remembering something of the forgotten past.

In this volume, we have chosen to focus upon Green's (1997) "Dead mother" paper, followed by an extensive examination of his theory of representation, the work of the negative, his theory of mind, and, most important of all, their clinical implications. These stand out and endure at the heart of his contributions.

We shall miss André Green, but we will continue to draw upon and benefit from all that he has left us and led us to consider. His distillation and vision of psychoanalysis remain to inspire us to struggle and debate with him and with each other as we attempt to explore the mysteries of the mind and of human relations.

References

Bion, W. R. (1970). *Attention and Interpretation*. London: Heinemann.

Botella, C., & Botella, S. (2005). *Psychic Figurability. Mental States Without Representation*. London: Routledge.

Freud, S. (1911c). *Psycho-analytic Notes on an Autobiographical Account of a Case of Paranoia. S. E.*, 12: 3–82. London: Hogarth.

Freud, S. (1920g). *Beyond the Pleasure Principle. S. E.*, 18: 7–64. London: Hogarth.

Freud, S. (1923b). *The Ego and the Id. S. E.*, 19: 3–66. London: Hogarth.

Freud, S. (1927e). *Fetishism. S. E.*, 21: 147–157. London: Hogarth.

Green, A. (1975). The analyst, symbolization and absence in the analytic setting (on changes in analytic practice and analytic experience)—in memory of D. W. Winnicott. *International Journal of Psychoanalysis, 56*: 1–22.

Green, A. (1997). The dead mother. In: *On Private Madness* (pp. 142–173). London: Karnac.

Green, A. (2005a). *Key Ideas For A Contemporary Psychoanalysis. Misrecognition and Recognition of the Unconscious*, A. Weller (Trans.). London: Routledge.

Green, A. (2005b). *Psychoanalysis. A Paradigm For Clinical Thinking*, A. Weller (Trans.). London: Free Association Books.

PART I
REMEMBRANCES

CHAPTER ONE

In dialogue with André Green

René Roussillon

M y journey of psychoanalytic thinking has long been shared with a few "special companions", some of whom, like Winnicott or Bion, I have known only from their books, while others I could meet and also have exchanges and debates with. André Green was one of these special companions, one of those with whom, whatever I thought, said, or wrote, I continued the dialogue. For many French psychoanalysts of my generation, Green was one of those—but there are not so many—with whom it was interesting to think and discuss, one of those who illuminate the path ahead. I do not think I have ever ventured to write an article or explore a question, whether clinical, metapsychological, or technical, without finding out first what Green had thought or said about it.

I am not, however, what one might call a "disciple" of Green, or a pupil; moreover, I do not think that it is a good policy for a psychoanalyst to be a disciple or pupil, and if it sometimes happened, rarely enough, it is true, that I did not agree with his propositions, his thinking has always elucidated my own.

Green himself pointed out that the major lesson he learnt from his adventure of encountering Lacan's thought was that of not contenting oneself with travelling endlessly down the well-trodden paths of what has already been thought, of the belief that one has thought about everything, or of the "right-thinking" transmitted by psychoanalytic orthodoxy or by a type of master. Psychoanalysis only remains alive and vibrant if it is constantly re-examined, if the adventure of thought that it represents, the exploration that it implies, are constantly renewed.

When he tries to think about the relationship of the creator with the societies in which he is immersed, Bion describes the figure of the mystic. I would not say that Green was a mystic, as this word has a particular connotation in French that does not really suit him; on the other hand, I would use the characteristics that Bion associates with it. Psychoanalysis cannot do without its establishment, but, at the same time as it becomes institutionalised psychoanalysis, it is in danger of losing the crux of its essence, of becoming "psychoanalytic ideology". That is why the psychoanalytic project must be re-examined constantly and cannot cease to explore the question of its foundations.

Conversely, the impact of a thinker or of a body of thought also supposes that it belongs to the established societies, which wrestle with it while transmitting it. This supposes that the creator occupies a particular position, at once sufficiently inside the establishment so that his thinking has its maximum impact and, at the same time, sufficiently independent of the established orthodoxies, thus sufficiently outside, so that, freed from established ideas, he can pursue his own creative exploration. A complex alchemy has to be achieved here and a particular posture maintained in order to avoid splitting and to preserve independence of thought.

Green achieved this alchemy marvellously and he knew how to walk the ridgeline that it implies. His thinking never ceased to draw on Freud's own thought, to explore it more deeply, and, thus, found its place within the French-speaking psychoanalytic tradition; at the same time, by drawing on Bion and Winnicott to elucidate his own clinical experience, he was constantly venturing well beyond the limits fixed by it.

I do not think it is possible to reflect on his scientific contributions by separating them from the different institutional, political, and epistemological "dialogues" that he engaged in throughout his life, because, in fact, we find the same attitude on these different "fronts". I am, therefore, going to present a few of the areas of dialogue and reflection in which he was involved.

Dialoguing with the limit and the
other fields of the human sciences

A creator in the world of clinical psychoanalysis, however intrinsically pertinent his creation is, must, if he wants to leave a lasting imprint, link his name to the exploration of a particular clinical problem: for Melanie Klein, it was child psychoanalysis; for Bion, groups, psychosis, and transformational processes; for Winnicott, the world of the baby and early childhood. Green, and it was an interest he shared with Anzieu, his co-reporter of the CPLR of 1970, linked his name to the question of the borderline states of the psyche.

This question and what it implies, at both the metapsychological and the clinical level, is, to a lesser or greater extent, always present, sometimes openly, sometimes implicitly, in his different reflections, even when they seem to be far removed from the question of limits or from the threat to identity that it poses for the life of the subject. It was here that the crux of the effort had to be made, both in France, in the dialogue at a distance with Lacan—a dialogue that never ceased completely at any point during his life's work—and on the international stage, in the array of studies on narcissism which occupied the foreground of the stage of psychoanalytic reflections.

It was *the* major question of psychoanalytic research and exploration, largely anticipating both the evolution of the demands for psychoanalysis which would characterise the last quarter of the twentieth century and the beginning of the twenty-first, and their dialectic with social evolution and the particular mode of handling the narcissistic organisation that was becoming such a common feature of clinical work. It was the question in the light of which all the others would be revisited, the question that was at the centre of both dialogues and debates, and even the struggle for the defence of clinical psychoanalysis.

In these different fields, Green knew how to ride the most promising wave by placing the accent on the question of the particularities of *représentance* (see my remarks below) and of affect (and the non-distinction affect representation in relation to the psychic representative of the drive) in extreme modes of functioning and psychic states by exploring their effects in the problem of artistic creation, and even by examining their effects on the neurotic economy itself, and, finally, by regarding them as the interface of encounters with the other fields of the human sciences.

For exploration of the problem of limits does not confine thinking to the edges of borderline patients alone; it opens up a field that covers the most diverse aspects of clinical psychoanalysis: it is a new paradigm for psychoanalysis and not a regional advance that concerns only a certain number of limited clinical entities. It was a question on the basis of which the narcissistic component of each of the modes of psychic functioning would be explored in greater depth. Green even felt, beyond the question of limits, that the current studies on melancholy and autistic processes were paving the way for a new paradigmatic evolution, the next one, no doubt, once all the lessons of the previous one had been sufficiently drawn.

The question of limits encounters, and is dialectalised with, that of the sexual and the first forms of drive life, the drive impulses, as much as it is rooted in the body and certainly the biological itself; its pivotal point, Green sensed early on, taking up a fundamental aspect of Anglo-Saxon psychoanalysis, was to be sought around affect, its composition and its forms. The new paradigms in view in the case of autism and melancholia will extend, as we can already sense in contemporary studies, to explorations of sensory-motricity and its place in the process of symbolisation.

The burning question of the autistic paradigm, which, as we know, has unleashed the anger of the sworn opponents of clinical psychoanalysis and obscurantism, leads me to make another remark. Green always considered, and in this he was faithful to a Freudian tradition, that psychoanalysis should be in dialogue with the other disciplines of the human sciences. In his article of 1970 devoted to "repetition", he offers very profound thoughts on the biological anchoring of double effects while emphasising this particularity of the first processes of life: the fundamental processes revealed by genetics, which represent the first operations of DNA. DNA with the double helix, before the transfer RNA and the messenger RNA, begins by providing itself with a copy of itself, by fabricating a double of itself. Since the discovery of efference copies[1] in modern neuroscience research and of the famous mirror neurons, the question of reflection and double representation in biological processes has been constantly highlighted.

But this anchoring in the processes arising from biology was, no doubt, a form of legacy from his medical training; this reminder of the biological body was not the only dialogue or *excursus* that Green allowed himself. His work is regularly dotted with references to linguistics (in his studies on language), to mythology, even to certain studies in developmental psychology, not to mention his immense knowledge of the artistic field, and others that I have forgotten. Green did not fear dialogue with related fields, knowledge of which could enrich psychoanalytic thought. A strong anchoring in clinical work underpins his identity sufficiently for there to be no need to be afraid of encountering other disciplines, provided, of course, that one continues to practise and to be open to exploration.

It was in this same spirit that, when he took over the reins of a psychoanalytic society, he inaugurated in France, in 1989, colloquia open to the general public, proposing that psychoanalysis and its debates should no longer be reserved only for clinicians and their work sessions within psychoanalytic societies. He had foreseen, then, that psychoanalysis was going to make its entry into "politics", that it was going to become an object of social debate, a situation we are very much faced with now.

Dialogue on the politics of psychoanalysis

This leads me to the question of the "politics of psychoanalysis" in which Green also distinguished himself.

It was also necessary to re-establish dialogues with the other psychoanalytic societies, dialogues that had been interrupted in France by the various splits of 1953, 1963, and 1968, to show that the psychoanalysts of diverse persuasions could engage in dialogue together, that psychoanalysis remained one in spite of its theoretical diversities, and that the various forces could be united for the social struggles that were looming.

Opening up a dialogue within psychoanalysis itself by organising a congress in 2002 devoted to the encounter with the other psychoanalytic societies and with the clinical workers from the different fields of psychic care was a way, was it not, of trying to hone the tools with which psychoanalysis would try to defend itself?

In this sense, too, if the current and coming generations continue to draw the lessons of openness that he proposed, Green's legacy will, no doubt, continue to be active for many years to come.

Whatever one might think of Green's sometimes difficult character, he did not cease to open up fields of encounter and dialogue, either within the psychoanalytic community or with the other sciences of man and of his forms of expression.

One cannot, in fact, reduce his contributions to the exploration of the question of limits and of the forms of narcissistic suffering with which this question is crucially bound up, or even to language and its relation to the psychoanalytic situation. For they also concern the absolutely crucial question of creation in its diverse forms, but also of the diverse forms of production of the human imagination, myths, dreams, etc.

To be quite honest, none of the fields of expression of conscious and unconscious psychic life and of their metapsychological theorisation escaped the delight of his explorations and the wisdom of his propositions. When Green turned his attention to the clinical practice or theorisation of a particular field, it at once promised a significant advance and announced a renewal of the question. His thinking was creative and exerted itself in all the domains in which a psychoanalytic approach promised to be pertinent. Green was a "generalist" of clinical and psychoanalytical thinking, a generalist in the sense that his contributions covered the whole field, but also a specialist of each of these fields in so far as, when he ventured into one of them, it was always with a good knowledge of the existing studies concerning it, even when he did not take the trouble to mention them or cite them in detail. There is no lack of choice, therefore, when it comes to paying tribute to his prodigious activity and to his immense scientific creativity, and I must say, for my part, that I have never engaged in reflections on one of the fields covered by psychoanalytic thought without first informing myself about what André Green had produced there.

I have no doubt that many future studies will stress the fecundity of his diverse contributions, but, in these troubled times for contemporary psychoanalysis, it is another aspect of his presence in the international community that I want to turn my attention to now: what I would be tempted to call his "politics of psychoanalysis", a policy of openness and a policy of open debates. But the man remained faithful to himself, for what I am going to summarise briefly concerning the positions and actions of Green in his "external" politics of psychoanalysis is merely the transposition of the positions that he also held within the internal politics of psychoanalytic thinking. He was one of those who, at a time when they were strongly opposed by many French psychoanalysts, opened up psychoanalytic reflection to a number of Anglo-Saxon or Latin-American psychoanalysts whom he knew as a consequence of his extensive travelling. Opening up French psychoanalysis to the most stimulating work of psychoanalysts from elsewhere was the same process as the one we are going to discover now in his endeavours to open psychoanalytic societies to the socius.

In 1989, when he was president of the Paris Psychoanalytic Society (SPP), he initiated and inaugurated the colloquium at UNESCO, the first of the "Colloquiums of the SPP president". This colloquium marked a turning point, in as much as it was the first large-scale colloquium, the first "official" colloquium of the SPP that was open to a wide public sympathetic to psychoanalysis, to practitioners who did not belong to the component societies of the IPA, and which was organised for, and orientated towards, the clinicians engaged in the domain of psychic care who sought, in psychoanalytic thinking, reference points for reflecting on their own endeavours in the various clinical fields in which they were operating.

André Green had clearly foreseen the dangers hovering over a psychoanalysis that was timid, turned in upon itself, holed up in an ivory tower, and which refused dialogue with society in general and the debates that this implied. To hell with a psychoanalysis that was in danger of becoming nothing more than an introverted "dusty psychoanalysis", and of continuing to consider itself as a psychoanalysis that was idealised by an intelligentsia in control of cultural life; it was necessary both to explain and present its new developments and, at the same time, to accept possible controversies with those who were beginning to contest the field of clinical practices.

When the danger became even clearer many years later and, in the same spirit, he was once again at the origin of a vast colloquium that brought together not only the majority of the analysts from the French component societies of the IPA, but also from societies of the Lacanian movement. It was necessary to re-establish the dialogue interrupted by the various splits of 1953, 1963, and 1968 and to show that psychoanalysts of different schools could engage in dialogue together, that, in spite of its diversities, psychoanalysis remained one, and that it was possible to unite forces for the social struggles that were imminent.

One might have wished things had been different, and that the evidence provided concerning the therapeutic and clinical relevance of psychoanalysis had exempted it from the epistemological and ideological struggles that traversed the social field, but we know that this was not the case. The politics of burying one's head in the sand proved catastrophic and Green was always, in contrast, at the forefront of a politics of psychoanalysis that accepted dialogue, when it was possible, with those who held alternative positions, or one of those who led the epistemological fight and crossed swords with those with whom dialogue was not possible and who had engaged in a process of murdering clinical psychoanalytic thinking.

Dialogues and debates with the advocates of cognitive–behavioural therapy (CBT), dialogues and debates with certain theoreticians of the neurosciences, with developmental psychologists (in particular with Daniel Stern), with linguists, anthropologists, and so on. These dialogues and debates presupposed a sufficiently good knowledge of the studies produced in other disciplines; one can engage well in a debate only with what one knows, and the position of taking others to task without knowing their work, a method that certain "enemies" of psychoanalysis often use, is foreign to Green's approach, which involved working in detail and as much as was necessary on the texts of the advocates of disciplines with whom he took part in debates and dialogues—as far as this is possible, of course.

In these cases, Green developed arguments; he did not get involved in sterile hate and accusations, but, rather, sought to continue to think, even if he became polemical and even if his tone could be sharp in response to the attacks of others to which psychoanalysis was subjected. This position requires work; it involves continuing constantly to go further into the foundations of psychoanalytic metapsychology, continuing to explore the clinical aspects of psychopathological entities, not only of those that are the most classical, but also of those that find new forms of manifestation or are at the origin of new forms of clinical work. This was also a lesson given by Green, one he said he had learnt from the debates with Lacan and Lacanian psychoanalysis, which is that the work involved in continuing to think about psychoanalysis and its extensions must continue; the clinical thinking arising from psychoanalysis will only maintain itself if psychoanalysts continue to explore their tools for thinking, their method and their settings more deeply, if they continue to work on elaborating the concepts necessary for clinical exploration.

However, such a position supposes that one is ready to learn from others, to be enriched by their contributions. Green was also ready to learn from other disciplines—linguistics, anthropology, philosophy, and even the neurosciences—with which he entered into dialogue, and to integrate what they could contribute to psychoanalysis, provided that, and herein he was faithful to a Freudian tradition, these contributions could be "repatriated" into psychoanalytic metapsychology. Moreover, he never hid his sensibility to the limits of psychoanalysis, as can be seen from his last books, where he dwells on some of his failures. Learning from failure without idealising clinical psychoanalysis for a moment implies both continuing to seek to make clinical advances, without using an established dogma to settle the question, and also having sufficient confidence in the fruitfulness of the process not to be afraid of recognising the areas where further work is necessary.

Green was also very present regarding another crucial aspect of the relations between psychoanalysis and society, that which is called, no doubt awkwardly, psychotherapy. One must not confuse the necessities of a training process for psychoanalysts (the classical treatment is irreplaceable here) with the constraints of the concrete practice of psychoanalysts, who necessarily sometimes venture far from the standard setting of the classical treatment. One of the dangers that hangs over the development and future of psychoanalysis is unquestionably the risk that it will fall back on the model of the classical couch/armchair setting with at least three or four sessions a week, and that the other forms of what Green called the work *of* psychoanalysis or the work *of the* psychoanalyst find that they are more or less disqualified. In this area, too, Green's positions are remarkable and adapt to the requirements of a psychoanalysis for the twenty-first century.

Green cannot be accused of either ignorance of the foundations of psychoanalytic practice or of discrediting it in any way, and it is in this respect that the position he took was important and contains a lesson that must be noted. Nevertheless, he was also sensitive to the fact that many psychoanalysts have ventured into settings that differ from the standard setting while, at the same time, continuing to work as psychoanalysts and without in any way reneging on their identity as psychoanalysts. Like Anzieu, in his time, with the concept of "transitional analysis", he was one of those who thought that psychoanalytic practice was not totally subjected to the first cradle of its practice, the standard setting, and that it could inspire the action of clinicians well beyond its modification in the form of the classical face-to-face setting, which is often the only alternative envisaged. Wherever psychic suffering is expressed, at the bedside of patients at the end of their lives, with patients suffering from psychosomatic illness, in prisons where we can meet violent delinquents, rapists, murderers, or drug addicts, in the settings suitable for the psychic treatment of psychosis or autism, in short, wherever it is possible to practise clinically, psychoanalytic listening has its degree of pertinence and the psychoanalyst has his place; indeed, he is often the only one who is able to initiate the clinical approach that is necessary. Naturally, both the particularities of the forms of expression of the psychopathology and the conditions of the clinical encounter must be taken into account, but a work *of* psychoanalysis is possible and one that in no way reneges on the essence of psychoanalysis or its foundations. This is an essential struggle both for the present and the future of psychoanalysis, and Green was also on that front.

On the path of the interface of psychoanalysis both with other disciplines and with society, Green, following a line that I believe to be genuinely Freudian, laid down a number of markers which, it is to be hoped, will continue to serve as a lesson and to illuminate those who have responsibilities for the politics of psychoanalysis.

The theoretical dialogue

I can now turn to my personal theoretical dialogue with Green.

In 1970, the third volume of the *Revue française de psychanalyse* was devoted to the death drive and repetition, and it was there that I came into contact with Green's thought for the first time. I recall that reading it was an epistemological shock for me. The shock was first one of being confronted with a theory of the subject as process, of a subject who could only be grasped secondarily through his process of production, a subject in movement, never completely identical to himself, a subject who could only conceive of himself retrospectively, through a reappraisal. What a liberating effect for thought and being; the subject did not have to identify himself immediately. Sure of himself from the outset, immobile in his concern to be, and to appear, a subject of mastery, he had to "produce" himself, just as we say that an actor "produces" himself when he acts.

The shock was then to discover the manner in which this "production" was articulated with reproduction in two senses. Reproduction as re-presentation, as creative repetition, but also reproduction as the very model of the living, just as the founding DNA reproduced itself. I was familiar with Lacan's work on the signifier and was discovering the importance of the Freudian theory of representation, its pertinence and its complexity. But Green did not content himself with reminding us of the theory of representation; he inserted it into an intelligibility of the living and articulated the psycho-logics with which I was beginning to familiarise myself with the very foundations of the bio-logics. He drew parallels between the representation of the human psyche and "the first operation of the living", the duplication of the DNA chain, the double helix schema. Before every "transfer", before every "message", DNA had first to produce a copy of itself, to re-present itself.

Green, thus, outlined a sort of logical continuum between soma and psyche. This seemed to me at the time absolutely essential and luminous, and I am still persuaded that this is so. Of course, I knew of Lacan's remark on the "mirror" effect which transformed into gregarious grasshoppers the form of the solitary grasshoppers immersed in a world of gregarious grasshoppers, and also of his remarks stressing how, in the process of embryogenesis, certain cells adapted their structure depending on the point of the embryo on to which they were grafted, but the import of Green's remark went far beyond these "regional" and, when all is said and done, "anecdotic" effects; he was establishing a foundational process.

The living, biological and psychic, represents itself; it reproduces and produces itself through, and thanks to, representation, and it is around the notion of representation that we must look for the essence of psychic reality, of the reality of the mind, of its fundamental laws. Subsequently, I often based my teaching with students of psychology and psychoanalysis on this remark, which made it possible to articulate biological reality with psychic reality, which brought into play the same basic logic at different levels, and brought them into correspondence with each other.

The second important moment was in 1973, when, faced with the task of caring for psychotic patients and with my disarray and dissatisfaction with the theorisations available at the time, at least those I was aware of, I discovered *L'enfant de ça*. Beyond the reminders of the theory of Bion's thought which it contained, beyond the idea of a listening which needed to shift its emphasis from the "contents" towards the "containers", and of the very processes of the *pensoir* (thinker) of which I already had an intuition, Green introduced the notion of the necessity to form the conception that one represents or does not represent. He saw this notion as an essential feature in the failure of the psyche of psychotic patients. Deeply unsatisfied with my readings of the psychoanalytic works of the period in France devoted to psychosis, often centred on hallucinatory wish fulfilment alone, or the "omnipotence" of patients, which was of very little use in listening to patients, I found in my reading of *L'Enfant de ça* the concept "meta" which I was lacking, a concept that would enable me to vectorise differently my listening to the psychotic and borderline states I was confronted with in my psychoanalytic practice.

The living, the biological, re-presents, as we have known since 1970; it is self-regulating and informs itself in order to regulate itself, but Green's concept makes it possible to go one step further: psychic life must represent the fact that it represents or fails to represent the fact that it represents; it must "meta-represent", that is its fundamental characteristic, its essential function, the one that governs all the others. The whole problem of consciousness has to be revisited in the light of this proposition, re-examined in the light of this form of reflexivity. Psychoanalysis does not only concern the process of symbolisation; it concerns the symbolisation of symbolisation, the manner and conditions necessary for symbolisation to take possession of itself. The biological–psychic articulation can then continue to acquire greater precision and refinement. The psyche "theorises" itself, it tries to represent itself, to take possession of itself through this self-representation. The living is satisfied with representing and informing itself through this type of self-presentation; the psyche must be apprehended as this specialisation of the living and of its representative function which is characterised by the self-representation of representation itself, by the self-possession of the representative function and the totality of its effects.

As a result, even if it did not magically transform the facts of the complexity of listening to psychotic or borderline patients, I began to listen to the desperate manner in which the patients tried to represent the fact that they could not represent, that they were unable to grasp subjectively that their psyche represented earlier states, that they "suffered from a form of reminiscence", that they suffered from a representation presenting itself as an actual, hallucinated perception.

The first version of my article of 1978 concerning the treatment of Liccio, a young psychotic patient, was a direct effect of this new way of listening to the psychotic states of the psyche; it is focused on the way in which this young man was trying to represent the fact that he could no longer represent (himself). I must say that, notwithstanding the immense interest that I took at the time in discovering Winnicott's contribution, this was only fruitful against the background of this concept, which I owe to my reading of Green. The current advances in neuroscience, those with which a certain degree of dialogue is possible (those of Edelmann and the re-entrant circuits, of Frith and the notion of meta-representation that he proposes, those of Jeannerod in Lyon and the concept of agentivity which is a variant of it, or even those of Damasio in the USA), will simply confirm experimentally this fundamental intuition of Green who "revolutionised" the question of consciousness and even that of the unconscious, replacing it with the notion of the representation of representative activity, conscious and unconscious. This is where, in my opinion, the decisive step was taken, making it possible to centre psychoanalysis on the question of symbolisation understood as the conscious representative activity of being a representative activity and, thus, differentiated from a representation presenting itself as a "thing in itself".

Winnicott, whose work is so profoundly useful clinically concerning the "fear of breakdown" (1974), in fact merely put forward the hypothesis which, for me, makes the concept of absence of representation, and absence of representation of the absence of representation clinically useful. Green and Winnicott, thus, immediately made intelligible Freud's article "Constructions in analysis" (1937d), which was only available in French later on. I often find myself regretting, when I am reading certain current psychoanalytical contributions, that the decisive advances of the period did not have such an impact that it would be impossible today to circumvent them.

The concept of the representation of representation opened up the possibility of revisiting the question of paradox and paradoxicality in the narcissistic organisation, a question to which I devoted my first book. The duplication of representation provides a way out of the potential impasses generated by the paradoxes of narcissism and of the relationship of the subject with himself. It opens out towards an analysis of the "theories" that the psyche tries to propose of itself; it opens up the analysis of the forms of the "clinical approach of the theory" which I was beginning to explore. In fact, it makes a whole epistemology of psychoanalysis possible, and also makes it possible to outline how and why symbolisation is the royal road for overcoming the impasses of narcissism itself.

My companioning of Green's thought continued, but I also began to find my own way: the paradoxicality of narcissism and that of its elaboration.

Since my first encounter with the concept of representation of representation, things had evolved, thanks to my clinical experiences, at the level of my understanding of the interest of this notion, regarding which I began to differentiate two forms in relation to the two registers of representation proposed by Freud. Through my work with the borderline and psychotic states of the psyche, it appeared to me that the question needed to be divided into two parts and that there were two "issues" concerning representation, two phases that it was important to differentiate, that of the word-presentation of representation or of the absence of representation, but also that of the thing-presentation of each of them. At the beginning of the 1980s, therefore, I differentiated the thing-presentation of representation from its word-presentation. My hypothesis led to my articulating the notion of pliable medium, arising from Milner's clinical work, with the notion of representation of representation. The pliable medium seemed to me to be the "thing" the experience of which was the basis for the thing-presentation of representation; this was the starting-point for my reflections on primary symbolisation and its conditions/preconditions. I am not sure that Green followed me on this point. It is true that while one of the sources of my reflections was my psychoanalytic practice in the strict sense, the essential part of the clinical experience that underpinned my thinking was derived from many years of experience of practising psychoanalytic psychotherapy with psychotic patients whom I saw in the psychiatric sector. This was in addition to my reflections on my experience at the university of supervising the clinical and research work of many clinical psychologists, psychotherapists, and psychoanalysts working with issues related to early childhood (autism, infantile psychosis, severe cognitive dysharmonies, etc.) or with destructured social situations (drug addicts, homeless people, etc.).

I do not know if these practices are comparable to that of "standard" psychoanalysis; the place of the apparatus of language no doubt modifies things considerably, even if language tries to take up again pre-linguistic psychic states, but I know that my thinking was as deeply influenced by this clinical experience as it was by that of the borderline states of subjectivity which I share more directly with André Green. The practices and the type of clinical problems with which these confront us play a fundamental role in our conceptual developments. I think, however, that there is no incompatibility between the developments I am proposing and the later developments of Green's thought; it is more a question of different formulations linked to preoccupations, which, if they have many points in common, none the less have their differences.

Thus, to explain one of the points of the debate, if the notion of negative hallucination, which Green was the first to highlight, has always seemed illuminating to me clinically, it has also often seemed to me that it was in danger of being torn, in his conception, between the notion of a "framing structure of representation"—where it signifies a form of actualisation of the "representation of the absence of representation" necessary so that representation can occur; it is only "hallucinated" through the return of the thing-presentation to the hallucinatory realm—and the contrary notion arising from the clinical observation, frequent in psychotic or borderline states (Schreber and the "Wolf Man" are the two main examples to which Green refers), of an incapacity to represent the absence of representation, where hallucination takes the place of the failure of representation linked to the failure of the function of the primary object as a framing structure of representative activity. That was why I personally preferred the reference to the thing-presentation of the absence of representation, which I differentiate from the psychotic hallucination that results from the absence of representation.

In reflecting on my memories of the history of my internal dialogue with Green's thought concerning representation, I must now turn to the other side of the theory of representation, to its negative, which was constantly present in my earlier reflections but as yet unformulated. Insisting on the theory of representation also implies reflecting on the clinical experience of its failure, that is to say, on the modes of functioning of the psyche which are established when representative activity is unable to take possession of itself, on the modes of non-symbolic linking, those that result from the forms of negativity of subjectivisation. Here, again, the internal metapsychological dialogue with Green was decisive; it concerned in particular the "turning point of 1920" and the second metapsychology which, precisely, relativised the place of representation (I would prefer now to say the place of the self-possession of representation and the richness of the "solutions" thus offered to the psyche) and opened up the question of psychic solutions outside representation, or which short-circuited the work of symbolisation.

My report of 1995 (Roussillon, 1995) does not cease to pursue the dialogue with Green on these points and the place that must be given to the object in the establishment of the type of solution of linking, symbolic or non-symbolic, that the subject ends up adopting. In this instance, the dialogue took place orally, in so far as this kind of occasion makes it possible. Although I have always regretted that it was not published, it emphasised the importance of "motor" solutions of evacuation of what was unable to find a suitable representative status in the psyche, and the importance of the first modes of processing instinctual drive life, those that precede, or take the place of, representative activity. On this point we were completely in agreement.

Subsequently, I thought for a long time that, on another point, a divergence had appeared; it perhaps resided in a different degree of optimism between us. In *La folie privée*, Green seems to believe in the existence of evil, evil that is a fundamental fact, whereas for me this evil is but the effect of a failure of the construction of a "double" primary homosexuality, a failure of the primary tunings and adjustments that impede the construction of the subject's capacity to form a conception of his representative activity. Our theory of the early stages of life and their impact on psychic organisation seemed to diverge here.

It is not that I consider that the child is innocent of all basic destructivity; like Winnicott, I think that "primary love" is ruthless, but I think that, in *ad hoc* environmental conditions, the child's primitive destructivity will find the means to put itself in the service of creative processes, and it is important for me to understand which factors favouring such an evolution might have been missing in his early development or in the deferred effects that he experienced later on in life. So, I give importance not only to the fact of trying to provide the analysand with "the response that ought to have been that of the object", as Green writes, but, in addition, it seems essential to help him to form a conception of what was lacking and could not take place in his history. I am far from certain that Green followed me along this path or that of always taking into account, in the analysis of a psychic process, not only the movement of the subject, but also the responses and reactions of the significant people in his history; that, in any case, is how I have understood Winnicott's propositions concerning the "use of the object". Another way of saying all this would be to say that the processes of evacuation or of desymbolisation cannot be total, that one can always, even if it takes time and might present considerable difficulties, find the subject trying, even in the worst cases, to signify something of his historical or current subjective experience, and, thus, trying to appropriate himself even if it is in the most unlikely way possible.

To conclude, I recently came across a text by Green in a collation volume (Richard & Urribarri, 2005) devoted to representation in which he developed the notion of psychical representative of the drive. Before the opposition between affect and representation, before their differentiation, there are psychic states which attest, none the less, as if on the threshold of meaning, to a first attempt to communicate to the other something of subjective experience, something of "the primary matter of their psyche", even if they are trying to evacuate at the same time. Perhaps, before it becomes representation "for a subject", representation presents itself as this undifferentiated mixture of representation and affect, this intermediate form between representation and affect.

The dialogue continues now *post mortem* and on a basis that Green formulated to me one day as follows: "My ceiling is the floor of the analysts of your generation".

Note

1.   "Efference copies" is a biological term from neuroscience used to designate motor control.

References

Freud, S. (1937d). Constructions in analysis. *S. E.*, 23: 255–270. London: Hogarth.

Green, A. (1970). Répétition, différence, replication. *Revue Française de Psychanalyse, 34*, PUF.

Green, A. (1972). Note sur le processus tertiaire. *Revue Française de Psychanalyse, 36*: 407–411.

Green, A. (1973a). On negative capability, a critical review of W. R. Bion's *Attention and Interpretation*. *International Journal of Psychoanalysis, 54*: 115–119.

Green, A. (1973b). *Le discours vivant*. Paris: PUF.

Green, A. (1974). L'analyste, la symbolisation et l'absence. *Nouvelle Revue de Psychanalyse, 10*: 225–252.

Green, A. (1976). Un, autre, neutre : valeurs narcissiques du même. *Nouvelle Revue de Psychanalyse, 13*.

Green, A. (1983). *Narcissisme de vie, narcissisme de mort*. Paris: Ed. de Minuit.

Green, A. (1984). *Le langage dans la psychoanalyse*. Paris: Les Belles Lettres.

Green, A. (1988). La pulsion et l'objet, préface à Brusset, *Psychanalyse du lien* (pp. i–xx). Paris: Le Centurion.

Green, A. (1990). *La folie privée. Psychanalyse des cas limites*. Paris: Gallimard.

Green, A. (1992). *La déliaison*. Paris: Les Belles Lettres.

Green, A. (1993). *Le travail du Négatif*. Paris: Ed. de Minuit.

Green, A. (1995). *Propédeutique*. Seyssel: Champ Vallon.

Green, A. (1999). Sur la discrimination et l'indiscrimination affect-représentation. *Revue Française de Psychanalyse, LXIII*(1): 217–272.

Green, A. (2000a). *La diachronie en psychoanalyse*. Paris: Ed de Minuit.

Green, A. (2000b). La position phobique centrale. *Revue Française de Psychanalyse, 64*(3): 743–771.

Richard, F., & Urribarri, F. (Eds.) (2005). *Autour de l'oeuvre d'André Green. Enjeux pour une psychanalyse*. Paris: PUF.

Roussillon, R. (1978). *Paradoxes et situations limites de la psychanalyse*. PUF, 1991.

Roussillon, R. (1995). La métapsychologie des processus et la transitionnalité. Rapport au 55ème congrès des psychanalystes de langue française. *Revue Française de Psychanalyse, LIX*(spécial congress): 1351–1519; 1705–1718.

Winnicott, D. W. (1974). Fear of breakdown. *International Review of Psychoanalysis, 1*: 103–107.

CHAPTER TWO

The place of André Green in contemporary psychoanalysis: a personal remembrance*

Jean-Claude Rolland

I had the opportunity to debate and discuss with André Green intensively and at length, first in the IPA working group on Borderline States (along with William Grossman, Otto Kernberg, Gregorio Kohon, Jaime Lutenberg, Elizabeth Spillius, and Fernando Urribarri)[1] and then, immediately afterwards, within a seminar on the same theme that we led together in Paris and Lyon.

While the debate with André was exciting and prolific, it was not always easy. Those close to this demanding thinker will understand that his enthusiasm, much like that of Freud in correspondence with his first disciples, could quickly turn into irascibility. For both men, such wrath and its associated intransigence were in part a reaction to the contempt shown for psychoanalysis by even cultured people. It also no doubt reflected the vigilance needed to maintain the purity of psychoanalytic thinking in the face of ideas, even amongst analysts, that tended to separate themselves and stray from essential psychoanalytic doctrines.

---

* Translated from the French by Dr Jenny Heller, with the assistance of the editors.

André Green was a true heir and disciple of Freud. His contributions revived and re-actualised core principles of Freudian thinking, increased the effectiveness of psychoanalytic practice, clarified obscure Freudian theory, followed up upon leads and intimations that Freud himself did not have sufficient time to fully work out, and, in reconsidering some points, brought them to the beginning of some resolution. The concept of the negative, as Green (1999) fashioned it, deepened significantly the concept of the unconscious, elaborating upon its economic and dynamic conditions and offering to the analytic view of the unconscious something akin to what perspective brought to painting between the thirteenth and fourteenth centuries: a depth that orders the multitude of lines and planes in pictorial space.

In the superficial layers of the psyche as described in the initial years of psychoanalytic practice and as encountered in neurosis with its typical cures, the formations of the unconscious can reveal themselves through multiple disguises and easily overcome their negative character. However, when deeper layers are reached, as happens in prolonged treatments and from the start with borderline patients, the unconscious always asserts its negativity more stridently and forces us to conclude that negativity is an entity to be reckoned with, one that possesses its own forms of psychic expression.

The latter are strange, worrying, and difficult to conceptualise. One must stop not only to consider the words that name them, but must also attend to what they conjure up. One has to go beyond the manifest, and immerse oneself in the opacity of the analytic experience: an unconscious formation that can be glimpsed in a dream, for example, no sooner perceived than denied, its "appearance" ephemeral and uncertain.

Such phenomena create as much doubt as conviction. They engender dread and blur those points of reference that ensure the identity of the actors involved in the scenario. For this analytic formation to concretise itself in a stable and recognisable configuration so that it can be represented as an oedipal object previously violently and traumatically repressed, infinite temporality crossing through psychic layers and a notable transformation of the psyche of the two actors are required. The cure must labour in every sense of the word to oppose the work of the negative and reverse its effect. However, the unconscious formation can manifest itself by a more radical negativity resulting in an obstinate silence, in unexpected and definitive thoughts. (André spoke of the "central phobic position" (Green, 2000) or a massive refusal of contact.)

There is no indication that will allow one to think whether something rather than nothing will happen. Yet, this negative that the transference solicits is a fact that analytic listening must pick up, support, decipher, and, at a certain point, understand. The worrying and the deceptive are, in the eyes of the analyst as in those of the patient, the first masks displayed by the formations of the unconscious. When extracting themselves from negativity, they direct themselves towards representation, replacing a compulsion to repeat with a compulsion to represent (Rolland, 1998).

André taught us that the analyst must neither become offended by, nor experience, despair in the face of the work of the negative in the unconscious, as it is our "daily bread". Although a first encounter with the negative might be in the form of the patient's powerlessness before it, the negative is, nevertheless and paradoxically, needed to initiate the treatment. As with ordinary psychic material (e.g., resistances), the analyst must learn to recognise and welcome its appearance in the cure.

The strongest homage I can offer to André is the recognition that his thinking, so vivacious, so convincing, provided me with the theory needed to understand this and with a technique based on the contemporary clinical tenets that he espoused. If our debates during his life were often conflictual, they nevertheless remained respectful, friendly, and even affectionate. Their purpose was to challenge us to revive our research in the quest for still deeper understanding.

Now that André is no longer with us, they can only take a different form. The sadness, the pain at having lost this friend, this guide, this teacher, compels us to silence our disagreement. During this period of grief, we want only to honour the memory of the departed one, not to judge his work, something that will come later.

I miss André. His disappearance leaves me alone and deprived, as I continue to face the scientific task we had begun, but have yet to accomplish.

The word "contemporary" often recurs in André's writing, and in the title of his books. The first thing to recognise him for is that he forced psychoanalysis to enter into the modern world, as much in its theory as in its practice and to transcend the limits of being merely a product of the nineteenth century, as Freud, who was a creature of his time, had fashioned it. André's interest in borderline and psychotic states, rather than in only typical neurotic cures, his insistent references to, and development of, later Freudian concepts, such as the death instinct or negative therapeutic reaction, attest to this movement.

André knew how to recognise that Freudian discourse contained a previously not perceived modernity, which had been left in its latency, and to this current he gave another life. By the same token, he perceived previously unexploited resources in the therapeutic potential of the analytic method. In imposing his thinking (he had the required qualities: enthusiasm, authentic charisma, and a rare gift to communicate with diverse audiences), he also gave new voice to that of Freud. This can be seen in his ever-growing influence in Anglo-Saxon countries and in South America.

André was able to combat the inertia, fear, and conservatism, which always threaten any science or institution. One cannot be an analyst after him as one was before. André emphasised the importance of the frame in borderline and limit states; he also advocated the necessity for the patient to internalise the space offered by the frame and the need for the analyst to use the opportunity of the frame to expand his listening and his psychic functioning.[2]

The analytic frame, in effect, closes a space: one that defines individuality and serves as an internal boundary, revealing the division between what the subject recognises as himself and what he has excluded through *refoulement*, splitting, and other forms of "negativisation" (defensive exclusion).[3]

There is one point where I differ from André, which, unfortunately, his death did not allow us to further explore. It has to do with the enigma, intellectually exciting and crucial for the understanding of psychoanalytic process, of deadly suicidal challenges that threaten borderline patients. For the latter, the loved object, due to the cathexis of a forbidden oedipal libido, is under primary repression, abolished in its form and shape. The object remains conserved in the unconscious like a dead person in an Egyptian tomb, whose mummification might lead one to believe that he is not dead.

This concept is difficult to grasp, because, like primal words that always contain a double meaning, they call for operations which are uncommon and difficult to imagine. It seems that the most effective way to describe this process is to imagine an introjection, or incorporation of the object into the ego, in such a way that it loses its quality of being a separate object and becomes confused with the substance of the ego. André named this operation *desobjectalization* and linked it to the establishment of a "negative narcissism" related to the death instinct.[4]

In contrast, I see suicidal potential in patients with borderline states as the consequence of the decoupling between the object and its libido. In isolating itself from its object, the libido is transformed from an affective "colour", dominated by love and thirst for life towards a more negative, hateful, and destructive concept. It is possible to describe this operation as a revolution in one's psychic economy that dismantles the power of a democratic institution and reinforces the authority of a tyrant thirsty for blood and cruelty.

Here is my main divergence from André: I am opposed to the dichotomy between the life instinct and the death instinct, and favour instead a theory that entails a single instinct which, depending on the hazard of traumatic history, turns itself either towards pursuing life and self-preservation or towards death. This transformation under primary repression (*Urverdrangung*) will decide the destiny of the subject and will affect, more or less strongly and definitively, a more or less important part of his instinctual capital. Isolated from its responding object, affect appears to occupy alone all the field of the unconscious. This is what brought Freud to represent the id as a pure instinctual cauldron. I think that here Freud was incorrect.

The practical and theoretical heart of this debate is about how to extract the unconscious formation from its negativity and how to restore vitality and engagement in life and in objects in a subject reduced to too much narcissism. The figure of the object as reality has imposed it on the subject's mind, has to be recognised; at least its features have to be reconstituted in a sufficiently convincing way. Such a case of "epiphany in the appearance of the object" is required in the treatment of borderline and psychotic patients, in whom the compulsion to repeat is only appeased when the traumatic memory that generated it is exhumed. What characterises the psychotic process, like the one that leads to the borderline state, is that, under the power of psychic pain and later in its psychogenesis, the subject absolutely freezes his memory and violently amputates his history.

Notes

1. See Green 2007 for a collection of essays summarising the work and various points of view of these group members.
2. See Green (1997), *On Private Madness*. One should also refer to the important work published under his direction *Les voies nouvelles de la thérapeutique psychanalytique, le dedans et le dehors* (Rolland, 2006) published by PUF. I developed at length what Green brought to this subject in Rolland (2015).
3. In French analytic discourse, *refoulement* refers to the barring of ideas and representations from consciousness, as opposed to repression, which refers to the barring of affects (Sechaud, 2016, personal communication).
4. The formation of André Green's thinking on these essential points spreads over many years with its most important stages in *Narcissisme de Vie, Narcissisme de Mort* (1983) and *The Work of the Negative* (1999).

References

Green, A. (1983). *Narcissisme de Vie, Narcissisme de Mort*. Paris: Editions de Minuit.

Green, A. (1997). *On Private Madness*. London: Karnac.

Green, A. (1999). *The Work of the Negative*. London: Free Association Books.

Green, A. (2000). The central phobic position. *International Journal of Psychoanalysis, 81*: 429–451.

Green, A. (Ed.) (2007). *Resonance of Suffering*. London: IPA.

Rolland, J. C. (1998). *Guérir de mal d'aimer* [Recovering from the sickness of loving]. Paris: Gallimard.

Rolland, J. C. (2006). "Névrose de destin", troisième partie (pp. 901–909). Sous la direction d'André Green, *Les voies nouvelles de la thérapeutique psychanalytique, le dedans et le dehors* [New ways of psychoanalytic therapy, inside and outside]. Paris: PUF.

Rolland, J. C. (2015). For André Green. *Revue Française de Psychoanalyse, LXXIX*(3): 824–835.

Sechaud, E. (2016). Personal communication.

PART II
THE DEAD MOTHER

CHAPTER THREE

Re-membering the dead mother

Howard B. Levine and Anna Migliozzi

" *T he starting point of this work is contemporary clinical experience*"
(Green, 1997a, p. 169, our italics). With these words, we can
infer that Green regards clinical experience as the point of
departure for psychoanalysis, setting the foundations for the dialogue
between practice and theory, demonstrating the often "cubist" nature
of psychic reality and affirming the powerful potential of our discipline to get at the "inner truth" of lived experience.

"The dead mother" paper is an ambitious work that reflects a
dense and complex creative process, in which Green (1997a) formu-
lates new ideas, adds different inflections and meanings to classical
concepts, and seeks to preserve dialectical tensions, rather than definitively resolving them. The paper is metapsychological and method-
ological, as well as clinical and its style of discourse is enigmatic and
sometimes obscure. It ranges far beyond the description of a particular syndrome and explores and expands upon certain undeveloped
intimations in Freud's theory and their implications for the analytic
situation and cure.

Seen in the light of Green's subsequent work, this paper appears as
a way station in the evolution of a number of key ideas that are only
here in the process of being worked out: for example, the work of the

negative, a theory of psychic representation, the differences between primary[1] and secondary repression, and between destructivity and aggression, the framing structure (*structure encadrante*), the dialectical tension between objectalising and disobjectalising functions, etc.

As Urribarri (2014) noted, rather than attempting to offer a seamless psychoanalytic discourse or new ideological system, Green offers us "a new disciplinary matrix, an articulation of certain central questions, certain ideas and guidelines to guide research . . . [and] recognise and address the specific challenges of the current stage" (translated for this edition) of development of analytic theory and practice.[2]

Green (2005) has often lamented that too many psychoanalysts take refuge in their own school of theory, failing to discuss their underlying concepts and assumptions. In contrast, he seeks here to foster a genuine communication between diverse currents of thinking and a deep discussion of the principles underlying the main theoretical standpoints governing contemporary psychoanalysis.

We borrow the term "cubist" from art to describe the three dimensional approach Green takes to Freudian theory, integrating it with the work of contemporary psychoanalysts, such as Winnicott and Bion, in what we consider a deliberate attempt not to be definitive or dogmatic, adhering to a specific school of thought, but, rather, *synthetic*, describing a subjectivity of the mother-object which renders her an alive psychic participant in the relationship between the mother and child.

For Green (2005), the art of psychoanalysis lies in the analyst's ability to piece together a narrative based on what both the analysand and analyst bring to the session. Similarly, neither clinical evidence nor theoretical formulation is able to stand alone or move forward without the other. Each depends upon a reflexive process of discovery and rediscovery that is at the core of the analytic process. The dialectic tension that exists between them defines and preserves the unique specificity of psychoanalysis, rendering it neither a science nor a religion, while, at the same time, affirming that the most effective way to understand the human psyche is through construction and narration in retrospect: in Freudian terms, *après coup*.[3] It informs Green's dialectical pairing of drive and object, life narcissism and death narcissism, objectalising and disobjectalising functions, and is central not only to the understanding of Green's "Dead mother" paper, but to its methodology as well.

Confronted by his own unexpected recollection of Freud's (1900a, p. 583) dream of the "beloved mother", Green (1997a) takes into consideration the way in which we try to explain the world through the stories that we tell to ourselves and others about ourselves and the way in which we recover early memory from a *synchronic* rather than a diachronic point of view.[4] In reflecting upon the process through which the "Dead mother" paper came to be, Green offers a crucial observation about the construction of meaning and how it grows out of the analytical process.

> I have known of these [Freud's] dreams for many years, as well as the commentaries to which they have given rise. One and the other were imprinted in my mind as significant memory traces of something that seemed to me to be obscurely important, without my knowing exactly how or why. These traces have been recathected by the discourse of certain analysands whom, at a given moment, I was able to hear, though not before. Is it this discourse that permitted me to rediscover Freud's written word, or is it the cryptomnesia of this reading that made me permeable to my analysand's words? (Green, 1997a, p. 172)

Green then adds that "nothing is more mysterious than . . . a registered meaning which remains in abeyance in the psyche while awaiting its revelation" (p. 172), a revelation that is far more than "A lost meaning refound" (pp. 172–173). This "meaning-in-waiting" is perhaps best seen as a "potential meaning, which only lacks the analytic— or poetic?—experience to become a veridical experience" (p. 173).

In his subjective description of the process of memory, Green himself experiences the recovery of that which has been repressed and the therapeutic action of analysis, categorising each of these as constructive, intuitive activities—like poetry—in which meaning is acquired through *après coup*: experience, discourse, reflection, and hindsight.

As such, all the pieces of the story begin to fall into place in a psychoanalytic presence and present which describes traumatic events previously experienced but never before narrated. ". . . the mutative interpretation is always retrospective. It is in the aftermath that this theory of the lost object is formed, and acquires its unique, instantaneous, decisive irrevocable and basic characteristic" (p. 147).

Thus, Green challenges us to dig deeper into our clinical experiences, in which our discipline is rooted and from which it is nurtured, ultimately allowing us to reconsider, confirm, and move beyond our known theoretical boundaries.

In this chapter, we offer a close reading of "The dead mother" paper, place it into the context of the trajectory of Green's subsequent writings, and raise certain themes that we believe require expansion and further explication. In particular, we:

- explore what might seem to be certain contradictions and/or paradoxes in Green's formulation;
- examine Green's elaborations of fundamental Freudian theoretical concepts such as narcissism and primary repression;
- discuss his investigation of the subjectivity of the object and its relation to the drives;
- contrast the clinical syndrome of the dead mother with the classical description of melancholia as elaborated by Abraham (1968a,b) and Freud (1917e).

"The dead mother"

Green refers to "The dead mother complex" as a particular syndrome characterised by detachment from the emotional world, feelings of futility, and a state of mind marked by a profound sense of emptiness where things are always "not enough". The presenting complaints of these patients revolve around dissatisfaction in work or love: feelings of loneliness, emptiness, impotence, and narcissistic fears of abandonment.

The depression that is so central to the dead mother complex does not reveal itself at first and is only exposed after treatment has begun, through "a revelation of the transference" (Green, 1997a, p. 148). In fact, rather than displaying clinically overt depression, the patient's life might have been marked by a precocious and hypertrophied sexuality or intellectual activity. The latter, when combined with innate intelligence or artistic ability, can disguise its defensive or desperately compensatory aim and seem, from the outside, to be a highly active, adaptive, and successful form of functioning.

In the course of treatment, however, when the transference depression does appear, it marks a return to a previously unrecognised infantile depression that had a specific configuration: "*it takes place in the presence of the object, which is itself absorbed by a bereavement"* (p. 149, original italics). We might describe this as a simultaneous bereavement of both mother and child related to a morbid series or sequence of losses and pathological grief of an exceptionally primitive kind. The cause of this maternal bereavement might vary, but its consequences for the development of the child are severe:

> What comes about then is a brutal change of the maternal imago, which is truly mutative. Until then, there is an authentic vitality present . . . which comes to a sudden halt, remaining seized from then on in the same place, which testifies to a [previous] rich and happy relationship with the mother. The infant felt loved . . . (p. 149)

For the child, there is a loss of the mother's affective attunement and vitalising engagement that is sudden, massive, and *for a longer period than can be tolerated.* It is a catastrophe that carries with it "the loss of *meaning"* (p. 150, original italics), as well as love, leaving in its wake " a *cold core"* (p. 150, original italics).

The child's responses could include self-blame, premature triangulation in which the mother's attachment to the father is mistakenly blamed for the cause of her sudden withdrawal, an unsuccessful turning towards the father as a substitute mother figure, vain attempts to resurrect and revive the mother's emotional presence, and a panoply of distress signals, including anxiety, agitation, insomnia, and night terrors. When the duration of mother's emotional unavailability exceeds the child's capacity to sustain her internal image, then the child's ego resorts to another level of response: *"decathexis of the maternal object and . . . unconscious identification with the dead mother"* (pp. 150–151, original italics).

Green makes clear that the dead mother complex does *not* refer to

> the psychical consequences of the real death of the mother, but rather to that of an imago[5] which has been constituted in the child's mind, following maternal depression, brutally transforming a living object, which was a source of vitality for the child, into a distant figure, toneless, practically inanimate, deeply impregnating the cathexes of certain patients whom we have in analysis, and weighing on the destiny of their object-libidinal and narcissistic future. Thus, the dead mother, contrary to what might one think, is a mother who remains alive but who is, so to speak, psychically dead in the eyes of the young child in her care. (p. 142)

Green offers two plausible descriptions of the cause of the "death" of the mother. One is of an imago that has disappeared without a trace (decathexis; primary repression) and, whether dead or alive, captures and holds hostage the infant's libido and, therefore, obstructs the possibility of any new object investment. The other, perhaps a consequence of the captured libido, involves a sense of reality that is constructed to confront the absence. This reality precludes investment in anything that is present or actually obtainable and is predicated upon absence itself.[6] This means that in order to maintain and stabilise a sense of self and existence, these patients must cling to the half of the proverbial glass that is empty and continually efface (*negative hallucination*) any psychic trace of the presence of a potentially satisfying object, including memories of the once "good enough" mother.

With respect to the problem of mourning, Green suggests that, symptomatically, the complex is initially marked by narcissistic difficulties rather than "recognized depressive symptomatology" (p. 142). Recall that, according to Abraham (1968a,b) and Freud (1917e), "recognized depressive symptomatology" implies melancholia and revolves around destructive rage towards the object and the vicissitudes of aggression turned inward upon the self. For Freud and Abraham, this, too, was a problem of "narcissistic difficulties", but at a much higher level. In melancholia, concomitant to identifying with the frustrating absent object, libido is drawn back into an intact self. There, it is preserved, can be liberated in the mourning process, and eventually reinvested in a new object. In the dead mother situation, the very intactness of the child's self is threatened, or even shattered, by decathexis. According to Green, the aggressiveness and rage that might appear as a result are neither primary nor motivational. They appear as secondary phenomena.[7]

What is crucial is the decathexis caused by the emotional unavailability and depressive preoccupation and withdrawal of the maternal object. Green introduces the subjectivity of the mother into the equation, especially the specific emotional quality of her investment in her caring. Thus, the mother is not an abstract entity but, rather, an active player in the drama having her own emotional life. In this light, Green clearly incorporates the Lacanian emphasis upon the subjectivity of the object.

It is important to emphasise that, for Green, the "mother" that is lost is an entity of the infant's *psychic reality*; she is metaphorical and approximate and cannot fully be described or captured in words. Hence, the term "mother" stands in for, and includes, a growth enhancing, emotional atmosphere contributed to, and/or created by, the real object, as well as the object itself: "her smell, her skin, her look and the thousand other components that 'make up' the mother" (p. 148).

This "mother" is more than the real world, external object whose emotional withdrawal precipitates decathexis and the resulting syndrome, more than the external object mother combined with the internal and symbolic imago of the child's specific mother. The mother of the dead mother complex is also *actual*—in the sense of an irreducible, untranslatable, enigmatic presence—a "primal" or "originary" object, perhaps akin to a preconception waiting to be met by a realisation (Bion, 1970).

The mother that Green refers to is part of an ensemble—mother, external object, real object, etc.—that is a fundamental building block of what will become the infant's self. Thus, Green's insistence that the dead mother complex is different from Freud's melancholia, in that it "does not concern the loss of a real object" (p. 148), although the external "fact" of a real separation may coincidentally exist.

The sudden and inexplicable loss of all this, inexplicable in part because of the infant's limited level of abstract comprehension (p. 150), can produce "blank . . . states of emptiness" (p. 146) and "a 'blank' anxiety which expresses a loss that has been experienced on a narcissistic level" (p. 146).

The term, "blank" (*blanche* in French, which may also be translated as "white"), is significant in Green (e.g., 1997a, 2005). It is associated with decathexis, negative hallucination, psychic voids, and tears in the fabric of the psyche and is contrasted with absence, which can leave a trace of its continuing presence in the mind.[8]

Green goes on to say that "The decathexis, which is principally affective, but also representative, constitutes a psychical murder of the object, accomplished without hatred" (Green, 1997a, p. 151).

He adds,

No instinctual destructiveness is to be inferred from this operation of decathexis of the maternal image. Its result is the constitution of a hole in the texture of object-relations with the mother, which does not prevent the surrounding cathexes from being maintained. (p. 151)

Green notes that some degree of maternal care continues despite mother's affective withdrawal. This care may be dutiful, perfunctory, and accompanied by the mother's belief in her ongoing capacity to love her child, even though her love is damaged or absent. The problem might not be what she does, but the affective tone of how she does it. That is, her provisions might be "correct", but "her heart is not in it" (p. 151).

On the child's part, there is often a desperate, almost obligatory response: an attempt at a primary mode of mirror-identification, a "reactive symmetry. . . . A mimicry, with the aim of continuing to possess the object (who one can no longer have) by becoming, not like it but, the object itself" (p. 151). This identification is unconscious and "cannibalistic" (p. 151), more of an attempt to preserve the object and one's self than an oral aggressive retaliation. It ties the child to a futile, repetitive, unconscious attempt to cling to and/or be the "dead" mother. In practice, it "evokes a hunt in quest of an unintrojectable object, without the possibility of renouncing it or of losing it" (p. 154) or of replacing it with another object. The child's "objects remain constantly at the limit of the ego, not wholly within, and not quite without. And with good reason, for the place is occupied, in its centre, by the dead mother" (p. 154).

Finally, Green adds,

> when the analyst succeeds in touching an important element of the nuclear complex of the dead mother, for a brief instant, the subject feels himself to be empty, blank, as though he were deprived of a stop-gap object, and guard against madness. *Effectively, behind the dead mother complex, behind the blank mourning for the mother, one catches a glimpse of the mad passion for which she is, and remains, the object, that renders mourning for her an impossible experience.* The subject's entire structure aims at a fundamental fantasy: to nourish the dead mother, to maintain her perpetually embalmed. This is what the analysand does to the analyst: feeds him with the analysis, not to help himself to live outside the analysis, but to prolong it into an interminable process. For the subject wants to be the mother's polar star, the ideal child, who takes the place of an ideal dead object, who is necessarily invincible, because not living, which is to be imperfect, limited, finite. (p. 162, our italics)

This formulation places the subjectivity of the object at the centre of the problem and locates Green as working in the tradition of

Winnicott and Bion, each of whom attempted to emphasise the existence of the actuality and unknown subjectivity of the object (p. 164).

Primary repression and decathexis

Green's reference to primary repression[9] in the dead mother paper, which he links to Winnicott's (1971) description of decathexis, is a proposed expansion and filling in of Freudian theory. The decathexis he describes seems to be a kind of "primal decathexis" that includes erasure from the mind—foreclosure, ejection or effacement (*Verwerfung*)—perhaps taking with it a piece of the psyche or at least disrupting the capacity for psychic functioning. It seems to go beyond the decathexis of secondary repression, which is a stripping away of consciousness (conscious cathexis), while maintaining the shape of the space reserved for the repudiated ideational content (the framing structure). It might also be seen as some form or transformation of the repudiated ideational content itself.[10] What remains unclear in Green's paper is whether it is the type of the repression (primal) that is responsible for disrupting the framing structure, the timing of its occurrence (before the framing structure is securely in place), or the unfortunate combination of both that is responsible for the damage done.

The description of decathexis that Winnicott brought forward in discussing the conditions under which the transitional object might lose its meaning is clinically evocative and central to Green's thinking.

> If the mother is away over a period of time which is beyond a certain limit measured in minutes, hours, or days, then the memory of the internal representation fades. As this takes effect, the transitional phenomena become gradually meaningless and the infant is unable to experience them. *We may watch the object becoming decathected.* (Winnicott, 1971, p. 15, quoted in Green, 1997b, p. 1074, Green's italics)

What Winnicott is describing is a psychic death that is a "fading away", rather than an active murder. Green seems to agree and yet, contradicts himself, because, as we have seen, he also describes the psychic death of the mother as "a *murder* without hatred" (Green, 1997a, p. 151, our italics). He will subsequently comment that for the infant, "After a certain limit of time, the mother is definitely dead, whether absent or present. This means no contact can be re-established when she is back" (Green, 1997b, p. 1074).

Thus, Green implies the danger of a failure of object constancy. The mother who might return, even if possessed of some degree of aliveness, might not be emotionally perceived as the same as, and continuous with, the mother who was lost.

It is a matter of the mother's subjectivity, her bereavement or internal preoccupation and emotional absence that constitutes her death.

> The mother's blank mourning induces blank mourning in the infant, burying a part of his ego in the maternal necropolis. To nourish the dead mother amounts, then, to maintaining the earliest love for the primordial object under the seal of secrecy enshrouded by the primary repression of an ill-accomplished separation, of the two partners of primitive fusion. (Green, 1997a, pp. 167–168)

Ordinarily, we assume that an overly frustrating or disappointing object turns into a "bad object" or remains in the psyche as an object of cold indifference. In either of these cases, even at the expense of a persecutory presence, the psyche remains intact. (See Bion's (1970) description of the absent breast becoming a persecutory 'no-thing'.) However, following Winnicott (1971), Green seems to be making a more extensive claim that there is a category of greater loss or destruction of all trace of the object and, with it, a disruption of psychic functioning and/or unravelling of part of the self—that is, decathexis produces a "fading of the internal representations" (Green, 1997b, p. 1074) of the once alive and vitalising maternal imago—and that the symptoms that follow amount to an *inner representation of the negative*. That is, ". . . 'a representation of the absence of representation' . . . which expresses itself in terms of negative hallucination or in the field of affect, of void, of emptiness or, to a lesser degree, futility, meaninglessness" (Green, 1997b, p. 1074).

So, there is the fading away of the representation of the once present but now missing, affectively vital and vitalising object, and in its place *there is a reorganisation of that which reality sense will be based upon, so that the gap becomes the substrate of what will feel and be deemed to be real.*

According to Green (1997b)

> it is the bad object that never goes away . . . The bad thing has to be there, and if it is not, it is this absence equated with void and

emptiness that becomes real, more real than the existing objects that are around. (p. 1075)

The absence, failure, loss of meaning, unravelling, etc. that are associated with this line of reasoning seem to fit well in relation to Green's "blank" series—negative hallucination, blank depression, *psychose blanche*—and the metaphor of torn fabrics and psychic voids.

> . . . the non-existence, will become, at some point, the only thing that is real. What happens afterwards is that even if the object reappears, the realness of the object is still related to its non-existence. The return of the presence of the object is not enough to heal the disastrous effects of its too long absence. Non-existence has taken possession of the mind, erasing the representations of the object that preceded its absence. This is an irreversible step, at least until treatment. (Green, 1997b, p. 1082)

The emphasis here seems to lean heavily towards an *economic* point of view that rests upon assumptions of traumatic disruption of vulnerable psychic structures, capacities, and developmental movements and their consequences upon not yet well-established psychic organisation and functioning.[11]

In connection with these processes, Green suggests that there is an instinctual de-fusion that takes place between Eros and the destructive instincts, also described as a shift in the balance between life narcissism to death narcissism. This weakens erotic, libidinal ties to objects and, thereby, liberates aggression and sadistic rage. However, as noted above, in Green's view, this is a secondary phenomenon, perhaps a misdirected self-preservative attempt, rather than a primary aetiological determinant. In this, we can perhaps see an echo of Freud's (1911c) description of the dynamics of psychosis, where the primary cause of psychosis is a withdrawal of cathexis from reality and the symptoms ordinarily associated with psychosis, delusions, hallucinations, etc., are miscarried restitutive attempts.

Summary and discussion

The mother's bereavement and internal preoccupation with something other than the emotional love and care of her baby is the initiating event triggering the dead mother syndrome. It extends Winnicott's conceptual focus on the actuality of early external object relations (the infant's facilitating environment) and continues to help redress a potential over-focus on the intrapsychic.

Green's explanation of how the maternal object captures, retains, and freezes the libido of the infant reverses the usual description in which the ego of the self is the active agent in response to deploying or retaining libidinal investment. In essence, this is a radical theoretical position for Green to adopt, one that prefigures his later (e.g., Green, 2005) conclusion that the drive and object have to be considered as a dialectical pair: each one stimulating and revealing the other.

Although Green did not reference it in this paper, Abraham (1968b) had earlier offered a tentative movement in this direction, implicating the subjectivity of the object when he described certain melancholic patients as having suffered from excessive attachment due to the mother's encouragement of the breastfeeding experience. Abraham believed that the resulting over gratification produced a fixation on the breast eventually leading to an "incorporation" towards "being the object".

The dead mother concept targets the emotional world of the patient and includes the subjectivity of the object. In that way, it places subjectivity of the mother at the centre of the problem. The mother's bereavement, or other form of internal preoccupation, leads to an actual affective loss and, consequently, a decathexis and fading of internal representations. This fading, or its consequences, can be clinically expressed as affects of emptiness, blank affect, negative hallucination, and a sense of futility and meaninglessness. Taken together, they reflect "a representation of the absence of representation". Above all, the patient has a pervasive sense that something is "not there". It is for this reason that the vitality and activity of the analyst in the analytic relationship proves essential as an element in the cure.

As Green (1997b) asserts,

> All that refers to a lack: absence of memory, absence in the mind, absence of contact, absence of feeling alive—all these absences can be condensed in the idea of a gap. But that gap, instead of referring to a simple void or to something which is missing, becomes the substrate for what is real. (p. 1075)

"Identification" with the mother is so primitive that it goes beyond wanting to be *like* the object, or even wanting to possess the object, to wanting to *be* the mother. In conjunction with this over-identification with the imagined object of the mother, the baby desperately attempts to recapture the mother's affective attention.

Green describes a condition of *oversaturation*, "a mad passion". There is no room in the ego for a new object, because all of the child's libido, all of the potential "receptor sites" in which a new object may be placed, is already and forever taken up by the imago of the dead mother. Unlike situations of mourning and melancholia, where libido once invested in the now lost object is withdrawn into the ego from which it can then be eventually redeployed, here, the emotions are tied up and entombed with the dead mother object and eventually "disappear".

For the patient, the sense of reality and a sense of self come to revolve around the gap itself, rather than around memories of objects who were once present but are no longer there. As a result, any competing presence is apt to be felt as overwhelming, destabilising to reality and sense of self, and evoke the spectre of the dead mother: a prelude to madness, annihilation, and despair.

Notes

1. Laplanche and Pontalis (1974) prefer the term "primal" rather than "primary", but the English translation of "The dead mother" paper uses the term "primary" and so we will continue that usage in this chapter.
2. This quote is from the eulogy for Green delivered by Urribarri and reprinted in Urribarri, 2014.
3. Freud's term *nachträglichkeit* is often discussed by way of use of the French term *après-coup* that was introduced by **Lacan** (1977) in 1953. As Faimberg (2005) has pointed out, this added the meaning of "retrospective modification" to the term, in contrast to Strachey's notion of "deferred action", the two meanings then pointing in opposite directions in relation to the arrow of time.
4. As Freud (1899a) indicated in his "Screen memories" paper, it is perhaps more accurate to say that we *re-member* rather than recover memories.
5. Note here his reference to the "*death*" of an imago.
6. Green would prefer the term, "lack" to that of "absence". In Green's work, the term "absence" is reserved for a situation where the external object is not present, but a representation of that object exists and

is held within the mind. "Lack" or "void" is used when the external object is missing and the psychic representation of that object disappears or is extinguished.

7. In his later work, Green (2005) will distinguish between "aggressivity" and "destructivity". The former

> is linked to sadism and attached to the stages of the evolution of the libido . . . In destructivity, it is the narcissistic dimension that prevails . . . [D]estructivity does not necessarily imply contact with the object. On the contrary, disinvesting the object can involve the satisfaction of destroying it by making it feel that it does not exist. (p. 72).

Green adds that this satisfaction differs from the *jouissance* and libidinal pleasure involved in sadistic aggression, dominance, and control.

8.
> The category of "blankness"—negative hallucination, blank psychosis, blank mourning, all connected to what one might call the problem of emptiness, or of the negative, in our clinical practice—is the result of one of the components of primary repression: *massive decathexis, both radical and temporary, which leaves traces in the unconscious in the form of "psychical holes." These will be filled in by recathexes, which are the expression of destructiveness which has thus been freed by the weakening of libidinal erotic cathexis. Manifestations of hatred and the following process of reparation are manifestations which are secondary to this central decathexis of the maternal primary object . . . [T]his view modifies analytic technique because to limit oneself to interpreting hatred in structures which take on depressive characteristics amounts to never approaching the primary core of this constellation.* (Green, 1997a, p. 146, our italics)

Note, too, the similarity to Kohut's (1977) description of "empty depression", its distinction from melancholia and to Kohut's insistence that the rage associated with empty depression is not a primary determinant of the syndrome, but is a reaction to environmental failure.

9. For most analysts, the term "repression" (*Verdrangung*) usually refers to what Freud called *secondary repression*, in which the forces that prevent an unacceptable, anxiety producing idea from becoming or remaining conscious (wish, memory, phantasy, or perception) consist of a repulsion coming from the ego or superego joined with an attraction exerted by already repressed unconscious elements. The origin

and ideational nature of the initial or primally repressed (*Urver-drangung*) ideas, however, were never elaborated upon by Freud (Laplanche & Pontalis, 1973, pp. 333–334).

10. This is a very complex and controversial matter that revolves around what Freud (1915e) means when he says that "word presentations" do not exist in the system Ucs., but only exist in the system Cs.-Pcs. The question of whether fully saturated ideational representations of any kind exist in the unconscious remains unsettled and, although it lies at the heart of a profound uncertainty in the dead mother paper, it cannot be addressed or resolved here.

11. Although Green might not agree, this perspective implies that dead mother patients are similar to the "slaves of quantity" described by de M'Uzan (2003).

References

Abraham, K. (1968a). Notes on the psycho-analytic investigation and treatment of manic-depressive insanity and allied conditions. In: *Selected Papers on Psycho-Analysis* (pp. 137–156). London: Hogarth.

Abraham, K. (1968b). The first pregenital stage of the libido. In: *Selected Papers on Psycho-Analysis* (pp. 248–279). London: Hogarth.

Bion, W. R. (1970). *Attention and Interpretation*. London: Heinemann.

De M'Uzan, M. (2003). Slaves of quantity. *Psychoanalytic Quarterly, 72*: 711–725.

Faimberg, H. (2005). *Après-coup*: revisiting what has been real. In: *The Telescoping of Generations: Listening to the Narcissistic Links between Generations* (pp. 108–116). London: Routledge.

Freud, S. (1899a). Screen memories. *S. E., 3*: 299–322. London: Hogarth.

Freud, S. (1900a). *The Interpretation of Dreams. S. E., 4–5*. London: Hogarth.

Freud, S. (1911c). *Psycho-analytic Notes on an Autobiographical Account of a Case of Paranoia. S. E., 12*: 1–82 London: Hogarth.

Freud, S. (1915e). The unconscious. *S. E., 14*: 159–215. London: Hogarth.

Freud, S. (1917e). Mourning and melancholia. *S. E., 14*: 237–258. London: Hogarth.

Green, A. (1997a). The dead mother. In: *On Private Madness* (pp. 142–173). London: Karnac.

Green, A. (1997b). The intuition of the negative in *Playing and Reality*. *International Journal of Psychoanalysis, 78*: 1071–1084.

Green, A. (2005). *Key Ideas for a Contemporary Psychoanalysis*. New York: Routledge.

Kohut, H. (1977). *Restoration of the Self.* New York: International Universities Press.

Lacan, J. (1977). *Écrits: A Selection,* A. Sheridan (Trans.). New York: Norton.

Laplanche, J., & Pontalis, J.-B. (1974). *The Language of Psychoanalysis.* New York: Norton.

Urribarri, F. (2014). Eulogy given at the funeral service for André Green, Paris, France. In: *Dialoguer Avec André Green. La Psychanalyse Contemporaine Chemin Faisant* (pp. 133–136). Paris: Les Editions d'Itaque.

Winnicott, D. W. (1971). *Playing and Reality.* London: Tavistock.

PART III
REPRESENTATION

CHAPTER FOUR

Green's theory of representation revisited

Gail S. Reed and Rachel Boué Widawsky

A ndré Green identified representation as "the essential paradigm of psychoanalysis" (2005) and he wanted to make sure its status was recognised. "I have insisted in many of my writings", he declared, "on the necessity of conceiving of a new theory of representation" (2005, p. 126).

The theory he formulated to answer what he perceived as a definite requirement is the result of substantial clinical and theoretical observation, as well as immersion in, and thoughtful study of, other psychoanalysts' work. He did not shirk new readings of Freud in France and England, North and South America. Most importantly, beside Lacan, he was conversant with those he called "the Anglo-Saxons," meaning Bion and Winnicott, and he was familiar with them before other French-speaking psychoanalysts had begun to study them (2005, p. 134) and had become interested in their ideas.

To frame this discussion around Green's concept of representation, however, requires that one follow Green's labyrinthine thinking as it appears in his equally complex writings. There are few straight lines here, but as one follows the subject of representation in Green's work, one can appreciate the extent to which Green's own clinical and theoretical research took place in the context of fierce debates among French and international psychoanalysts.

It will help to maintain some historical perspective. Green's thinking on representation is preceded by Freud's successive models, both
topographic and structural, Lacan's structural theory of representation, and, finally, Pierre Marty's findings on psychosomatics. The
latter, especially, inspired Green to think about unrepresented states
from a new and different perspective.

In *Le langage dans la psychanalyse* (1984), while still following
Freud's topographic model, (unconscious–conscious, thing–word
presentation), Green takes an important step: *he inserts drive theory
into the theory of language.* Referring to his own earlier work on
affect (1973), Green considers that the psychoanalytic cure is "living
speech", or, in French, *un discours vivant.* For him, aside from the
psyche, the field of representation includes three domains: the body
(soma), the world, and the other. These dimensions define his idea
of a field of representation and they do so by making it essentially
heterogeneous (Green, 2010, pp. 29–31).

The oft repeated Lacanian theory of the unconscious as "structured
like a language" could not embrace this passionate living speech and
Green, heretofore a favoured student of Lacan, moved on. In his now
broadened concept, "a general theory of representation" is based on a
model of the triple characteristics of language, to wit:

—of a double significance of sign and meaning;
—of a double representance of words (linguistic) and objects (extra-
linguistic);
—and of a double reference to external reality and internal (psychic)
reality. (Green, 2011, p. 17)

For Green, the drive moves affects through multiple levels and
layers of representation. Indeed, drives are a part of the representational system as both representatives and representations. Drives
represent internal movements from the psyche and are represented
through affects or memory traces.

It is important to recognise, however, that there are two kinds of
drive representatives involved in Green's thinking: the *psychical representative of the drive* and the *ideational representative of the drive.*

In what concerns the *psychical* representative of the drive, Green is
interested in the way in which, as he puts it, "instinctual excitation of
endosomatic origin reaches the psyche and manifests itself at the level
of the body". He maintains that the drive has "psychical representatives

that cannot be reduced to thing presentations". The manifestation of the drive is the "manifestation of the delegation of the demands of the body to the psyche". "In fact," he continues, "the drive itself is not knowable, only its representatives are knowable". These drives must be identified by "the presence of the psychical representative of the drive" that cannot be reduced to thing presentations (Green, 2005, p. 126).

The *ideational* representative of the drive, to the contrary, involves the part of the drive concerned with "representation in repression" (Green, 2005, p. 126). Here, the Freudian word-presentation can reconnect to phonic memory trace.

It would appear, though, that with these explanations Green has significantly complicated Freud's model of representation. He escapes the difficulty, at least to his own satisfaction, by including the role of the drives in representation. That is, he manages to keep the body close to the psyche.

There is, however, one major, fundamental requirement for this representational system to function: it is necessary to have a capacity to separate from the object and a capacity to bear the absence of the object in order to create a new object. Indeed, this requirement defines representation for Green.

"To represent" has many other related meanings for Green. It can mean "to make present in the absence of what is perceivable and which thus has to be formed by the psyche again". Green takes "making present" literally in relation to the moment when "something is evoked which was, but is no longer present, but which I make present once again differently by re-presenting it; at the present instant, in the absence of what I am speaking about, I represent" (Green, 2010, pp. 29–30).

For Green, "to represent" has yet more meanings: It can also mean "to associate", that is, "to establish . . . relations between representations", thus involving binding. In addition, it means the "activity of a subjectivity" that "takes up a position". Because "[a]n individual who projects or represents decides", Green contends, "[h]e reveals himself in relation to his representations", whether he "agree[s] to that" or "[doesn't] want to" (Green, 2010, pp. 30–31).

As he delved further into the treatment of borderline and other pre-psychic patients, Green found the concept of representation illuminating new aspects of his clinical work. In some borderline patients, for instance, psychic life seemed to suffer from a *deficit of representation*.

This idea of a deficit of representation also applied to patients who could only communicate through concrete, or "operatory thinking". The representational dimension of the neurotic psyche relying on a relative fluidity between drives and representatives did not seem applicable to these patients. This idea figured both in Green's interest in, and misgivings about, Marty's psychosomatic system.

Here, unlike many contemporary French analysts, and perhaps because of the unusual perspective he was able to adopt, Green recognised the pivotal importance of Freud's great shift from topographic to structural theory. In consequence, he saw the id as *unrepresentable* and the ego, partially unconscious, as able to mobilise its representatives. This was surely the source of his interest in psychosomatic patients and, thus, in Marty's theories.

Marty, after all, investigated patients who made the dangerous illnesses with which they were afflicted into flat, affectless conversations (mechanical thinking), ignored the inherent danger of medical problems by making their delivery monotone, unfeeling, robotic (essential depression), and performed many other deadening operations.

These patients certainly did not fit the descriptions of neurotic patients analysts had learnt from Freud how to treat, and neither did they resemble psychotic-like patients where the forms of psychosis were different from classic ideas of that malady. An analyst and psychiatrist, Pierre Marty had founded a group in which analysts could study psychosomatic patients and their treatment in the late 1940s. In 1963, after many years of research and the addition to his group of other talented members of the Paris Psychoanalytic Society, he published *L'investigation psychosomatique* (Psychosomatic Investigation), a book called by many the "founding act of psychosomatics as a strictly psychoanalytic discipline". In their writing, the four authors, David, de M'Uzan, Fain, and Marty himself, described "affectless psychosomatic symptoms and illnesses" (translated for this edition), including "essential depression, mechanical thinking, the mechanism of projective reduplication, and the economic perspective" (translated for this edition), all clinical discoveries derived from their work with psychosomatic patients. They described the death-like automatism of essential depression, and the mechanical existence of operative thinking. Some of what they described is very close to Green's description of blank (black) or white (blanche) psychosis (Marty et al., 1963).

Despite having great respect for Marty's psychosomatic work, Green nevertheless remained a sceptic and was inclined to question Marty's generalisations. If a patient used unbinding, had a concealed but prolonged depression, constantly sought evidence of low self-worth, mistrusted any thoughts that were not part of the real, and/or systematically annulled the narcissistic gratifications that could have been recognised, Green would be puzzled as to why that particular patient demonstrated so many symptoms familiar to psychosomatic researchers, yet did not qualify as having developed a psychosomatic illness. Indeed, with his long study of non-neurotic patients, Green had developed his own, more general and flexible, list of applicable symptoms. These are important, and, therefore, we present them as far as possible in Green's own words.

1. Green located these pre-psychic patients with whom he was concerned on a continuum, from those distinguished at one end of the continuum by "fusional regression" and "object dependence" (Green, 1975, p. 6) and at the other end by the "supra normal" characters described by McDougall (1972).

2. The manner of the object relating of these patients, more specifically in their incapacity to separate from the object and the consequences of that inability, showed that these patients exhibited confusion between subject and object, with a blurring of the limits of the self (Green, 1975, p. 6).

3. They derived their mode of symbolisation from a "dual organization of patient and analyst" (Green, 1975, p. 6).

4. These patients required the analyst "to lend him/herself to the patient's fusional hunger" (Green, 1975, p. 6).

5. Indeed, they tended to mobilize four defences characteristic of certain psychic states to prevent regression. The four mechanisms are *somatic exclusion, expulsion via action, splitting, and decathexis*. The first two involve a "mechanism of psychic short-circuiting" (Marty et al., 1963, translated for this edition). The third, splitting, is familiar to us, and I will return to it (Green, 1975, pp. 6–7).

6. Unlike conversion, *somatic exclusion* is believed to be devoid of symbolisation.

7. *Expulsion via action* is its opposite, aiming to void the inner experience of painful psychic reality; it is the means by which the ego protects itself from disintegration (Green, 1975, p. 6).

The *effects* of the third, splitting, in Klein's sense, Green said,

> go from a protection of a secret zone of non-contact where the patient
> is completely alone (Fairbairn, 1940; Balint, 1968) and where his real
> self is protected (Winnicott, 1960a, 1963a); or again, which hides part
> of his bisexuality (Winnicott, 1971), to attacks on linking in his thought
> processes (Bion, 1957, 1959, 1970; Donnet & Green, 1973) and the
> projection of the bad part of the self and of the object (M. Klein, 1946)
> with a marked denial of reality. (Green, 1975, pp. 6–7)

Decathexis, the fourth defence, is an attempt at homeostasis. It is
achieved through a dangerous withdrawal of libidinal investment in
a "dead mother", too unresponsive, withholding, frustrating, and/or
unreliable to be related with as a reliable object. The frustrating and
disappointing object is no longer treated as such; instead, it is a depersonalised function, or group of functions; it is, says Green, "disobjec-
talised". In the place of a libidinally based object relation that
contributes to binding, emerges Green's version of the death drive.

The disobjectalising function, then, is both negative and destructive, part of a mental state where things that could connect instead
become disconnected, unbound, disorganised. These states extend
beyond Klein's formulations to the most primitive imaginable. The
disobjectalising function contrasts with a libidinal objectalising function that binds objects together, unites, and builds structure.

However, this defensive withdrawal is dangerous. It results, not in
a reparative depression like Klein's, but in a "primary" depression, one
of blankness, "a radical decathexis on the part of the patient who seeks
to attain a state of emptiness and aspires to non-being and nothingness" (Green, 1975, p. 7); for Green, this is the core of the pathological
negative. This blank psychosis, or negative hallucination, not only
does away with the representation of the object, but fixes the subject to
the negative as signifying the only reality.

Green believed that Winnicott had already "intuited" this negative
without having had time before his death to explore it at any length.
In "The intuition of the negative in *Playing and Reality*" (Green, 1997),
Green explored the traces Winnicott left and, in doing so, showed
Winnicott using the concept of decathexis just as Green had.

Green argued that to speak of the development of the transitional
area in the infant is to speak about the journey from the purely subjective, merged relation to the object gradually towards "objectivity", or

differentiation, at its end. "Let us remember", writes Green, that "the transitional space is not just 'in between,' it is a space where the future subject is *in transit*" (Green, 1997, p. 1072). What Green conceives is the metaphoric transversing of a space, a voyage in the sense of a process, leading towards separation. As Green, quoting Winnicott, continues,

> The infant can employ a transitional object [only] when the internal object is alive and real and "good enough" (not too persecutory). But this internal object depends for its qualities on the existence and aliveness and behaviour of the external object. "Failure of the latter in some essential function indirectly leads to deadness or to a persecutory quality of the internal object" (p. 9). After a persistence of inadequacy of the external object, the internal object fails to have meaning for the infant, and then, and then only, does the transitional object become meaningless too. (Green, 1997, p. 1073, citing Winnicott, 1971, pp. 9–10)

Or, as Winnicott says more directly, in describing the interaction between the mother and child elsewhere in his original article, if the mother is away too long "we may watch the object becoming decathected" (Green, 1997, p. 1074, citing Winnicott, 1971, p. 15). We have returned to the conditions favouring death, destructiveness, and blank and/or white (blanche) psychosis.

This blank psychosis, the ultimate product of the failure of the external object, is further defended against by a specific constellation of object relations, a splitting of the object into a persecutory object that intrudes and never goes away and a "good" object, that is, none the less, inaccessible and indifferent. This persecutory object is ever present. Thus, it is impossible to think of it as "not there", or to represent it in one's mind while it is not there as not being there. Representation, under these circumstances a necessity for differentiation and separation, is impossible. This lack of the capacity for representation in the face of the object's absence increases the terror of abandonment.

Another important clinical challenge posed by these patients, Green notes, is their inability to use the analytic setting as a facilitating environment: "they make a 'non-use of it' *so that the analyst is faced with the urgent need to understand 'the meaning of the setting itself*" (Green, 1975, p. 10).

In what might be most crucial for analytic technique, Green describes in more detail the need for the analyst to use his countertransference. In these patients who cannot use the setting and where it is "impossible to constitute absence", the analyst feels an internal pressure, as if the analytic situation were under threat. He is forced to "enter a world . . . which requires imagination from him" (Green, 1975, p. 10), then is obliged to transform the inner states evoked in him into words. This use of the analyst's psychic capacities for representation[1] (Green, 1975, p. 10) is the imaginative and intuitive work required of the analyst when treating those unable to represent the object in its absence.

This group of patients are those in whom exceedingly early development is compromised so that, for example, the unpredictable and too long absence of the external object destroys, through decathexis, the presence of a lively and creative intrapsychic object in the infant. The individual's necessary journey from the purely subjective to objectivity is impeded by the voids this event has created, and the subject's ability to become separate and to use the object (in Winnicott's sense) is similarly damaged.

We can imagine these patients longing for, but defending against, a fusional regression that risks encountering an objectless emptiness, the void of former non-gratification, which can lead to a death-like decathexis of anything lively or loving. This is a more primitive level of functioning than outward aggression.

To avoid that decathected state, defences turn psychic disturbance into unrecognisable physical illness, or into unreflective action. Or, the intrapsychic object is defensively split into good and bad, longed for and never attained, or, alternatively, intrusive and never gone. Because the part-object is always present, mostly as a persecutor, these patients cannot represent the object in its absence, therefore, again, cannot separate.

This splitting sometimes can look like triangulation when it is actually the self interacting with two halves of a split object divided by gender, so that one gender appears to abandon by being unattainable while the other intrudes and appears eternally persecutory. Green calls this "bi-triangulation" and is clear that this structure is not an oedipal triangulation, though it is often misunderstood and assumed to be one.

The aforementioned defences lead to discontinuities of the self; a patient presenting this general picture cannot easily put words to his suffering, cannot communicate what he lives.

Such a patient often cannot associate because voids stemming from failures in the environment cause discontinuities of the self that, in turn, interrupt the chain of associations which, in neurotic patients, allows us to infer unconscious content from displaced verbal material.

These patients need help recognising what they experience and feel, and the analyst must use his countertransference to articulate what these patients experience but cannot express.

Green had presented these ideas at an important IPA panel in London in 1975, with Anna Freud as one of his discussants, but, despite several attempts, had never been able to persuade Marty to discuss their diverging ideas in public. Then, a conference was scheduled, and Green and Marty met privately to discuss a possible programme. This private meeting stimulated in Green's mind a series of trial titles, most of them unsatisfactory to him. One version emphasised Winnicott's "in between zone" and was also closer to Green's conviction that "the language used reflects the ideology that is behind the theory . . . precisely in the way the subject's pre-conscious representations reveal a sort of ideology that is constitutive of his mind" (Green, 2010, p. 3). Indeed, somato and psychic, psychosomatic, uniting and separating, posed, Green thought, "the problem of the 'pre-psychic'."

In fact, one important difference between Green and Marty was that all Marty's theoretical thinking, perhaps all his clinical thinking as well, inevitably came up against the difficulty put by Green as "the model of neurosis provided the sole term of comparison with psychosomatic praxis".

Green thus entertained another possible title: "the relevance of the theoretical model of neurosis in the face of non-neurotic and more particularly psychosomatic states" (Green, 2005, p. 3). The disagreements here were the most obvious, perhaps Green's way of focusing on the treatment of non-neurotic patients that responded to their needs and was therefore different from the way neurotic patients were treated.

This practised neglect might well have come from the fear that analysts would be forsaking Freud and the way he had taught us to see and understand. Green rejected this possibility. Rather, he saw movement in a direction that paralleled Freud's developing interests. That movement allows contemporary analysts, like Levine, to question "Is there experience, perhaps deriving from the soma . . . that is inscribed, somewhere, somehow, but not yet psychically represented? If so, how do we understand such inscriptions and speak about their impact?" (Levine, 2014, p. 277).

Green pointed out that borderline cases should no longer be elucidated by the application of the model of neurosis. (Others, especially
Kernberg in the USA, had already developed their own variations on
the concept of splitting as it would apply to the treatment of borderline patients and other patients with psychotic characteristics.) Green
himself, as early as 1975, had proposed a model specific to them:

> I envisage the mind in terms of its frontiers: I try to define it between
> the bounds or limits of psychical activity. I place the psyche between
> the soma on one side and reality on the other. And within the psychi-
> cal field I see two fundamental mechanisms: depression and splitting.
> By "depression," I mean a *primary depression* . . . a lowering of psychi-
> cal tonus, which I distinguish from neurotic or melancholic depression
> as we know them. (Green, 2010, p. 4)

What is being described is something akin to Green's blank screen
(blanc) or white (blanche) psychosis.

On the side opposite from psychosis, Green contended,

> we have *splitting* . . . a fundamental activity of mental life, because it
> is with splitting that differentiation begins. The possibility of dividing
> the universe in two is the first psychical act by which it can be signi-
> fied: good–bad, inside–outside, etc. In short, all the essential pairs that
> underlie mental life imply a fundamental (I do not say primitive) and
> matrix process of splitting. To these fundamental splits, underlying
> the mind, others must be added. The split psyche/soma—which is part
> of normal experience—can take a very pathological turn. This is what
> we observe in psychosomatics. (Green, 2010, p. 4)

Marty contended that

> in the structures he treats there is a sort of reduction of the whole
> psychic field, that is, of the inner world, with, on the other hand, a
> hypercathexis of the factual and of reality, which seem to play a very
> important role. In other words, the psychosomatic patient puts his soma
> and external reality in communication, while crushing everything that
> pertains to mind. I have argued that the mind can be considered as an
> intermediate formation between these two poles. (Green, 2010, p. 5)

Green continues,

> However, should this crushing of the psychic field be seen in relation
> to neurosis rather than in relation to the non-neurotic structures, that

is, to forms akin to psychosis or the borderline cases where, precisely, another mode of functioning than neurosis obtains, and where the mind avoids this crushing by employing other defensive manoeuvres? Go crazy or die: this is the dilemma in which borderline cases are caught, in my view. (Green, 2010, p. 5)

Green had heard de M'Uzan allude to the workings of psychosomatic mechanisms in the individual, and particularly heard him mention the role of defence in preventing awareness of "certain psychoses" or "certain borderline dilemmas". He realised that he was encountering precisely the concepts that had escaped him in his title search. "It was a case of ideas coming back through the window after being refused entry via the door", he wrote. Only then was he able to think about the theoretical concepts he was missing and find a satisfactory title for the encounter with Marty: "The return of the *theoretical repressed of psychosomatics*" (Green, 2010, p. 5). This title would focus the attendees on what was missing from Marty's psychosomatic theory. However, it became impossible to discuss these ideas with Marty himself because Marty died before the conference could take place.

A clinical example: Colette Jeanson-Tzanck (1993)

Among the many very difficult examples of treatments of non-neurotic patients of his own that Green describes in highly condensed form, one comes upon a case treated by a student, Colette Jeanson-Tzanck. Green recounts this case in somewhat more detail, a possibility because Green had sat in on weekly case discussions and had a better memory of the case material than he had of older material of his own. The patient was understood to be suffering from psychosomatic difficulties by virtue of her physical symptoms and her tendency to operatory thinking—hence the warning by the referring supervisor to make "no interpretations". We will discuss only the reorganising intervention suggested by the title.

We imagine, from remarks by Green, that the treatment took place more than ten years before the article's publication in 1993, when the author, Colette Jeanson-Tzanck, was a student and was participating in a study group in which Green also participated. The example "shows", remarks Green, "that psychosomatic psychopathology cannot be reduced to the conception that is proposed [by Marty]" (Green,

2010, p. 16). When she was presented with this patient, a case of haem-
orrhagic proctocolitis, she was told "no interpretations, but apart from
that, feel free to use your intuition". Green comments unfavourably on
the "double bind implicit in these instructions" as they pertain to the
countertransference and which, no doubt, follow Marty's psychosomatic theory of treatment.

Indeed, her patient had traits "corresponding to what Marty had
described" remarks Green, meaning operational thinking and an
operational life: the patient arrived, had nothing to say, lived with her
parents and sister, slept in the same room with them all, and found
this arrangement "was not practical". The illness "wasn't practical
either". Owing to the proctocolitis, she had to go to the toilet during
the night and often very quickly. The toilet, however, was far from her,
and on the landing. As a child, she had one frightening memory. She
had seen her mother fall down a sewer hole in the street one day when
she was five. She did not ask herself if that memory was true or not.
There were fireworks that night, so things were exploding from top
and bottom (Green, 2010, pp. 16–17).

Her mother was intrusive and "overly present". She sometimes had
strange fears for her mother's body, but she did not know how that
affected her. She had insatiable curiosity concerning what was outside.
The less internal space she had, the more she felt obliged to use external space. "Her clothes never fitted her, they were either too large or too
tight" (Green, 2010, p. 17). She was also incapable of arriving on time.

As to the technique of treatment, the advice not to give interpretations surely derived from what was understood to be normal psychosomatic practice, where the therapist accepts the patient's flat
"operational" tone, assuming the patient to be using language not
only with no affect, but also with no symbolisation. It was likely to be
the intervention of Green that had the therapist [i.e., Jeanson-Tzanck]
utilising "colourful turns of phrases, such as speaking of a violent
presence of emptiness" in the patient. Green adds the admonition that
". . . you must take interest in the void when working with psychosomatic patients; if you do not, you cannot understand them because
that is what psychical space consists of" (Green, 2010, p. 18). One uses
language to establish a frame around the void which enables analyst
and patient to explore both frame and contents.

The patient also gives the impression that there is a sort of reality
brimming to the full. (This is the "hypercathexis of reality" of which

Marty spoke.) Next, it is again probably Green who suggests that the therapist adopt "an attitude that consisted in adopting a technique of binding, in linking ideas together" (Green, 2010, p. 18). Linking leads to representation. For this patient, that path transverses a profusion of dreams that "were highly charged, indicating a very important level of instinctual violence, with signs reading 'danger of death' in the manifest content" (Green, 2010, p. 18). In one dream, someone reproaches the patient for closing a door too noisily. After reporting the dream, the patient then adds "'You know, I shut the door very gently!' . . . she defends herself against an accusation in reality, as if the dream were the extension of a reality conveying a hostile parental superego." Green concludes from this example that "instead of having a conscious mind and an unconscious mind, we have two realities: a neutral reality and a malevolent or absurd reality" (Green, 2010, p. 18). Most importantly, Green sees "a confusion between perception and representation". In the dream narratives, there is

> the insistent presence of white. Everything is very white, the white makes everything seem larger, there are no walls, there are columns, and the white makes everything seem larger and it is as if there were mirrors reflecting everything endlessly, mirrors which reflect nothing but white. This *representation of the absence of representations* is indicative of the considerable field occupied by negative hallucination. (Green, 2010, pp. 18–19, *my italics*)

Jeanson-Tzanck notes this only "in passing" Green says, but for him, voids and gaps and negative hallucinations deserve the utmost attention. They are evidence of tears in the fabric of the mind and Green insists that it is absolutely impossible to understand "the functioning of a psychosomatic structure if one does not make use of the notion of negative hallucination" (Green, 2010, p. 19).

Negative hallucination signals the dominance of the void, where nothing is linked and no meaning can thus be discerned, where there is no meaning because there is no distinction between frame and content.

Finally, additional space for bathroom and sleeping became available and the family managed to acquire it and were rearranging and bringing order to their newly configured living spaces. In sessions, the patient gave precise explanations of everything that was happening. Then

> from a certain moment on, she [the patient] no longer knew what was happening, she could not co-ordinate her movements any more, there were surprising gaps, holes . . . In one session, she was in disarray, she could not see what was missing at all . . . Everything was blank, and the date when they were due to move in had faded into the distance. Katia [the patient] asked herself what was missing. Jeanson-Tzanck said to her: "I think the bottom shelf in the cupboard is missing and that the hammer is still on the windowsill; the paintwork also needs touching up." And Katia replied, her face lighting up, "Goodness". (Green, 2010, p. 20)

From that time on, the patient was able to wonder what someone else was thinking and feeling and to speculate about it.

Green thought the interpretation brilliant "because the configuration of the domestic space had been conserved and the place of the objects had not been negativised". In other words, the material suggested that "the fundamental experience is the alteration of a sort of mnemic ego capable not only of registering events, but of conserving them, of linking them together by giving them a meaning". This ability to conserve in turn permitted "an experience of temporal and spatial continuity" that the therapist might recognise as having been supplied once again by the transference after having been temporarily lost. The transference functioned to preserve and/or renew continuity, that is, it functioned as a frame, or, in Bion's words, like a container. As Green pointed out, "this absence of a frame for conscious experience" explains why representation was not immediately operative (Green, 2010, pp. 20–21).

These are complex and important insights into primal areas of the mind. Obviously, both the tear in the fabric of the mind and the potential damage to the container are metaphors. Green would argue that at least some of the most operational-sounding language hides such symbols. Both frame and container stand for what must be supplied by the mother's arms or presence, too often disappointing by its absence in the past, or too overwhelmingly invasive. What is necessary is something that endows the home and the heart with caring again but without overwhelming and dangerous fusion. It is the therapist who creates this missing connection through his/her interpretations. Spatial and temporal continuity is at stake.

Conclusion

This discussion of framing and containing brings us back to the question of representation. Clearly, for Green, to represent means something very explicit. It means, in Green's words, "to make present in the absence of what is perceivable and which thus has to be formed by the psyche again" (p. 29). The idea of making present is to be taken literally

> in relation to the moment when it occurs, when something is evoked which was, but is no longer present, but which I make present once again differently, by re-presenting it; at the present instant, in the absence of what I am speaking about, I represent. (Green, 2010, pp. 29–30)

For Green representation is an act of substitution for what or who is absent. Thus the mind represents what is absent but also establishes relationships between representations. Indeed, to represent has many linked meanings, the most significant clinically is the one connected to the analytic cure.

The implication of this operation in the psychoanalytic treatment is that the cure is not only about the work on the unconscious and conscious representations (content) but ultimately on the very work of representation, namely the act of producing meaning.

Note

1.   For more information on the function of representation in Green, see Levine et al. (2013), Chapters One and Two (pp. 3–41).

References

Green, A. (1973). *Le discours vivant: La conception psychanalytique de l'affect*. Paris: Presses Universitaires de France.

Green, A. (1975). The analyst, symbolization and absence in the analytic setting. *International Journal of Psychoanalysis*, 56(1): 1–22.

Green, A. (1984). *Le langage dans la psychanalyse*. Paris: Les Belles Lettres.

Green, A. (1997). The intuition of the negative in *Playing and Reality*. *International Journal of Psychoanalysis*, 78: 1071–1084.

Green, A. (2005). *Key Ideas for a Contemporary Psychoanalysis: Misrecognition and Recognition of the Unconscious*, A. Weller (Trans.). London: Routledge.

Green, A. (2010). Thoughts on the Paris School of Psychosomatics, A. Weller (Trans.). In: M. Aisenstein & E. Rappoport de Aisemberg (Eds.), *Psychosomatics Today: A Psychoanalytic Perspective* (pp. 1–45). London: Karnac.

Green, A. (2011). *Illusions and Disillusions of Psychoanalytic Work*, A. Weller (Trans.). London: Karnac.

Jeanson-Tzanck, C. (1993). Une intervention réorganisatrice dans la psychothérapie d'une "vie opératoire". *Revue française de psychoanalyse*, 57(1): 135–146.

Levine, H. B. (2014). Beyond neurosis: unrepresented states and the construction of mind. *Rivista Psiconanal.*, 60(2): 277–294.

Levine, H. B., Reed, G. S., & Scarfone, D. (2013). *Unrepresented States and the Construction of Meaning*. London: Karnac.

Marty, P., de M'Uzan, M., & David, C. (1963). *L'investigation psychosomatique*. Paris: Presses Universitaires de France.

McDougall, J. (1972). L'antianalysant en analyse. *Rev. Fran. Psychoanal.*, 36: 167–184.

Winnicott, D. W. (1971). *Playing and Reality*. London: Tavistock.

PART IV
THE WORK OF THE NEGATIVE

CHAPTER FIVE

The negative and its vicissitudes: a new contemporary paradigm for psychoanalysis

Fernando Urribarri

The positive: the negative of the negative.

André Green used to say that for him, psychoanalysis was essentially a way of thinking. One can see this in his writings, where "the negative", which he considered to be his most original contribution to contemporary psychoanalysis, is always at the Freudian core of his dialectical approach. For example, he wrote, "The psyche is the relation between two bodies, one of which is absent" (Green, 1990a, p. 274).

Green was always enthusiastic when he found, usually inspired by clinical experience, a new theme to expand his investigations on this topic. As his friend Pontalis once told me, "André is driven by clinical passion". For instance, right after my collaboration with him on his book *Illusions and Disillusions of Psychoanalytic Practice* (Green, 2011), which focused on the radical negativity at play in treatment failures, we started working on the preparation of another book. Its proposed title was to be "The Positive: The Negative of the Negative", and its aim was to elucidate the creative and transformational capacity of the analyst and the analysand in their psychic work.

Key Ideas for a Contemporary Psychoanalysis: Misrecognition and Recognition of the Unconscious (Green, 2005a) had been written on the basis of a long series of conversations we had in September 2001 (transcribed by his secretary, edited as a text by me, rewritten by Green, and then revised by us both). Since then, I collaborated with him on the preparation and edition of his subsequent books. The method he invented was that I would first present him with a review of his previous writings in relation to themes on which he wanted to work (several of these texts formed the basis of the prefaces or post-scripts that André decided to include in these books). This allowed him to begin to contextualise his new hypotheses, review previous ideas, and organise the themes of his current interest. He usually began with a spontaneous discourse beginning with his major new ideas. This discourse took the form of (nearly) free associations in which clinical narratives or vignettes were combined with "evenly suspended theorisation" (as Piera Aulagnier used to call it). My role was to take note of these novelties and later interrogate their relation to his previous conceptualisations and those of other authors, to formulate questions regarding possible contradictions or inconsistencies, and ask him for further development of certain proposals. We used this method—which Green called "dialogical thinking"—to work on "The positive: the negative of the negative". The present chapter is a panoramic overview of some of the initial notations that we used to start placing this theme in the frame of his previous elaborations.

Let me begin by presenting the general evolution of Green's think-ing following the guiding thread of his texts on the negative, narcis-sism, and the death drive. As I do so, I shall also highlight Green's legacy in relation to his project of offering us a new contemporary paradigm for psychoanalysis. These notes, which now prioritise his work on the negative, follow the model of historical periodisation of Green's works that I proposed in 2011 in the Postscript to *Illusions and Disillusions* (Green, 2011; Urribarri, 2011)[1] and later developed in the prologue to *La Clinique psychanalytique contemporaine* [Contemporary Psychoanalytic Clinical Work] (Green, 2012). Summarising, I propose to consider three main periods in his long intellectual travels.

During the 1960s, 1970s and 1980s, Green created and consolidated an innovative programme of investigation centred on patients at the limits of analysability, studying their representational functioning (and dysfunctioning) in the analytic setting. The major result of this stage was the construction of a model of borderline states and narcissistic disorders (presented in his books, *Life Narcissism, Death Narcissism* (Green, 2001b) and *On Private Madness* (Green, 1986). Consequently, advances were also made towards the innovation of technique and variations of the setting required for treatment of these patients.

From the mid-1980s and throughout the 1990s, the spotlight was on the renewal of metapsychology in order to advance beyond the limitations of Freudian and post-Freudian theoretical models. As a result, new concepts were introduced of which the most innovative were the work of the negative and the theory of thirdness. These two theoretical axes converged in the elaboration of an original metapsychology and the conceptualisation of the analytic setting as the epistemological and technical foundation of the analytic method. This work is advanced in his books, *La causalité psychique* [Psychical Causality] (Green, 1995c), *Propédeutique. La metapsychologie revisitée.* [Propaedeutics: Metapsychology Revisited] (Green, 1995d), and *Time in Psychoanalysis* (Green, 2002).

Finally, Green arrived at what he called "the turning point of the year 2000". In this last stage, he proposed a new contemporary paradigm aimed at overcoming post-Freudian fragmentation by building a new, pluralist and complex, theoretical–clinical disciplinary matrix that he hoped would address what he felt was the crisis of psychoanalysis. This project promoted a programme of investigating variations in practice and the extension of the clinical field accomplished in the previous decades. In order to do so, Green (2005a) gathers his main ideas and places them at the service of those who want to construct a "psychoanalysis of the future". Simultaneously, in *Psychoanalysis: A Paradigm for Clinical Thinking*, Green (2005b) advances elaborations on the work of the negative, exploring the radical destructivity of non-neurotic functioning and the creativity of the analyst's psychic work needed to combat it.

The work of the negative

In the 1960s, Green published his first papers, which evidence the three major characteristics that structured his Freudian thinking: a profound and anti-dogmatic reading of Freud, a critical and creative elaboration of post-Freudian contributions (mainly those of Lacan, Winnicott, and

Bion), and the exploration of the relation between theory and clinical work needed to understand and address difficulties that lay beyond the neuroses. The theme of the negative is present in this work from the outset, and soon acquires its first and most original, general elaboration.

An early and exemplary work by Green was his intervention in the famous Bonneval Colloquium (1960), which brought together for the first time since the 1953 split analysts of the official analytic society (SPP) and followers of Lacan. The latter were represented by Laplanche and Leclaire, whose presentation was discussed by Green in "L'Inconscient freudien et la psychanalyse contemporaine" (The Freudian unconscious and contemporary psychoanalysis) (1962).

After appreciating the elegance and coherence of his colleagues' work, Green criticised the reductionism of the Lacanian model:

> In contrast to Lacan's position, ours tends to place more value on the role of drives: their economic aspects, basic organization and aims, while also considering the structuring role of repression, to grasp the subject's manifestations in the conflict between positivity (drives) and negativity (defenses). Actually Lacan's reconstruction of Freud is built upon grounds that differ radically from those of the founder of psychoanalysis. Lacan seems to follow a particular desire: to find an ontological status for psychoanalysis based on philosophical consistency, which requires the reinterpretation of a whole aspect of Freudism: everything that is usually labelled as biologistic. In spite of the impasses to which this apparently leads, it seems to me to be indispensable to preserve it, since this perspective is the only attempt to give psychic reality *body* without reifying it. (Green, 1962, p. 379)

In his 1964 paper on obsessional neurosis, Green proposed the idea of "negative identification" in these structures, in which identification with a parental figure takes up only the object's prohibiting, persecutory aspect. Two other early texts advanced ideas on the negative: "The constitution of parental imagos: negative hallucination of the mother and primary identification with the father" (Green, 1995a) and "Lacan's object (a) and Freudian theory: convergences and questions" (Green, 1995b). At the end of the latter, Green criticised the limitations of the Lacanian notion of "lack" and proposed the mechanism of negative hallucination in order to explain the conditions necessary for the process of symbolisation.

"Primary narcissism: state or structure?" was the first major paper, with a truly original contribution by Green (2001a[1967]). At its centre is the theme of the negative, conceived and developed in all its heterogeneity. Green took up the problem, left open by Freud, of the relation between narcissism and the second drive duality, formulating a novel dual theory of narcissism as a structure (rather than a simple libidinal state). There, Green proposed a "positive narcissism" (formulated by Freud as libidinal cathexis of the ego) along with a "negative narcissism" to explain the role of the death drives in the structuring, functioning, and dysfunctions of the ego.

Lacan, who was a great reader, immediately recognised the originality of this theorisation that went beyond his mirror stage model of positive narcissism. He publicly attacked Green—in the famous Seminar and in the Lacanian review *Scillicet*—denying Green the right to publicly respond and defend his paper. This provoked the rupture of their relationship after seven years of close and intense interaction in the Seminar (where Green was the first of his generation to be invited to give a lecture) and in the small private group of disciples that discussed with Lacan the articulation of his theory with practice.

It is also important to underscore the difference between metapsychological concepts of positive and negative narcissism (or life narcissism and death narcissism), on the one hand, and psychopathological or clinical categories such as those of normal or pathological narcissism as proposed by Otto Kernberg, on the other. As described by the title of Green's book (2001b), which includes the 1967 article, "Life narcissism, death narcissism", he postulated a dialectical relation of complementary opposites: the narcissistic structure is structured and functions on the basis of interplay between life and death drives. Here, Green refers to "the work of death", although he subsequently renamed it "the work of the negative".

By deepening and revising the Freudian perspective, Green defined the death drive in terms of its functions of unbinding, decathexis, and unweaving representational fabrics and libidinal objects. On the one hand, he recognised the radically destructive potential of the death instinct, although he rejected the Freudian hypotheses of its biological grounding, teleological character and automatic functioning. On the other hand, he attempted to think about modes of functioning of the psychical apparatus that both co-operate with, and antagonise, life drives.

Green put these conceptual tools to work to theorise the key notion of the "framing structure" of primary narcissism: the foundation of the psyche's basal unit. It is this containing structure, which establishes primary separation from the fusional object (in the Freudian perspective). For Green, primary subject–object difference is the result of a double work of the negative that corresponds to two different dimensions. First, there is a "double reversal" of drive movements (turning to the ego and reversal into the opposite), which creates a circuit of self-cathexis, closed upon itself, as well as a boundary between inside and outside. In this way, Green theorises on the interiorisation of (fusional) maternal support, which later becomes the core container function of the psychical apparatus.

The second process is the "negative hallucination of the mother" achieved by de-cathecting the (fusional) hallucinatory perception of the mother. This de-cathexis creates an empty, potential space for the representation and cathexis of new objects. In this process, negative hallucination, understood as the condition and complement of the positive hallucination (of satisfaction experience), is defined as a "representation of the absence of representation". This definition is later replaced by more precise definitions that differentiate more clearly between container and contained in the representational process. However, it is worth recalling this reference to absence as a condition of symbolisation. In the negative hallucination, the primordial function of "the work of death" is to "absent" the mother. In other words, the negative hallucination creates the "blank screen" on which the representational "film" and figurative flow can be projected and framed.

This inaugural text of André Green's thinking conceptualises three major aspects of the work of the negative. First, the operations of unbinding inherent to the death drive enable separation from (and, therefore, substitution for) primary objects, and differentiation within psychic spaces and representational processes. Second, the identification mechanisms establish the origin and ground of renunciation of satisfaction as a psychic value and source of pride. Green points out that the Ideal is "the negative of the drive". Last, but not least, are the defence mechanisms (movements of halting, containing, and diverting sexual drive discharge). Beyond these three major dimensions the work of the negative corresponds, in a broader sense, to all psychical *work*—to all the operations that, directly or indirectly, say "No" to direct drive discharge.

These ideas on the negative, enriched by Green's very personal reading of the writings of Bion on thought, lead to a theory of "blank psychosis" presented in his book, *L'enfant de Ça [The Child of That/Id]* (written in collaboration with Donnet, 1971). The action of the death drive "empties the head" and, thus, the negative produces a psychosis without delusion, marked by severe disorders of thought, a consequence of the de-cathexis of the representational and emotional process.

This structure of blank psychosis is uncovered during an extended, single interview with a patient named Z (transcribed and analysed word by word, focusing special attention on countertransference) (Donnet & Green, 1971). Its study yields the theorisation of a unique, failed form of the Oedipus complex: bi-triangularity, composed of two dual and simultaneous relations with an impotent, good paternal object and an omnipotent, bad maternal object. The subject is fixed to the invasive but "negative reliable" (always present) malignant object. *The Fabric of Affect in the Psychoanalytic Discourse* (Green, 1999b), a book that earned widespread recognition, explains in detail Green's differences from Lacan. In contrast to Lacan's theory, which denied theoretical status to affect when it defined the unconscious as being "structured like a language" and asserted that it was composed homogeneously of linguistic signifiers, Green postulated the "heterogeneity of the psychoanalytic signifier". In so doing, he deepened Freud's distinctions between diverse types of representations and affect, revised post-Freudian contributions (e.g., Hartmann, Klein) and proposed personal conclusions.[2]

Green also distinguishes two modes of functioning of affects: bound to the representational chain or unbound from it and consequently interfering with symbolisation and overwhelming the associative channel. The unbound mode generates the unrepresentable dimension of the affects. The theme of the unrepresentable (and of unrepresentable states) as a central issue of the theory of the negative is henceforth described in three aspects: as pure psychic energy (the psychical representative of the drive, the id's drive motion, unconscious affect) and, therefore, heterogeneous and irreducible to representation, as the unrepresentable but complementary opposite of representation, that is to say, de-cathexis at the service of Eros which creates the blank (absence or spacing between elements), and, finally, death drive and negative narcissism: the negative's destructive aspect, the radical antagonist/enemy of representational binding and its mode of creating meaning.

The view of "analytic discourse" as being co-created by analyst and patient enriches the definition of the analytic object as "living discourse" (verbal and non-verbal communication charged with drive, composed of words, thing representations, images, affects, gestures, acts, etc.). Analytic discourse is also seen as determined by the setting, which makes it *"a supine word addressed to a hidden interlocutor"*.[3] This definition highlights the negative dimension of the setting, which limits action and perception while encouraging hypercathexis of representations and their intrapsychic and intersubjective transference.

The borders of analysability, and the expansion of the clinical field

"The analyst, symbolization, and absence in the analytic setting" (Green, 1975) was written for the 1974 International Congress in London. The Congress programme committee asked for contrasting papers by Leo Rangell (supported by Anna Freud) and Green, to serve as the basis for the plenary session on "Changes in psychoanalysis practice and experience: theoretical, technical and social implications". Bergman (1999) wrote that some debates determine the direction of the history of psychoanalysis and, thus, acquire the status of landmarks events. The London debate was one such landmark: one that can be seen—in my view—as the beginning of contemporary psychoanalysis.

In his London paper (later included in *On Private Madness*) Green (1975) proposed a dialectical view of the history of psychoanalysis, where the negative is also always at work. He stated that psycho-analysis was in crisis due to external conflicts (in the relation with society), internal conflicts (the post-Freudian fragmentation into Schools, whose decline is already visible), and serious new challenges in the clinical field derived from the already acknowledged predomi-nance of borderline cases (over neurotic cases), which had become the "typical" patients of the contemporary era.

In order to acknowledge—and attempt to overcome—the crisis of psychoanalysis, Green began by historicising it. His vision of the parallel evolution of analytic theory and technique led him to distin-guish three movements that corresponded to three theoretical–clinical models: Freudian, post-Freudian, and contemporary. His description of this last model—which implies a goal of overcoming the impasse and limits of the two others—constituted his initial formulation of the project for a contemporary psychoanalysis, conceived as a new programme of investigation: the study of borderline states and the dynamics at the limits of analysability, focusing on their representational functioning (and dysfunctions) within the analytic setting.

The 1975 paper presents at least four novelties: (1) after Freudian studies centring on the neuroses and post-Freudian studies focusing on the psychoses, a new type of "paradigmatic case" is defined: the borderline state; (2) the setting (or frame) is introduced as a technical and epistemological concept (i.e., the setting partly determines the construction of the analytic object, and so is foundational for the analytical process); (3) the representational process is defined as the basic psychic function, making it the True North of the analyst's listening.

The fourth novelty is the redefinition of analysability, which is no longer determined in relation to a psychopathological diagnosis of the patient's intrapsychic functioning. Instead, it is determined on the basis of the possibilities of the patient–analyst couple to institute a setting, establish an analytic relation, and create an analytic object. (The latter is a term derived from the field theory of Willy and Madeleine Baranger.) The limits of analysability are seen as determined on the patient's part by the limitations of the patient's representational capacity; on the analyst's part, they correspond to the limits of the analyst's analytic imagination (figurability) and working through of countertransference.

In this context, the setting becomes an "analyser of analysability". The need to modify technique with these patients is accorded a central place. Inspired by Winnicott's theory of the transitional, Green suggests the need to use—and if necessary modify—the setting as a potential space. Its variations are justified when they facilitate the representational process.

As Bergman (1999) wrote, "Green took the invitation to the London congress as the opportunity to create a new model to supplement Freud's model of neurosis[4] as the negative of perversion. The new theoretical model was based on borderline patients". Green points out that the work of the negative changes in borderline functioning: castration anxiety and repression no longer play a central role as the major mechanism of defence.

"The implicit model of borderline states lead us back to the duality of separation anxiety/intrusion anxiety. The patient suffers from the combined effects of persecutory intrusive objects and depression consequent of the loss of an object" (Green, 1975).

To deal with this double anxiety, the borderline patient depends upon four characteristic defence mechanisms: splitting, de-cathexis, expulsion through action, and somatisation. These four modalities of the work of the negative correspond to a predominance of negative narcissism and reflect the latter's pressure towards destructive delinking. These defence mechanisms "short-circuit" the process of representation and disrupt the binding work of Eros. As a result, the borderline transference is an unstable dynamic mixture of representable and non-representable transference movements.

The series of papers included in *Life Narcissism, Death Narcissism* (Green, 2001b) and *On Private Madness* (Green, 1986) develop and consolidate the original conception of the functioning and treatment of borderline cases. Green proposes that we replace the diagnostic category "borderline" with that of the more colourful, descriptive designation of "private madness", asserting that the latter is not a psychopathological classification, but is, instead, a clinical structure inherent in a passionate transference. That is, for Green, private madness is the expression of intertwined and conflicting life passions and death passions.

In his programmatic paper, "Passions and vicissitudes of passions", Green (1986) emphasised the difference between private madness and psychosis, noting the central role of archaic sexual drives in the former, which differs from the predominance of destructive drives in the latter. In so doing, he rejected the implicit post-Freudian model of psychosis as the most useful guide to the understanding and treatment of borderline states. Thus, Green openly disagrees with the psychopathological definition of borderline cases in American psychiatry and psychoanalysis based on a relation with certain psychoses, especially schizophrenia, and with the post-Kleinian theory of the "psychotic core", which he criticised throughout his work as a wrong answer to a real problem.

The dead mother

"The dead mother" (Green, 2001c) constructed a paradigmatic figure of contemporary clinical thinking and became a major reference point for what, within Green's system, is clinical work with emptiness or the negative. From the metapsychological perspective, the text states in its first and second sections its ambitious purposes: (1) to introduce a theoretical structural equivalent of the dead father concept for the maternal function and (2) to propose a "structural theory of anxiety", based on the differentiation between "red anxiety" (linked to the libidinal body, and the imaginary menace of a bleeding wound), black anxiety (linked to hate), and the "white or blank anxiety" (linked to a loss at the level of primary narcissism).

For the first time since 1967, Green revisited and developed his theory of the framing structure. In the section entitled "Metapsychological hypothesis", he conceptualised the failure in the dead mother complex of its ego structuring function, explaining how narcissistic trauma impedes the organisation of the framing structure, and describing the specificity of its central consequence: blank mourning. His theorisation of "negative narcissism (or death narcissism)" aims to clarify conceptually (and orientate technically) clinical work with what Green calls "the blank series":

> corresponding to the negative hallucination, blank mourning, the feeling of emptiness, understood as resulting from a massive and temporary decathexis of the primary object (expression of the destructiveness of the death drive) which has affected the structure of primary narcissism and has left marks in the unconscious in the form of psychic holes. (Green, 2001c)

This extraordinary article, his most internationally recognised text, combines, conjugates, and condenses the diverse theoretical–clinical axes or perspectives developed up to that time (and announces others to be developed over several decades). As occurs with other densely complicated, albeit "successful" texts, simplified readings are quite frequent, and tend to complex concepts into the commonplace. It is worth indicating some of his original force-ideas that tend to be overlooked in this type of reading. (See also Levine and Migliozzi, this volume.)

The complex of the dead mother does not present as an overtly depressive clinical picture, but is revealed in the transference, generally after a long period of treatment. It assumes the form of a "transference depression" (a term coined as an equivalent of transference neurosis) based upon a previously unrecognised infantile or childhood depression.

The "dead mother" is not a version of Winnicott's not "good enough mother". In contrast to the latter, Green gives to destructivity and psychosexuality a central role, articulating and elucidating the complex using his notions of narcissism and the representation processes. For instance, the "impossible mourning" is not only due to narcissistic negative identification with the depressed mother, but also to the failure of separation from her as an *incestuous* object. The dead mother is the object of timeless, unrenounceable, archaic "mad passion" (private madness). Green states that the ultimate technical key of the analysis of the dead mother complex concerns the "frozen love" that preserves the maternal imago in a kind of hibernation in which the (erotic and thanatotic) vampirist position alternates between subject and object. Frozen love keeps the maternal imago occupying the framing structure and, therefore, interferes with symbolisation and mourning: this is one of the reasons for the blank mourning. Clearly, this mode of theorising is very far from that of Winnicott.

In the dead mother complex, the trauma is provoked by the massive, unexpected, and inexplicable loss of maternal love of a mother who is still physically present but is affectively absent, emotionally "frozen" with her child, because of her mourning. Green states that if cathexis is what makes life meaningful, the maternal massive de-cathexis of the baby breaks his feeling of life continuity and aliveness. Deadness at the core of this complex is the bi-product of the negative identification with the depressed mother, the internalisation of her emptiness, and the blankness provoked by the mother's emotionally withdrawing from the child inducing his de-cathexis of representative processes as a means of defence.

The main clinical difficulty encountered is that any direct interpretation of this complex provokes a blanking out of thought and/or feelings of emptiness. Thus, Green questioned both the technical adequacy of the Kleinian systematic interpretation of transference, and the distant and silent attitude of the classic Freudian analyst (the so-called "rule of silence", which is followed in France by Lacanians and non-Lacanians alike).

The alternative technique developed by Green, which is an original synthesis of four models—the Freudian model of dream interpretation, the Winnicottian model of playing, the Bionian model of reverie and containment functions, and post-Lacanian historicisation—is mainly based on what he calls the "interpretative process" that spreads out along several sessions. In his paper "Silence in psychoanalysis" (1990a), he describes that process as the co-construction of an intersubjective dialogical matrix, based on the prioritisation of the analytic couple's cathexis of the work of representation. The aim of this process is to make thinkable the subject's conflicts and foster the precondition for transference interpretation by helping to build a consistent and competent preconscious functioning.

The next step in Green's elaboration of technique appears in "La capacité de reverie et le mythe étiologique" [The etiological myth and the reverie function] (Green, 1990b), and is probably one of the clearest descriptions of the historicising dimension in his original clinical thinking. There, Green enriches his vision of the interpretative process by articulating it within an enlarged conception of construction (shared with other post-Lacanian authors such as Piera Aulagnier and Jean Laplanche) as *construction of the history of the analysis*, asserting that the latter helps to create an intermediate zone that is a necessary bridge for the interpretative process to address the consequences of early pre-verbal traumas.

> What does the analyst's listening consist in? First, in understanding the manifest content of what is said, a necessary precondition for all that follows; then, and this is the fundamental stage, in *imaginarising* the discourse: not only imagining it, but also including in it the imaginary dimension, construing what is implicit in such a discourse differently, in the *mise-en-scène* of understanding. In the following step, the analyst will unbind the linear sequence of this chain by evoking other fragments of sessions: recent ones (perhaps of the last session), less recent ones (from months ago), and, finally, much older ones (such as a dream from the beginning of the analysis). The analyst has to be the archivist of the *history of the analysis* and search the records of his *preconscious memory*; to this end, he will call his associations to mind at all times. Such is the backdrop against which the analyst's capacity for reverie is developed. Such capacity grows in the final step, that of *rebinding*, which will be achieved by selecting and recombining the elements thus gleaned to give birth to the countertransferential phantasy, which is supposed to meet the patient's transferential phantasy. (Green, 1990b, pp. 416–417, translated for this edition)

The work of the negative in the analyst's listening processes is central: in the unbinding of manifest content movement and in the latency of the preconscious memory (potentially open to memories from all periods of time). One can perceive in the above quotation—from a paper devoted to both an homage and a serious critique of Bion's notion of reverie—the decisive differences between the post-Freudian notion and use of countertransference (the central concept of technique, centred in the "unconscious communication") and Green's contemporary redefinition and utilisation of it as part of a more complex view of the listening function.

Revisiting the metapsychological foundations

The 1990s were characterised mainly by potent conceptual innovations and the systematisation of Green's general theoretical–clinical conception. This introduced two "meta-concepts", or conceptual axes. The first, in 1989, was that of *thirdness*, which renewed his view of symbolisation, in the sense that it enabled the articulation and deepening of a number of previously proposed "tertiary" notions, such as the "theory of generalised triangulation with substitutable third" (a third object called "the other of the object" that is not necessarily the father) the "tertiary process", etc.

The negative is at the heart of thirdness. The major background for this conceptual (or meta-conceptual) axis is in his extensive Report: "Le langage dans la psychoanalyse" [Language in psychoanalysis] (Green, 1984), in which he returns to, develops, and radically deepens the notion of "tertiary processes". In 1971, the latter were introduced to explain the analyst's "normality" and reflective thought as processes establishing relations and complementarity between primary and secondary processes. In 1984, Green postulated that tertiary processes are the foundation of symbolisation as a dynamic and transformational process, which, in its minimal, triadic form may be summarised by the sequence "cathexis–decathexis–re-cathexis". In this way, the poeisis of meaning and signification finds its root and motor in positive and negative movements of the drives.

> Lacan was wrong when he linked the symbolic to language—since it's actually to the psyche that the symbolic is consubstantially joined . . . What Lacan tried to do was to surpass Freud in the conceptualisation that the latter essayed when he opposed the primary and the secondary processes. However, this kind of "improvement" through the

Symbolic excluded not only the signified but the affect. We proposed a different solution. We postulate the existence of relationship mechanisms between the primary and secondary processes, which circulates in both directions: we call them tertiary processes and attributed them to the preconscious of the first "topographical scheme" and to the unconscious Ego of the second. Therefore, the symbolic order is based not on language, but on all the bindings–unbindings–rebindings that operate in the three agencies of the psychic apparatus. (Green, 1984, translated for this edition)

In this study dedicated to elucidating the status and functioning of language in psychoanalysis (in contrast with Lacanian extrapolation of psychoanalysis from linguistic theories), Green developed a meta-psychological elucidation of the analytic setting that, to my knowledge, is unique in the history of our discipline.

To continue with our guiding thread, we note that the thinking of the negative finds its place in the definition of language itself in the setting, in the sentence that states, "the analytic word un-mourns language". The explanation of this sentence is simple in the context of French psychoanalytic culture. It implies that the patient's verbalisation in transference produces a hyper-cathexis of repressed representations that redeems Hegel's maxim (quoted by Lacan), "the word is the death of the thing".

A short time later, Green published what he considered to be his most original book, *The Work of the Negative* (1999a). His elaboration of its structuring and destructuring dimensions ranged from the most "abstract" speculation on destructive drives to the most "concrete" consideration of extreme situations in clinical work, and included a complete revision of the defence mechanisms and the conception of the ego. The first three chapters situated the idea of the negative historically in the works of Hegel, Lacan, Bion, Winnicott, and, especially, Freud. The fifth chapter corresponded to his short 1984 lecture, "Death drive, negative narcissism, de-objectalizing function", in which he presented the latter concept for the first time, placing it in the series of the negative. The following chapters presented diverse innovative developments revealing the heterogeneity of the field of the negative: negative therapeutic reaction in the light of narcissism and masochism, splitting (from disavowal to subjective dis-commitment in borderline cases), the hallucinatory and negative hallucination, and sublimation.

Two and three years later, "La causalité psychique" [Psychical causality] (Green, 1995c) and *Propédeutique* (Green, 1995d) responded to the expectations of many readers who wanted an integrated presentation of André Green's theoretical thinking. In these writings, we find the "new Greenian metapsychological foundations" (to paraphrase Jean Laplanche's book title) that are composed, schematically, along five axes: (1) the drive–object pair, which articulates the intrapsychic with the intersubjective (in its centre are the notions of the objectalising and the de-objectalising functions as modern reformulations of the Freudian theory of life and death drives); (2) the generalised theory of representation, which expands Freudian theory so that it includes the body, affects, thought, otherness, and the social; (3) an expanded topography—in which the limit is a concept—that articulates the double conflict, ego–id and ego–object/Other; (4) thirdness: a meta-conceptual axis that ranges from the theory of "open triangulation with a substitutable third party" to third party processes; (5) the work of the negative.

The turning point of the year 2000

The "turning point of the year 2000" (an expression coined by Green) is distinguished by the project for a new contemporary paradigm needed to overcome what Green and many others felt to be the crisis of psychoanalysis.

> The historians of psychoanalysis may mark the beginning of the 2000s by designating in our discipline what I propose to call the turning point of the millennium. Today, when some anxiously await the death of psychoanalysis, I, for one, see signs of a rebirth. (Green, 2006, translated for this edition)

Green pointed out that the crisis of post-Freudian psychoanalysis is a "melancholic" one that carries the mark of interminable mourning for Freud's death. In a symptomatic way, each important post-Freudian author has attempted to replace him as the leading figure, and each militant movement has tried to revive the original situation of the pioneers and the founding father. Ego psychology, self psychology, the Kleinian and Lacanian movements have repeated the same process which consists in establishing their own reductionist model, transforming it into dogma, generalising a particular technique, and idealising the leader of their school. The project of a new contemporary paradigm, according to Green, aspires to go beyond this repetitive dynamic.

> Here is the programme on which we should reflect. We should forge pathways between the foundations of the psychoanalysis and the limits of the analysable, forcing our thought to move between contradictory polarities, to respond to the need to imagine today what analytic practice is, across the whole field and the various situations offered by the experience. (Green, 2000, p. 46, translated for this edition)

Green's aim was to collectively construct and use a new disciplinary matrix, to articulate certain questions and certain key ideas to orientate a theoretical and clinical work, and to give the conceptual frame to a renewed programme of investigation that recognised the specific challenges of the contemporary era. For instance, the end of "the kingdom of the couch" (Green), and the rise of face-to-face and other setting variations.

His contemporary disciplinary matrix is founded on four axes. The first is a contemporary reading of Freud, "critical, historical, and problematic" (Laplanche, 1981), which again establishes Freudian metapsychology and method as the foundations of psychoanalysis. The second proposes a critical and creative synthesis of the major post-Freudian contributions, as well as openness to pluralistic dialogue with the diverse current tendencies. The third corresponds to an expansion of the limits of analysability, an extension of the clinical field that considers "non-neurotic structures" the paradigmatic cases in today's practice. The fourth is a "tertiary" clinical model integrating Freudian models (centred on transference) and post-Freudian models (centred on countertransference), based on the concept of analytic setting (supported in turn by the analyst's "internal setting").[5] In this new model, Freudian vocabulary is also established as a *lingua franca* and common ground.

The book, *Key Ideas for a Contemporary Psychoanalysis: Misrecognition and Recognition of the Unconscious* (Green, 2005a), presents the project of this new paradigm, for which Green summarises his major contributions and places them at the service of the collective work programme required for its construction. It is worth emphasising that

Green (at that time the most highly recognised and translated living psychoanalyst) does not promote any "Greenian" school or discourse, but a contemporary theoretical–clinical model—Freudian, pluralist, complex, extended, cosmopolitan. In 2008, he persevered in his attempt to promote this project and the international group collaboration it required, by editing the extensive collective volume, *Les voies nouvelles de la psychanalyse* [New Roads in Analytic Therapy] (Green, 2008).

Green also continued his own investigations and reflections on themes of personal interest—for example, *Time in Psychoanalysis* (Green, 2002) and *Psychoanalysis: A Paradigm for Clinical Thinking* (Green, 2005b). Aside from their different themes, we find here his interest focused on two main questions: radical negativity in non-neurotic structures and the analyst's creative psychic work. Both questions lead to explorations that deepen his conceptualisation of the work of the negative, a subject that is also explored in other important books, such as *Pourquoi les pulsions de destruction ou de mort?* [Why Are There Destructive or Death Drives?] (Green, 2007) and *Illusions and Disillusions of Analytic Work* (Green, 2011), where he introduced a new reflection on "the interiorization of the negative".

In *Time in Psychoanalysis*, the dimension of the work of the negative that structures temporality is elucidated as a condition of "heterochrony", as Green studies the problem of unconscious traces of traumatic experiences that could not be re-cathected (to create a representation) because of the pain and disinvestment they automatically provoke. He also offers a thorough revision of the repetition compulsion, which is redefined as the "murder of time". In this context, the old idea of unconscious psychical holes provoked by de-cathexis of the blank series is revisited in relation to the theory of the unrepresentable.

In his succinct article, "Death in life" (Green, 2005b), included in *Clinical Thinking*, Green summarises his agreements and disagreements with Freudian postulates on the death drive. To overcome problems in connection with the latter term (and the biological, teleological, and mechanical ideas associated with it), Green proposed to refer to "destructive drives oriented internally or externally". His new metapsychological foundations led him to rethink the question in the double, intrapsychical, and intersubjective perspective. Green redefined the destructive drives as resulting from failure in the relation with the primary object, seeing them not as a permanent force, but, rather, a destructive potential, activated by excessive frustration in the vital, erotic "dialogue" with objects, a force whose aggressive aspect aims to deny the importance (and even the existence) of the object. In its extreme, negative narcissistic form, the destructive drive also aims to eliminate the very source of the drive.

The second thematic axis of this period corresponds to a renewed reflection on clinical work, and the development of a contemporary clinical model (see Urribarri, 2007). This axis is expressed through introduction of the notion of "clinical thinking". "Clinical thinking is defined as the original and specific mode of rationality emerging from practical experience. It corresponds to the work of thought set into motion in the relation of the psychoanalytic encounter" (Green, 2005b).

In this context, the notion of the analyst's "internal setting/frame" emerges as the seat of the analyst's psychical work in the session. It attempts to integrate evenly suspended attention, countertransference, and analytic imagination, based on consideration for the specific role of tertiary processes in listening and the analyst's work. The analyst needs a maximum of psychical vitality and creativity to sustain and overcome situations at the limits of analysability—those in which the unrepresentable and destructivity dominate the transference scene.

Green also takes into consideration the creative dimension of the work of the negative in order to introduce a new dimension of tertiary processes in clinical thought that he calls "the virtual". He links the latter to "negative capability" (a term from Keats quoted by Bion): that designates the ability to wait and to place understanding of the material into latency, calling this "the most fruitful and creative form of the work of the negative". Green concludes that interpretation depends on

> working through, which is an activity with a delayed effect (après-coup). [Therefore] it is best for it to emerge as aperture of the latency in which it was being kept. At that moment we see a kind of "positivation" of the negative or transformation of the negative into the virtual. With this precise movement, the [analyst's] unarticulated unconscious thought is articulated when it is spoken and accesses the level of language. (Green, 2005b)

This idea of a "positivation" of the negative is an example—a key one—of what the projected next book, to be entitled "The positive: the negative of the negative" was seeking to thematise. Sadly, its author could not finish it. Perhaps this theme may became an inspiration for us to develop the next part of his great legacy, as we strive to build the psychoanalysis of the future. I hope this overview of his vast work and the other essays in this volume might contribute to that immense and important project.

Notes

1. Green himself used this scheme for his 2011 article, "From private madness to pulsations of destruction. 20 years of On private madness" (RFP).
2. In Green's formulation, the term signifier—which he did not continue to use in future texts—is not a linguistic element, but a mere transport of psychical force and meaning. Affect is defined by Green as a "mode of primary symbolization" (like the affective opposition between pleasure and unpleasure). In this line, he inscribes affect in a view of the process of signification as being defined by a "logic of heterogeneity", determined by relations of irreducible and productive tension between force and meaning, the economic and the symbolic, the structural and the historical.
3. Green defined analytic discourse as that of a supine (lying down) speaker addressed to an unseen interlocutor.
4. "The model of neurosis" is an epistemological concept that Green coined to point out what he calls "the theoretical implicit model of (every) practice".
5. On the evolution and construction of Green's contemporary clinical model, see Urribarri, 2017.

References

Bergman, M. (1999). Changes in psychoanalysis practice and experience: theoretical, technical and social implications. In: G. Kohon (Ed.), *The Dead Mother: The Work of André Green*. London: Routledge.

Donnet, J.-L., & Green, A. (1971). *L'enfant de Ça* [The Child of That/Id]. Paris: Editions du Minuit.

Green, A. (1962). L'Inconscient freudien et la psychanalyse contemporaine. *Les Temps Modernes, 195*: 365–379.

Green, A. (1975). The analyst, symbolization and absence in the analytic setting (on changes in analytic practice an analytic experience). *International Journal of Psychoanalysis, 56*: 1–22. Reprinted in: *On Private Madness* (pp. 30–59). London: Hogarth Press, 1986.

Green, A. (1984). Le langage dans la psychanalyse. In: *Langages rencontres Psychanalytiques d'Aix-en-Provence 1983* (pp. 19–250). Paris: Les Belles Lettres.

Green, A. (1986). *On Private Madness.* London: Hogarth Press.

Green, A. (1990a). Le double limite. In: *La Folie privée.* Paris: Gallimard.

Green, A. (1990b). La capacité de reverie et le mythe étiologique. In: *La Folie privée. Psychanalyse des cas-limites.* Paris: Gallimard.

Green, A. (1995a). The constitution of parental imagos: negative hallucination of the mother and primary identification with the father. In: *Propédeutique.* Paris: Odile Jacob.

Green, A. (1995b). The logic of object (a) and Freudian theory: convergences and questions. In: *Propédeutique.* Paris: Odile Jacob.

Green, A. (1995c). *La causalité psychique.* Paris: Odile Jacob.

Green, A. (1995d). *Propédeutique. La metapsychologie revisitée.* Seyssel: Editions Champ Vallon.

Green, A. (1999a). *The Work of the Negative.* London: Free Association Books.

Green, A. (1999b). *The Fabric of Affect in the Psychoanalytic Discourse,* A. Sheridan (Trans.). London: Routledge.

Green, A. (2000). Le cadre psychanalytique. Son intériorisation chez l'analyste et son application dans la pratique. In: A. Green & O. F. Kernberg (Eds.), *L'Avenir d'une disillusion* (pp. 11–46). Paris: Presses Universitaires de France.

Green, A. (2001a)[1967]. Primary narcissism: state or structure? In: *Life Narcissism, Death Narcissism.* London: Free Association Books, 2001.

Green, A. (2001b). *Life Narcissism, Death Narcissism* London: Free Association Books, 2001.

Green, A. (2001c). The dead mother. In: *Life Narcissism, Death Narcissism.* London: Free Association Books.

Green, A. (2002). *Time in Psychoanalysis.* London: Free Association Books.

Green, A. (2005a). *Key Ideas for a Contemporary Psychoanalysis: Misrecognition and Recognition of the Unconscious,* A. Weller (Trans.). London: Routledge.

Green, A. (2005b). *Psychoanalysis: A Paradigm for Clinical Thinking,* A. Weller (Trans.). London: Free Association Books.

Green, A. (Ed.) (2006). *Unité et diversité des pratiques du psychanalyste. Colloque de la Société Psychanalytique de Paris*. Paris: Presses Universitaires de France.

Green, A. (2007). *Pourquoi les pulsions de destruction ou de mort?* [Why Are There Destructive or Death Drives?]. Paris: Panama.

Green, A. (2008). *Les voies nouvelles de la psychanalyse* [New Roads in Analytic Therapy]. Paris: Presses Universitaires de France.

Green, A. (2011). *Illusions and Disillusions of Psychoanalytic Work*, A. Weller (Trans.). London: Karnac.

Green, A. (2012). *La Clinique psychanalytique contemporaine*. Paris: Éditions d'Ithaque.

Kohon, G. (Ed.). (1999). *The Dead Mother: The Work of André Green*. London: Routledge.

Laplanche, J. (1981). L'angoisse. *Problématiques 1*.

Urribarri, F. (2007). The analyst's psychic work and the three concepts of countertransference. In: A. Green (Ed.), *Resonance on Suffering* (pp. 165–186). London: Karnac.

Urribarri, F. (2011, 2010). Postscript. Clinical passion, complex thinking: towards the psychoanalysis of the future. In: A. Green, *Illusions and Disillusions of Psychoanalytic Practice*. London: Karnac.

Urribarri, F. (2017). On clinical thinking: the extension of the clinical field towards a new contemporary paradigm. In: R. Perelberg & G. Kohon (Eds.), *The Greening of Psychoanalysis: André Green's New Paradigm in Contemporary Theory and Practice* (pp. 133–150). London: Karnac.

CHAPTER SIX

The death drive and the work of the negative in André Green's work: metapsychology, clinical practice, and culture*

Cláudio Laks Eizirik, Luciane Falcão, and Zelig Libermann

Introduction

In an interview given to Dominique Eddé, published in the book *La lettre et la mort* (Green, 2004), when asked about the fact of being internationally renowned for his ideas on affect, Green says, "And if it is ever necessary to define me as the man of something, I'd say I'm the man of the drive. The drive that necessarily includes the affect" (p. 49, translated for this edition).

The broad and deep contact with André Green's scientific work authorises us to consider him one of the contemporary psychoanalysts who best articulated Freud's ideas with current psychoanalysis, portraying it through complex thinking. Green was capable of putting Freud's ideas into motion, broadening the way of seeing psychoanalysis, enabling new perceptions regarding the construction of the psychic apparatus, especially that of borderline or non-neurotic cases, which represent the typical patients of our time.

---

* Translated by Patrizia Cavallo.

His thinking helps us understand fundamental Freudian concepts and their relation with the ideas of post-Freudian authors (referring both to the convergences and to the divergences) and with the problems of psychoanalytic clinical practice.

Green's work is located in a metapsychological dimension that involves two complementary notions: a model of mental functioning and clinical thinking. One of the main elements of his thinking is the concept of drive, formulated by Freud, and the articulation of the drive–object pair, that is, the drive assembly, as he called it, without which we could not think about metapsychology. This drive assembly enables the construction of the representational frame. In his last book published while still alive, *Du signe au discours*, he wrote,

> As for the unconscious representation, a double system of representation exists. Thing-representation and object-representation, which promote satisfaction, arise from the external world. While the psychic representative of the drive that demands satisfaction arises from the body. As long as we do not understand the coalescence between these two kinds of inscription, nothing can be understood about psychoanalysis. (Green, 2011b, p. 43–44, translated for this edition)

According to Green,

> Freud's originality lies in having established a relation between the drive and affect system (affect intended as drive discharge) and language . . . And I absolutely do not believe that we can dispense with it [the concept of drive]. (1990d, p. 35)

One of the central elements of Green's work is exactly the value he confers on the concept of drive: the ideas regarding the life drives and the death drives and the references to the drive–object pair: the drive assembly (Green, 2002b).

Setting out from the new drive dialectic presented by Freud in *Beyond the Pleasure Principle* (1920g), Green developed a theoretical outline that allows us to understand the life and the death (or destructive), drives, in terms of the psychic functions they perform (objectalisation and disobjectalisation, respectively) and, based on these functions, use them in clinical practice in connection with the role of the object beyond its purely biological aspects.

In this context, Green also proposes changing the theoretical framework regarding the death, or destructive, drives. In the dynamics and heterogeneity of the psychic apparatus, the death drive is a force that will act as a disinvestment, that will disobjectalise and will not allow representational paths to be psychically constructed.

The idea of the death drive as a disinvestment force extends the debate beyond the issues of aggression, destruction, sadism, etc., linked to this drive force. Disinvestment as an expression of the death drive made the connection with another mental phenomenon possible, which was studied in depth by André Green, that is, the work of the negative, both in the field of the individual's functioning and in his or her collective expressions, such as destructiveness and evil.

Considering the above, this chapter aims to point out the connection of the phenomena of evil and destructiveness in Green's work, taking as a starting point the study on the drives and on the death drive and their connection with the work of the negative.

The drives

As Freud himself said, the theory of the drives represents a mythology of psychoanalysis (1933a, pp. 57–80), and the death drive is a concept that "received little acceptance even among psychoanalysts" (Freud, 1937c, p. 246). Maybe for this reason, several generations of post-Freudian psychoanalysts have considered the drive as a purely biological notion and as being solipsistic in nature. However, André Green's conceptions contributed to emphasise the psychic aspects contained in the concept of drive, its integration with the object relations theory and, mainly, to restate its clinical application.

First, while highlighting Freud's idea (1915c) that the drive is located between soma and psyche, Green (1990a) considers it a concept that must be understood "according to processes of transformation of *energy* and *symbolisation* (force and meaning)" (p. 146, translated for this edition, original italics) and, therefore, it would be the first element of a process that starts in the body and reaches thought. The drive is a part of the phenomenon of representation, which Green (1990d) considers almost a synonym of psyche: "One cannot build anything without conceptualising this mixture of force and meaning through the mediation of *representance*" (Green, 2000, p. 31, original italics).

This psychic aspect of the drive stands out in his elaboration regarding the action of the life drives and the death drives, a development that help us integrate Freud's complex ideas, which can be found first hand in the text *Beyond the Pleasure Principle* (1920g), and the difficulties that we face daily when attending patients in whom the characteristics of negative narcissism predominate, the latter described by Green in his book *Narcissime de vie, narcissisme de morte* [*Life Narcissism, Death Narcissism*] (1983).

According to Green, the expression of the life drives and the death drives is characterised by processes of binding and unbinding, respectively. The primordial objective of the life drive is what he called objectalising function, that is, the capacity not only to create a relation with the object (internal or external), but to transform structures into objects, to attribute the status of object to that which has no quality, property, or attribute of object, on the condition that only one characteristic is maintained in the psychic work carried out: the significant investment, "even when the object is no longer directly in question" (Green, 1988a, p. 64, translated for this edition). The transformation of structures, which assigns them qualities and attributes of object, coincides not only with the idea that the ego may become an object of the id, but that even the investment itself could be objectalised (Green, 1988a; Libermann, 1999).

On the contrary, the death drive aims to perform a disobjectalising function through unbinding (Green, 1988a, p. 65). In such a way, the attack is launched not only against the relation with the object, but also against the ego and the investment itself that had been objectalised, that is, against the capacity to seek binding. Thus, the destructiveness of the death drive manifests itself through disinvestment (Falcão, 2015; Green, 2007a; Libermann, 1999).

Therefore, Green believes that apart from containing a psychic nature, the notion of drive is inseparable from the concept of object. The existence of the latter is not only defined by its presence in the real world. Because it is "only inside, also outside" (Botella & Botella, 2001, p. 125), it needs to be moved by the subject's investment: ". . . I would say that there is no object that is not invested and moved by the drives . . ." (Green, 2000, p. 10). However, Green goes further, showing us all the complexity of his thinking in articulating the theory of the drives and the object relations theory:

The construction of the object leads retroactively to the construction of the drive, which constructs the object. The construction of the object is only conceivable if it is cathected by the drive. However, when the object has been constructed in the psyche, this leads to the construction of the drive *après coup*, the missing object giving birth to the conception of the drive as an expression of the subject. One then sees that there is a possibility of conceiving desire or of being aware of the instinctual animation that has given birth to desire and to the object. (Green, 2000, p. 17)

Green believes that the inevitable separation between subject and object is accompanied by changes within the ego. The figure of the mother as primary object of fusion fades, leaving room for the ego to make its own libidinal investments. However, the image of the mother does not disappear completely. It persists, in this new moment, as a *representation of affect* (Green, 1973; Falcão, 2013) that provides security regarding the love of the object and also the possibility of bearing its absence. Thus, the possibility of creating an internal space emerges:

The primary object becomes a "framing-structure" for the Ego, sheltering the negative hallucination of the mother. . . . The space which is thus framed constitutes the receptacle of the ego; it surrounds an empty field, so to speak, which will be occupied by erotic and aggressive cathexes, in the form of object representations. This emptiness is never perceived by the subject, because the libido has cathected the psychical space. Thus it plays the role of primordial matrix of the cathexes to come. (Green, 2005a, pp. 165–166)

The above extract, referred to in "La mère morte" [The dead mother] (1983), also reflects a key topic addressed (1986, 1990a) throughout his work: the notions of borders, borderline states, and patients with non-neurotic organisations. We can consider that Green's contributions regarding psychic borders and borderline states represent a vivid example of his thoughts on the clinical usefulness of the concept of drive.

Green, in his model of the mind, proposed the idea of a psychic apparatus with a *double limit* structure (Green, 1990a,b), one that separates the inside from the outside and the other dividing the constituents of the internal world. This conception refers to the notion of spaces, of territories. However, in his opinion, dealing with spaces without considering what moves the psychic is equivalent to referring to lifeless spaces.

For this reason, he argues that the association between the topical and the dynamic points of view implies the notion of spaces animated by movements that circulate displacing borders: "Herein lies the problem of the drive . . . The problem with the drive is that it is an excitation that puts itself in motion and transposes a space" (Green, 1990d, p. 17).

This idea is in line with the role of id in Freud's structural theory. In contrast to the first topography, in which a model of bound energies predominates (Libermann, 2010), the id constitutes a perennial source of energy emission, "a chaos, a cauldron full of seething excitation" (Freud, 1933, pp. 81–111). It *pulsates* continually, demanding from the psychic structure a constant effort to direct both the energies striving in favour of the investment and those that struggle for unbinding.

The idea that the drive moves itself and transposes spaces represents an essential element for Green: the inseparable drive–object pair. Psychism is neither based predominantly on the subject pole nor on the exclusive vertex of the object. The vicissitudes of psychic life, the result of the inevitable matches and mismatches between the drives and their objects, are located between the intrapsychic and the intersubjective (Green, 2002b).

Death drive and the work of the negative in André Green's work[1]

In 2010, Green published *Illusions et désillusions du travail psychanalytique* [Illusions and Disillusions of Psychoanalytic Work], in which, after fifty years of psychoanalytic practice, he aims to reflect upon some of the least fruitful experiences of his *metier*, articulating them theoretically. Green describes some memories of disappointing experiences. According to him, despite being disappointing, these memories were not bad. He did not regret having treated those patients, even when he became impatient due to their resistance or obstinacy "in a period when I still ignored what I would later call the work of the negative" (2010, p. 172, translated for this edition).

The work of the negative is central in Green's work. Its essence is based on a double dimension: structuring (the hallucinatory realisation

of the wish) and destructuring (predominance of the negative hallucination of the mother). This double dimension goes from a more *abstract*
speculation on the drives to a more *concrete* consideration of borderline
situations—situations of clinical impasse. This psychic negative allows
a double simultaneous approach:

1. The negative of Freud's first topography: it belongs to a dynamic
    field of representations and psychoneuroses, implying a work of
    repression.
2. The negative of Freud's second topography: Green's focus, in
    which the emergence of the negative cannot be deduced from the
    causes of neurosis themselves or from personal history, such as
    repression.

In Green, the work of the negative implies grouping together
the mechanisms of repression, splitting or disavowal, denial, and foreclosure or rejection. The dynamicity of the framing structure of the
ego and the negative hallucination of the mother is essential in this
work. Green conceived the framing structure of the ego as "an enclos-
ing circuit that demarcates opposed spaces (internal and external) . . .
it could be regarded as a structure providing a frame for the psychical space, capable of gathering and inscribing representations as well
as making them interact" (1999, p. 280).

For Green, the mother is caught in the empty framework of negative hallucination and becomes a framing structure for the subject
himself. The subject constructs himself in the empty framework of the
negative hallucination of the invested object. However, the absence of
the mother may be represented and, therefore, become a part of the
subject's psychic structures. It is very clear that it is not the perceptive
apprehension of the mother that can be internalised, because it is
secondary and marked by her presence. We need to consider what
happened before this possibility. It is here that the intervention of a
process in the form of negative hallucination can be observed (Green,
1995a, p. 80).

In the paper "A metapsychological supplement to the theory of
dreams" (1917d), Freud states that the solution of the hallucination
problem should be preceded by that of negative hallucination. Initially,
Green addresses this idea from Freud and says that negative hallucination "is the obverse of that of which the hallucinatory realization of

the wish is one side" (2005a, p. 55). Progressively, he makes this proposition complex, condensing the original hallucinatory and the wish, such as absence. In his book *Le discours vivant* [The Living Discourse] of 1973, he broadens the concept and states, "Negative hallucination not as absence of representation, but as the representation of the absence of representation" (Green, 1973, pp. 335–336, translated for this edition).

In 2002, Green reviews the concept of negative hallucination and further develops his thinking:

> In the past I defined it as representation of the absence of representation, but such a definition is perhaps subject to ambiguity inasmuch as it tends to preserve a confusion between representation and perception. (Green, 2005b, p. 218)

Green insists that the negative hallucination has to do with perception:

> Negative hallucination is the non-perception of an object or of a perceptible psychical phenomenon. It is thus a phenomenon involving the erasure of what should be perceived. In the past I defined it as representation of the absence of representation. (Green, 2005b, p. 218)

For him, the representation of the absence of representation is both that which makes it possible to better understand the notions of the id and the death drive and that which operates in the work of representance and through which the impulses of the id transform themselves in ego investment, thus ensuring the permanence of representations. There is a fundamental transformational value here. Without this negative, only the quantitative would exist, only a permanent and violent motor or hallucinatory discharge.

At first sight, due to its perplexing nature, the representation of the absence of representation is a concept elaborated by Green and that, still today, is difficult to understand. Sara Botella (2013) reminds us that it is apparently contradictory, uniting representation and absence of representation. However, it becomes more accessible if it is understood less in its literal content than as an attempt to express, by rational means, something that it is not.

It would be a primordial hallucinatory entity, its heterogeneous elements being the hallucination of the wish and the hallucination of the absence, which feed on a dialogical relationship. The maternal object would then disappear as a primary object of fusion, leaving room for the framing structure of the ego, capable of sheltering representations. Cesar Botella emphasises that, with this form of inseparability, of hallucinatory absence and hallucinatory wish, the foundations of psychism could be seen as having a hallucinatory nature. As we shall observe, this extension of the primordial paradigm introduced by Green enriches psychoanalysis (C. Botella, 2013).

Until the end of his life, Green considered the work of the negative of paramount importance in order to think, from a clinical point of view, about cases characterised by a subjectal unbinding of the ego. To understand these patients, it is necessary to identify what he called the internalisation of the negative, that is, the early introjection of negative factors that lead the individual to prefer forms of destructive activity to the positive forms of the pursuit of pleasure (Green, 2011a).

Understanding Green's trajectory requires the reader to have a consistent grasp of Freud's thinking. For example, based on Freud's notion of drive dialectic, Green (2001) proposes studying the operations of the psychic apparatus, beginning with the work, movement, force and the drive's interrelationship with the object. In addition to primary decussation (*decussation primaire*),[1] Green introduces the double drive reversal (*double retournement pulsionnel*),[3] which he considers to be the basic model of psychoanalysis. It is during this period that Green proposes the notion of narcissism as a structure: narcissism as the scaffolding (*un échafaudage*) on which the psyche will structure itself and develop. Here we come face-to-face with a fundamental change in the theoretical framework of the death drive. In the dynamism and heterogeneity of the psychic apparatus in Green's conceptions, the death drive becomes a force that acts to disobjectalise and prevents the psychical constitution of representational paths. Attack and aggression, which Klein considers original elements, are secondary elements in Green's account of the psychic apparatus. Green extends and reformulates Freud's theory and includes a new dialectic: life narcissism/death narcissism. This death narcissism is related to the actions of the death drive (Falcão, 2015).

According to Freud (1920g), the original manifestation of sadism is an effect of the destructive drive, the first drive that seeks to destroy Eros's narcissistic relationship with its own self. Freud said that even a person's self-destruction will not be bereft of libidinal satisfaction. In 1924, Freud considered masochism the central expression of the death drive; aggression is projected outwards (according to the narcissistic libido model) (Freud, 1924c). Elaborating on Freud's idea, Green (2007b, pp. 62–64) believes that whatever has survived the internal attacks of the death drive and is not deflected outwards as aggressiveness remains in the ego and becomes a mortal residue which, during the individual's life, will support that person's self-destructive tendencies.

Thus, Green hypothesises an original destructiveness with two orientations—one inward, one outward. In summary: sadism attacks the other, and masochism kills the subject (Green, 2007a).

Examples of these phenomena can be found in clinical work with patients with suicidal tendencies, or patients who are sadomasochistic, borderline, or anorexic, as well as those with severe narcissistic pathologies. Their "triumph" in destroying their own analyses exemplifies the results of the disobjectalising function. And negative narcissism as an aspiration to reach level zero is another expression of this disobjectalising function. This function enters into action each time the objects of the psyche lose their status, when their originality disappears, or when they are no longer valued. Once this happens, the objects are eliminated. Disinvestment is crucial (Green, 1983, 1988a, 1999, 1995b, 2007a). Green (2007b) maintains that to disobjectalise is to begin an action that makes drive evolution lose its ability to deal with the object's most distinguishing traits (p. 62).

Unlike Freud and Klein, Green does not see the death drive as a self-destructive function that expresses itself primitively and automatically. For Green (2002c, p. 319), the death drive does not always exist in an active state—the death drive can be silent. However, in particular circumstances, the death drive can be active and expressed as a destructive force that does not necessarily find an outlet (Falcão, 2015, p. 464).

As we have seen, Green supported the hypothesis of an original destruction with a dual orientation. This destructivity is unconscious most of the time. When painful experiences invade the psyche and cause the pleasure principle to fail, they give rise to painful, non-representable experiences, and to the fear of the original agony. Thus, destruction takes over the psyche. Green understood that in these cases we are closer to what Marty and de M'uzan (1962, 1967) called disorganisations than to actual regressions (Green, 2007a, pp. 204–205).

Back in the 1960s, Marty and de M'uzan (1962, 1967) proposed substituting the term "death instinct" with the phrase "counter-evolutionary disorganisation" because he maintained that the death instinct is engaged when stimuli become overwhelming. Concerning nomenclature, Green (2002c) also proposes a substitution: instead of death drive, he suggests "destructive drive", where aggression is directed inwards and outwards. Outward aggression is merely a fraction of those destructive energies, because destructivity is also internal. For Green, violence is a form of hopelessness that expresses despair and rage at its own impotence. Questioning this, Chervet (2012) asks if the notions of negativity and destructiveness are not equivalent. He also asks whether the death impulse and the destructive impulse might be interchangeable—could we not substitute one for the other?

Theory and clinical practice

The metapsychological approach to the concept of drive had an important impact on the integration of clinical practice and theory, not only in the cases of borderline patients, but also for our understanding of areas with primitive functioning in patients with neurotic structures. We would like to highlight some aspects of this integration arising from Green's work that contributed to the understanding and to the analytic practice when dealing with patients with borderline organisations.

First of all, Green was one of the psychoanalysts who contributed to transforming the concept of borderline cases, which, historically, has been influenced by psychiatric descriptions that considered this condition a threshold of psychotic diseases. His theory taught us that patients with borderline states are not necessarily people on the verge of psychosis. Instead, they are individuals with a "not only autonomous, but relatively stable" organisation (Green, 1990d, p. 12), who, most of the time, will not develop a frank psychosis.

A second aspect to consider is that Green helps us understand a disconcerting behaviour of these patients both in analytic sessions and in their relationships out of the setting. Faced with the permanent feeling that they are not understood, accepted, or have their needs met and their complaint regarding the impossibility of participating in other aspects of the analyst's life, it is surprising and bewildering to see rejection emerge (both in the form of aggressiveness and extreme anxiety); this happens when, in some moments, there is an affective mobilisation in the patient caused by the feeling of being understood and being closer to the analyst; this reaction, in our experience, could not be entirely understood in terms of the unconscious feeling of guilt, contained in the phenomenon of the negative therapeutic reaction described by Freud.

To understand this point, Green proposes the expression "double contradictory anxiety" (Green, 1990d, p. 13), which involves both separation anxiety and intrusion anxiety.[4] This is a drama experienced by these patients: on the one hand, how to find the ideal distance that avoids the feeling of abandonment and the intense and endless mourning, and, on the other, the experience of being invaded by the object, which is felt as threatening to the subject's own identity.

Due to the lability of their sense of identity, such patients experience a permanent dilemma: they seek closeness in order to feel accompanied and, at the same time, they seek distance that might protect them against the threat of invasion that a relationship means to them. In the psychoanalytic relationship, this oscillation represents a challenge for the analyst. With regard to the capacity for acceptance, we often feel we are on a sort of roller-coaster in which a moment of closeness might just represent the prelude to a free fall accompanied by a feeling of threat to our own psychic stability. The intensity of this dilemma can be assessed if we consider the paradox regarding the presence or the absence of the object in reality:

> ... especially in relation to borderline cases, it is not enough for the object to be present to avoid separation anxiety – I would even say that separation anxiety reaches its maximum degree when the object is present – and that, in the same way, intrusion anxiety does not manifest itself predominantly when the object is present, but exactly when it is not. (Green, 1990d, pp. 13–14)

This paradox is related to the internal experience of the presence–absence duality of the object, which is structured in primary relations and associated to separation experiences, which, in borderline patients, are linked to the feeling that just the negative is real: "After an overly extensive phase, the absence of the object would correspond to a loss, causing indifference *regarding its presence or absence, since reality, from that moment on, will be identified with the negativization of the object* (Green, 2002d, p. 284, original italics).

The negativisation process of the object described above involves the creation of an empty space that we can consider a sort of antithesis of the previously referred concept of framing structure. Negativisation leads to the creation of a different blank space, a result of the tendencies of disobjectalisation or disinvestment (considered by Green an expression of the death drive, as we have noted above), which will be filled by chronic feelings of emptiness and, often, by hate of life and of others, bringing about another feature associated to borderline states: the rationale of hopelessness.

The difficulty in maintaining affective bonds provokes insufficient representations in the individual's mind, resulting in intense anxiety that might lead the subject to fill the empty space with concrete manifestations. The possibility of overflow always exists, and the symbolic activity, essential to the construction of the domain of the psychic, could be replaced by the hallucinatory or by manifestations directed at the body or the act. Thinking loses its place.

We can consider the disobjectalising function (Green, 1995a) as belonging to the transference–countertransference relationship if we remember that when the subject–object separation did not take place adequately, and at the proper time, the experience of destructiveness is immeasurable. Green reminds us that this happens when the threat of having love withdrawn is greater than the baby can tolerate. This occasions intense destructive experiences in the baby related to the threat of losing love. The reactions to this threat are desperate attempts to bring the intolerable situation to a close, that is, bi-directional channelling of destructive energy coming from the failure to distinguish between subject and object (Green, 2002c, p. 314). Internal anxiety and tension will be directed outwards but within the setting. The *darstellbarkeit* ("presentification") (Kahn, 2012)), or the work of psychic "figurability" (Botella & Botella, 2001) will arise in analytic sessions and make an initial inscription possible (Chervet, 2013).

Of course, there are oscillations between fusion/non-distinction moments and separation/distinction moments. These situations allow us to understand that much fusion and separation is linked to the responses of the object and to the consequences. As Green (2002c, p. 321) maintains, the destruction of the drive is widely dependent on the response of the object.

Falcão (2015), to paraphrase Green on the objectalising and dis-objectalising functions, proposed the term "psychic functions of the setting" for the possibilities of transformations arising from the objectalising function in the analytic process. The psychic functions of the setting are necessary for the analytic process to mediate libidinal functions, that is, to create connections, Eros, as well as the analyst's drive activity.

By contrast, when the death drive brings about drive diffusion within the treatment, we end up with the disobjectalising function of the analytic process, where disconnecting forces attack the analytic process, creating resistance or death itself. Which drive forces will win out in each analytic process? Given the drive antagonism of the psychic apparatus, how can we think about the criss-crossing and strengthening of the drive forces as a double drive reversal and a primary decussation (Green, 2001) within the setting? In the analytic process, should one consider clinical practice, transference, and countertransference to mean the return to one's self through a detour brought on by confronting the familiar other (Green, 1988b)?

Influenced by Winnicott (1969, 1971), Green (1995a) proposed tertiary processes in which one finds three objects, two separate objects and another object corresponding to the union of two objects: the analytic object, which is a third object. This is the analytic third, an important concept used by diverse authors in contemporary psychoanalysis, mainly corresponding to what was proposed by Baranger and Baranger (1961–1962) as the analytic field.

In clinical practice, we use various techniques in dealing with transference and countertransference. The mental functioning experienced in the setting guides the analytic process: the mental functioning of primary and secondary processes, based on the drives of the analyst and of the patient. However, analytic work must also be based on movement, on the demand for work, on fortitude, not just on the unconscious. The disobjectalising function is at work in interrupting the associative chain of discourse (Falcão, 2015). The ego fragments, and this paralyses the capacity to think thoughts (Bion, 1962). One avoids contact with the primary objects, which in the past attacked or abandoned the patient. The negative therapeutic reaction is an example of disobjectalising whatever previously functioned as a link. Green's dead mother syndrome (1983) offers us a clinical example.

Today, transference is understood as being based on the past, coming from the present, *hic et nunc* (here and now) and that which *transports* (Green, 2011a). However, on the same page, Green describes transference as a double act, addressing both the word and the object: Green proposes that all psychic movements are translated through the act of verbalisation. These movements bring with them something beyond the word that, none the less, infiltrates the path of the word (Falcão, 2015, p. 472).

Keeping in mind Green's notion of negative narcissism, we propose that death in life comes about and takes over—silencing and paralysing the libido, which stops its movements in the psychic apparatus since it cannot engage in a give and take with the other. Death narcissism is death in a non-life. It is psychic non-constitution, the analytic non-processes (Falcão, 2015, p. 473).

Another important contribution provided by Green's ideas that goes beyond non-neurotic patients is the fact that contemporary psychoanalysis deals more and more with the presence of the analyst's mind and the analytic field he or she builds with each patient (Baranger & Baranger, 1961–1962; Bion, 1962). In this sense, each analytic process constitutes a fluctuation between different mental states, or moments of understanding and non-understanding (Joseph, 1983). To understand these fluctuations, the shared fantasies of the field and the bastions that are present in every analysis, the notions put forward by Green and presented above are an indispensable tool also when working with neurotic patients, because now we can dive with them into deeper psychic waters and more primitive mental states. Current analytic practice would not be the same without all these relevant notions that Green left us.

Green's contributions to understanding evil and destructiveness in culture

In the introduction to *Pourquoi les pulsions de destruction ou de mort?* [Why Are There Destruction or Death Drives?] Green (2007a) states that he had always agreed with Freud about the death drive, but that it was only when writing this book that he began to understand for the first time some of the complex issues put forward by the hypotheses regarding this concept.

Green (2007a) insists that nothing will be understood of Freud's thinking if we omit the idea that the erotic libido is bound to the aggressive and destructive libido. He focuses on the study of primary masochism, primal sadism, and that which they will be directed at and drafts a scheme referring to Freud's idea:

Primal sadism = Primal (primary) masochism → outward ejection → death residue → reintrojected → secondary masochism

In this draft, we can observe Freud's idea according to which the destinies of sadism and masochism are different. Symmetry is interrupted, but the effects of primary masochism (which carries the thesis and the antithesis, life and death) represent a danger to the individual's survival and not only to his psychic life. Freud concludes that even self-destruction cannot be produced without libidinal satisfaction. Self-destruction is, then, chained to Eros. Here, there is the difficult issue of the drive renouncement that Freud addresses in *Civilization and its Discontents* (1930a). Sadism or masochism arise from death or destructive drives. Eros is their common enemy, with which they will ally in the future (Freud, 1930a; Falcão, 2011; Green, 2007a).

In the third part of his book *Pourquoi les pulsions de destruction et de mort?* (Green, 2007a), titled "La pulsion de mort dans le champ social – Le malaise dans la culture", André Green further contributes to this topic by giving continuity to Freud's ideas. He proposes studying the issue by dividing it into four parts: death drive in culture (1), primal parricide (2), recent discussions over the cultural process (3), and death drive and language (4).

In *Moses and Monotheism* (Freud, 1939a), the civilisation processes and the individual developments go together. They converge towards the idea of the father's death. For Freud, recognising this death involves the reduction of the narcissistic satisfaction of being better than those who refuse to become aware. In *Moses*, Freud does not mention the death drive, despite the death of the father being the most emphasised topic. It was in *Civilization and its Discontents* (1930a) that the role of the aggressiveness released by the external authority denying the subject primary drive satisfaction first appeared. In this work, Freud highlights that the source of anxiety lies in the authority that has not been internalised and then assimilated to the superego.

Concerning this part of Freud's work, Green talks about an enigma and tries to understand it. For Freud, it is necessary to define a basic conflict, that between the child and the authority that prohibits, the castrating father. According to him, the conflict between the child, dominated by drives that seek only satisfaction, and the obstacle to the drive gratification is a fundamental complex, causing the threat of castration and the formation of the superego, resulting in unconscious guilt and need for punishment. However, the source of the conflict is still an issue. Would it be engendered by the powers of the aggressive forces that constitute the destructive drives, or would it be enough just to cope with the intensity of the conflicts based on their phylogenetic reference or the ineluctability of their appearance? (Green, 2007a; Falcão, 2011).

Green considers the conclusion of *Moses*, which also represents Freud's last words, a strong argument against any kind of naïve geneticism that tends to give more importance to what is older. Green comments on the structural path adopted by Freud as follows:

> An amazing issue of today's psychoanalysis. Freud knows very well that the mother exists, but it seems that he wants to tell us the father is another thing! He is the progress of mental life; he is what enlivens cultural life and he is the reference that men need, when the time has come, to turn against him, rebel and sentence him to death. Nothing similar happens regarding the mother. It is not that matricide is ignored or incest even less. The murder of the mother is nothing other than craziness. . . . Now, the choice is castration anxiety and fear of the father rather than the maternal dismemberment and seduction. And more, there is also the veneration of the father, the respect due to him, the tributes that are paid to him. The father is the dead father. The dead mother is another thing: an infinite, constantly recurring depression against life. (Green, 2007a, pp. 175–176, translated for this edition)

Evil and destructiveness have characterised human history throughout the centuries, whatever culture we consider. To be convinced of this, suffice to examine the succession of tyrants and villains that have existed and exist at all latitudes; it might be tempting to see in them the origin of this mysterious and enigmatic force that psychoanalysis has shown to inhabit and be an integral part of the psychic functioning of each human being.

Why evil? This question has challenged and aroused the interest of many philosophers, poets, artists, and writers. At once, several important names come to mind: Shakespeare, Dante and Milton, Bosch and Swift, Sade, Goethe, Hugo, Nietzsche, Rimbaud, or even Baudelaire, who wrote the *Les fleures de mal* [The Flowers of Evil] (2011).

Arendt (2009) offers us an implacable insight regarding evil. According to her, concentration camps and the extermination instigated by totalitarian regimes are like laboratories in which the fundamental belief of totalitarianism—that everything is possible—can be observed. The camps are not only designed for the extermination of people and the degradation of human beings, they also represent the horrifying experience of eliminating spontaneity itself as an expression of human behaviour and transforming human personality into a mere thing. Therefore, for her, human nature itself is at stake; and it seems that these experiences are not intended to transform man, but merely destroy him, creating a society in which, consequently, the banalisation of the *homo homini lupus* is brought about.

Among those who managed to escape from this hell, Primo Levi, Jorge Semprun, Elie Wiesel, and Imre Kertész also reflected upon aspects of evil and destructiveness. Reading their books provides us with a documental, sharp, and, at the same time, reflective perspective not only on their terrible experiences, but also on more sinister aspects of human nature. Memory, oblivion, the impossibility of understanding, the doubt regarding the essence of human nature, and the need not to forget are some of the topics that emerge from these painful and moving stories.

André Green also confronts this issue and asks himself: "Pourquoi le mal?" ["Why evil?"] (Green, 1990c). He highlights that destructiveness, which expresses itself in murder without passion, plays a crucial role and is different from sadism. In a cold-blooded crime, the murderer kills his victims, that is, his objects, without touching them, as if he were trying to deprive them of even the masochist pleasure that might be obtained from their wounds.

Annihilation, by transforming someone into nothing, consists in a brutal and frequently unconscious disinvestment of someone with whom the murderer has been, even yesterday, connected by love or hate; someone who becomes, from one day to next, almost a stranger. This is different from the hate that does not diminish over the years in as much as it is interwoven with the erotic libido, sharing the passion that the latter provokes. Therefore, the cold and cruel monster of destructiveness becomes one with most traditional figures of evil. Evil, thus, is insensitive to the pain of the other: it ignores the suffering of the other or, on the contrary, tries to increase it, thus showing its narcissistic roots.

When Green addresses the Holocaust as the most complete form of evil, he refers to a kind of evil that arises from disobjectalisation due to the death drive. Sadism impresses us less than the efficiency of the performance, and the cruelty seems less terrible than the eagerness for the order and cleanliness in the extermination.

Green's view, which is similar to Arendt's, makes us think about the almost aseptic efficiency of Nazism (upon which he reflected again in 2010), but also about the current weapons of remote destruction or the games that currently excite teenagers and adults due to their extra-ordinary capability to provoke remotely aseptic deaths, or about a James Bond film, *Skyfall*; there is no possible empathy in this exercise of evil that stimulates certain current forms of war (Eizirik, 2014).

However, it is especially *Macbeth* (Shakespeare, 1994[1608]) that draws his attention. For Green, the most tragic figure of evil, and without any doubt the most impenetrable one, is Macbeth. Actually, we could say *the Macbeths*, uniting the royal couple in just one person. Macbeth's thirst for murder has no explanation. This incursion into Shakespeare's theatre gives us the opportunity to reformulate an observation that experience constantly confirms. The darkness of certain souls, or their propensity to evil, is a powerful stimulant to the imagination. He repeatedly stresses one of the reasons for being fasci-nated by evil: we realise evil excites us intellectually and affectively; it stimulates the creative imagination of those whose task it is to produce and mitigates the tensions of those who consume leisure.

Green records a spirit of chivalry in the battlefields of the past, in which there was some respect for the enemy, and contrasts it with the situation in football stadia today, where what counts is to destroy the opponent, no matter how; for Green, we are permeated by evil as a phantasmatic stimulant, which could be attached to sadism, to evil as blind and paranoid violence. It is enough to look at our stadia, at all latitudes, to realise how true his perspective is.

Four years later, Green (1992) resumes his study of *Macbeth*, which he describes as a tragedy of darkness. At a certain point in his work, he visually guides us, by saying,

> . . . You can only imagine Macbeth in the mists of the moorland, where each shadow that threatens and each leaf that moves fearfully announce the presence of an emissary of the devil under the rain falling from a leaden sky, through which neither the sun's rays nor light pass. (Green, 1992, p. 202, translated for this edition)

Afterwards, he reminds us about the frightening and sinister effects produced by Orson Welles in his film of *Macbeth* (1948), from which one leaves the cinema convinced of having passed through troubled times.

All those who have had the opportunity to watch Welles' film, like those who have read the dark pages of *Macbeth*, will recall the veracity of Green's description. Like that of Freud, Green's work often presents a literary strength that, beyond the psychoanalytic component, produces an aesthetic pleasure rarely found in other authors.

When he reflects upon his trajectory, Green (2011a) stresses the importance of "Why evil?", because that text instigates the reflection he will resume regarding the death drive. Here, it is worth noting that, in a more mature or late period, the evolution of his thinking follows a similar path to that of Freud. On the one hand, he shows the extent to which Freud adopted an increasingly radical position *vis-à-vis* the death drive and insisted on its central place in the second topography (there is no second topography without the death drive). On the other hand, he details his own positions regarding the death drive through a continuous dialogue with Freud, Winnicott, Klein, and Bion.

In *Time in Psychoanalysis: Some Contradictory Aspects* (Green, 2002a), the elaboration of a theory of psychic heterochrony gives rise to the study of the compulsion to repeat, as well as of the mutation of the psychic apparatus in the second topography. What Green writes there has become classic: that is, the discharge of repetition attempts to create a vacuum within the psychic apparatus, and it is in this sense that the compulsion to repeat is a murder of time. Green underlines the greater problem of the transition from a fixed and consolidated binding by its successive repetitions to another that is unknown, unpredictable, and capable of breaking the circle of eternal recurrence, but running the risk of renewing the trauma at the origin of the repetitive formation, which is more or less disorganising.

In a work carried out with a group of colleagues on bastions, surprise, and communication in the analytic field (Eizirik et al., 2012), our starting point was precisely those ideas in order to compare two clinical possibilities: on the one hand, we are condemned to repeat with our patients the dramas that have occurred in their lives up to now; on the other hand, there is space for the new, the unexpected and the surprising in each analysis.

As we have previously mentioned, with *Illusions et désillusions du travail psychanalytique* [Illusions and Disillusions of Psychnoanalytic Work] Green (2010) takes his thinking a step further, boldly and frankly dealing with the slightly unpleasant and somewhat controversial topic of the disillusions and difficulties of our clinical work. Indeed, more than one colleague commented that the book was a scandal. After describing several cases that can be considered, if not failures, those of patients particularly resistant to, or rebellious against, analytic action, Green states that these cases were characterised by more or less invalidating psychical events. When, in the patient's evolution, these sequelae that have marked the organisation of the psyche are seen to be long-lasting, one can observe what he proposes calling the internalisation of the negative. Green means that the psyche introjected these primary defensive reactions as a means of unconscious defence, altering the psychic organisation and preventing it from developing according to the usual models of behaviour imposed by positive experiences. In other words, in the end, the analyst concludes that an internal enemy, a fifth column, has taken over the reins of power. Maybe, we would have to reach these experiences through the analysis of transference.

However, in this book, Green (2010) also takes an in-depth look at certain social situations. By using a thorough reading of Vasili Grossman and Imre Kertész, he suggests the culture of the negative: it is not the result of introjection, but of the effect of a seizure of power of the negative as an expansion of the sadomasochistic process exerted by a subversive power that desires the submission of those it aims to enslave. Fanaticism, in the pursuit of what should be condemned and executed, is systematically supported against tolerance: it opposes the free exchange of ideas. Indeed, the truth is kidnapped, bound and gagged, silenced.

Therefore, it is now possible to see the difference between these two negatives: the first succeeded in reaching the unconscious, the second never tried it. This form of negative gathers accomplices, acolytes, specialists in terror, as well as suicidal individuals who sacrifice their lives in the hope of becoming martyrs. Language has now become the exercise of perversion. They are, after all, two forms of attack against the life of the spirit.

In this work, Green (2010) allows us to understand well the experience of totalitarian societies that exist still today, within which religious fundamentalism lends a hand to oppressive political regimes. For those who live in a continent where several military dictatorships have seized power in different periods of history and where despotic candidates repeatedly try to threaten the democratic stability that currently predominates, it is extremely important to be able to rely on a contemporary perspective such as that suggested by Green, who also follows in the steps of Freud, a thinker on culture (Eizirik, 2014).

If we think about our most difficult cases or about those who even rebelled against the analytic method, especially some painful self-destructive evolutions, if we think about a rigorous metapsychological formulation that is coherent with the whole theoretical set and its fundamental hypotheses, if we remember the successive periods of our history and social organisation, both those we have lived to the present and those told by survivors or even those who are part of the history of humanity, if we reflect upon the circumstances of our institutions, bursting with illusions, disillusions, and undeniable advances, we can only feel encouraged and stimulated to continue reflecting and pursuing each one of these paths enlivened by Green's great body of work.

Notes

1. The ideas presented in this chapter were originally discussed in Falcão (2015).
2. *Decussation*: Green uses the term metaphorically. It originally comes from neurology, meaning a crossed tract of nerve fibres passing between centres on opposite sides of the nervous system. Green presents a definition: "In 1967, in my study on primary narcissism, I postulated the existence of *primary decussation*, where the innermost and the outermost psyche of the subject crossed when exchanging places. The description of such a movement is necessary for understanding projection" (Green, 2005b, p. 221).
3. Green introduces this notion of double drive reversal as an expansion on Freud's hypotheses on defence, which consists of the drive being

turned around upon the subject's own ego and undergoing reversal from activity to passivity. The double drive reversal is dependent on the narcissistic organisation of the ego. The notion of the double reversal was introduced and developed for the first time by Green in 1967, in his essay "Primary narcissism: structure or state" (Green, 2001). This notion constitutes "a basic model of psychoanalysis" (Green, 1984, p. 162) and underlies implicitly or explicitly his developments on narcissism, playing, the subject of the unconscious, representation, and language.

References

Arendt, H. (2009). *The Origins of Totalitarianism*. Oxford: Benediction Books.

Baranger, M., & Baranger, W. (1961–1962). La situación analítica como campo dinâmico *Revista Uruguaya de Psicoanálisis, IV*(1): 3–54.

Baudelaire, C. (2011). *Les fleures du mal*. Charleston, SC: BiblioLife.

Botella, C. (2013). A obra de Green e a evolução do pensamento analítico. *Revista de psicanálise da SPPA, 20*(1): 29–37.

Botella, C., & Botella, S. (2001). *The Work of Psychic Figurability. Mental States without Representation*. New York: Brunner-Routledge.

Botella, S. (2013). Sobre o negativo psíquico na obra de A. Green. *Revista de psicanálise da SPPA, 20*(1): 67–73.

Bion, W. R. (1962). *Learning From Experience*. London: Tavistock.

Chervet, B. (2012). Pulsions de destruction ou de mort? Pulsion de destruction et pulsion de mort [Destruction or death instincts? Destruction and death instincts]. *Revue Belge de Psychanalyse, 60*: 89–92.

Chervet, B. (2013). Dualidade pulsional, trabalho do negativo e destrutividade. Premissas para uma reflexão sobre o assassinato fundador [Instinctual duality, negative and destructive work. Premises to a reflection on the founding murder]. *Revista de psicanálise da SPPA, 20*(1): 39–66.

Eizirik, C. L (2014). À propos du mal et de la destructivité: l'importance des contributions d'André Green dans la contemporanéité. In: B. Chervet, *André Green* (pp. 157–163). Paris: Société Psychanalytique de Paris.

Eizirik, C. L., Knijnik, J., Rispoli, A., Tofani, A. C., Mello, C., & Rubin, L. (2012). Baluarte, surpresa e comunicação no campo analítico. *Revista Brasileira de Psicanálise, 46*(1): 150–161.

Falcão, L. (2011). O pulsional, a destrutividade e a cultura. *Revista de Psicanálise da Sociedade Psicanalítica de Porto Alegre, 18*(3): 623–645.

Falcão, L. (2013). Representação-afeto na obra de André Green. *Revista de Psicanálise da Sociedade Psicanalítica de Porto Alegre*, 20(1): 139–155.

Falcão, L. (2015). Death drive, destructive drive and the desobjectalizing function in the analytic process. *International Journal of Psychoanalysis*, 96: 459–476

Freud, S. (1915c). Instincts and their vicissitudes. *S. E.*, 14: 109–140. London: Hogarth.

Freud, S. (1917d). A metapsychological supplement to the theory of dreams. *S. E.*, 16: 217–236. London: Hogarth.

Freud, S. (1920g). *Beyond the Pleasure Principle. S. E.*, 18: 3–64. London: Hogarth.

Freud, S. (1924c). The economic problem of masochism. *S. E.*, 19: 155–170. London: Hogarth.

Freud, S. (1930a). *Civilization and its Discontents. S. E.*, 21: 59–145. London: Hogarth.

Freud, S. (1933a). *New Introductory Lectures on Psycho-Analysis. S. E.*, 22. London: Hogarth.

Freud, S. (1937c). Analysis terminable and interminable. *S. E.*, 23: 211–254. London: Hogarth.

Freud, S. (1939a). *Moses and Monotheism. S. E.*, 23: 3–137. London: Hogarth.

Green, A. (1973). *Le discours vivant* [The Living Discourse]. Paris: PUF.

Green, A. (1983). La mère morte. In: *Narcisisme de vie, narcisisme de mort.* Paris: Éditions de Minuit.

Green, A. (1984). Le langage dans la psychanalyse [Language in psycho-analysis]. In: *Langages* [Languages], *Second Psychoanalytic Meetings of Aix-en-Provence.* Paris: Belles Lettres.

Green, A. (1986). The analyst, symbolization and absence in the analytic setting. In: *On Private Madness*, K. Lewison & D. Pines (Trans.) (pp. 30–60). London: Hogarth.

Green, A. (1988a). Pulsão de morte, narcisismo negativo, função desobje-talizante. In: A. Green, D. Widlöcher, J. Laplanche, H. Segal, E. Rechardt, P. Ikonen, & C. Yorke (Eds.), *A Pulsão de morte* (pp. 57–68). Rio de Janeiro: Imago.

Green, A. (1988b). La pratique fondamental de la psychanalyse [Fundamental psychoanalytic practice]. *Revue française de psychoanalyse*, 3(52): 569–593.

Green, A. (1990a). Le concept de limite. In: *La folie privée* [On Private Madness] (pp. 103–140). Paris: Gallimard.

Green, A. (1990b). Le double limite. In: *La folie privée* [On Private Madness] (pp. 293–316). Paris: Gallimard.

Green, A. (1990c). Pourquoi le mal? In: *La folie privée* [On Private Madness] (pp. 369–401). Paris: Gallimard.

Green, A. (1990d). *Conferências brasileiras de André Green – Metapsicologia dos limites*. Rio de Janeiro: Imago.

Green, A. (1992). *La déliaison*. Paris: Les Belles Lettres.

Green, A. (1995a). *Propédeutique. La métapsychologie revisitée* [Propaedeutics: Metapsychology Revisited]. Seyssel: Champ Vallon.

Green, A. (1995b). *La causalité psychique: entre nature et culture* [Psychic Causality: Between Nature and Culture]. Paris: Odile Jacob.

Green, A. (1999). *The Work of the Negative*, A. Weller (Trans.). London: Free Association Books.

Green, A. (2000). The intrapsychic and intersubjective in psychoanalysis. *Psychoanalytic Quarterly*, 69(1): 1–39.

Green, A. (2001). Primary narcissism: structure or state? In: *Life Narcissism, Death Narcissism*, A. Weller (Trans.) (pp. 48–90). London: Free Association Books.

Green, A. (2002a). *Time in Psychoanalysis: Some Contradictory Aspects*. London: Free Association Books.

Green, A. (2002b). L'intrapsychique et l'intersubjectif: pulsions et/ou relations d'objet. In: *La pensée clinique* [Clinical Thought] (pp. 37–76). Paris: Odile Jacob.

Green, A. (2002c). La mort dans la vie: quelques repères pour la pulsion de mort [Death in life]. In: *La pensée clinique* [Clinical Thought] (pp. 309–332). Paris: Odile Jacob.

Green, A. (2002d). *Idées directrices pour une psychanalyse contemporaine*. Paris: PUF [*Key Ideas for a Contemporary Psychoanalysis*, A. Weller (Trans.). London & New York: Routledge 2005].

Green, A. (2004). *La lettre et la mort*. Paris: Éditions Denoël.

Green, A. (2005a). *On Private Madness*. London: Karnac.

Green, A. (2005b). *Key Ideas for a Contemporary Psychoanalysis*, A. Weller (Trans.). London: Routledge.

Green, A. (2007a). *Pourquoi les pulsions de destruction ou de mort?* Paris: Panama.

Green, A. (2007b). Pulsions de destruction et maladies somatiques [Destructive drives and somatic maladies]. *Revue française de psychosomatique*, 32(2): 45–70.

Green, A. (2010). *Illusions et désillusions du travail psychanalytique*. Paris: Odile Jacob.

Green, A. (2011a). Les cas limite. De la folie privée aux pulsions de destruction et de mort [Borderline cases. From private madness to death and destruction drives]. *Revue française de psychanalyse*, 75(2): 375–390.

Green, A. (2011b). *Du signe au discours*. Paris: Ithaque.

Joseph, B. (1983). On understanding and not understanding: some technical issues. *International Journal of Psychoanalysis, 64*: 291–298.

Libermann, Z. (1999). Pulsão de morte e narcisismo. *Revista de Psicanálise da Sociedade Psicanalítica de Porto Alegre, VI*(1): 127–137.

Libermann, Z. (2010). Patologias atuais ou psicanálise atual? *Revista Brasileira de Psicanálise, 44*(1): 41–49.

Marty, P., & de M'uzan, M. (1962). La pensée opératoire [Operative Thought]. *Revue française de psychanalyse, 27*: 345–356.

Marty, P., & de M'uzan, M. (1967). Regression et instinct de mort. Hypothèses à propos de l'observation psychosomatique [Regression and death drive. Hypothesesconcerning psychosomatic observations]. *Revue française de psychanalyse, 31*(5–6): 1113–1126.

Shakespeare, W. (1994)[1608]. *Macbeth*. London: Penguin.

Welles, O. (Dir.) (1948). *Macbeth* (film). Los Angeles, CA: Mercury Productions.

Winnicott, D. W. (1969). The use of an object. *International Journal of Psycho-Analysis, 50*: 711–716.

Winnicott, D. W. (1971). *Playing and Reality*. London: Routledge.

CHAPTER SEVEN

Thought and the work of the negative

Marie France Brunet

Introduction

André Green's development as an author reflects an increasingly complex synthesis of the work of Freud and various post-Freudian contributors, especially Lacan, Winnicott, and Bion. Anchoring his research in contemporary clinical practice, Green created an ever-expanding, personal, and original theoretical model that contains its own concepts and offers unique contributions to psychoanalytic theory and technique. Foremost among these are the ideas formulated under the heading, "the work of the negative" (Green, 1993). The latter include Green's ideas about thinking, both in its normal/neurotic development and in the disturbances that occurred in what he called "limit cases", that is, borderline, psychosomatic, and other non-neurotic disturbances.

In the discussion that follows, I examine the work of the negative and the relation between Green's theories of thinking and those of W. R. Bion, revisiting certain ideas that already appeared in the book *L'Enfant de ça*, which Green co-authored quite early in his career with Jean-Luc Donnet (Donnet & Green, 1973). In addition, I explore Green's ideas about narcissism, emphasising what he called "negative narcissism" and its relation to the death instinct. Finally, I present clinical material to focus on the particularities of thought, negative narcissism, and the difficulties they can present in psychoanalytic work.

Thought and the work of the negative

In his book, *Le travail du négatif* [*The Work of the Negative*], Green (1993) summarises preliminary "intimations" of the negative in earlier psychoanalytic formulations, starting from the work of Freud and continuing with that of Lacan, Winnicott, Bion, Searles, and others, but it is to Green himself that we owe the originality of the concept. His work of the negative is conceived as a constitutive element of mental functioning and, indeed, of all psychic work. It includes a variety of activities that range, in their most positive aspects, from the support for psychic structure building to malignant, destructive qualities ("negative narcissism") found in the so-called "hard" (i.e., non-neurotic) cases. At its most adaptive, the work of the negative is responsible for limiting excessive "positivity" or "presence" of the drives, which must be "negativised", that is, evacuated, managed through defence mechanisms, or bound, so that they can become psychically usable. Without this negativisation, psychic development proves impossible and there is no chance of compatibility between possession and expression of the drives and being part of the human community.

Green conceives of defence mechanisms as modalities of thought and places them at the core of the positive pole of the work of the negative, gathering together repression, the first mechanism described by Freud, with those that were added later based on the vicissitudes of clinical practice (denial, splitting, disavowal, foreclosure). He considers this ensemble as "primary", because their function is the decision between a yes or a no; that is, whether or not a specific ideational content will be allowed to remain conscious or will be accepted or rejected by one or another psychic agency.

We must not forget that Freud emphasised that even when this work of the negative appears in the form of, or in relation to, ego mechanisms of defence, the latter remain rooted in instinctual functioning: "Affirmation—as a substitute for uniting—belongs to Eros; negation—the successor to expulsion—belongs to the instinct of destruction"

(Freud, 1925h, p. 238). Thus, we see that the work of the negative is not limited to the field of the ego alone.

We must also consider that these defence mechanisms are closely linked to sexuality, and were originally described by Freud in relation to it. Some are associated with archaic sexuality, an aspect emphasised by Green (2012, p. 177), who points out that post-Freudian studies of ego functioning and object relations have tended to diminish the place of sexuality in psychoanalysis. In contrast, even when sexuality acquires particular distorted or seemingly non-sexual forms, Green believes that it must be included in the clinical work with, and comprehension of, non-neurotic patients.

The various "primary" mechanisms of the work of the negative reflect a wide range of psychic movements. For example, repression has a conservative aspect even if it excludes certain representations from conscious awareness, because it allows binding and unbinding mechanisms to be followed by a rebinding in the unconscious. In contrast, the mechanisms of foreclosure—in which something has been "abolished" and, thus, excluded from associative chains—or disavowal and splitting—which operate on perception and disturb contact with reality—work to limit symbolisation, mutilate the ego, and destroy rational thought, allowing room for "mad" versions of the latter.

Symbolisation is conceived of by Green as an activity that gathers together binding–unbinding–rebinding processes and might involve the agency of the psychic apparatus. In contrast, the more disruptive work of the negative is associated with unbinding, and the death drive, which are conceived of as a kind of de-cathexis or disinvestment and are an important component of the process referred to by Green (1995) as disobjectalisation. However, it should be noted that de-cathexis and disinvestment may also be utilised as part of a progressive process, for it is not possible to consider evolution and change without disinvestment and displacement, understanding these as necessary preludes to the replacement of older objects or aims with the new.

Green proposes a personal conceptualisation of the psychic container under the name of "framing structure" (Green, 1983a), which he suggests results from the internalisation of the relationship with the primary object after the original fusional state. This achievement, which is related to the initiation of primary narcissism, requires the work of the negative (double return mechanisms—reversal against the self and turning something into its opposite-and negative hallucination of the mother by a disinvestment of the perceptive pole), but it can only be achieved "when the love of the object is secure enough" (Green, 1983a).

The framing structure takes in the primitive representations of the mother and will become the platform upon which all future investments will unfold. It is, therefore, fundamental to the process of objectalisation: Green (1995) sees the latter as the main expression of Eros and a necessary predecessor of the capacity for displacement. It should be considered as the first mediating structure between the drive and the object, one that allows the distinction inside/outside, helps to secure the achievement of primary narcissism, and provides a necessary foundation for the ego. Clinically, there is a correlation between the failure in the constitution of the framing structure and the difficulties certain patients experience in tolerating and making use of the analytic setting.

The issue of thought and its development makes an early appearance in *L'Enfant de Ça* (Donnet & Green, 1973) and occupied Green's attention throughout his *oeuvre*. This early text, which reflects Green's reading of Bion, with whom he had a personal relationship and a strong intellectual exchange, introduces the concept of white psychosis (*psychose blanche*).

Regarding the theory of thinking, Green often stated that after Freud, it was Bion who made the most significant contributions to analytic theory.

Freud said,

> The antithesis between subjective and objective does not exist from the first. It only comes into being from the fact that thought possesses the capacity to bring before the mind once more something that has once been perceived, by reproducing it as a presentation without the external object having still to be there. (Freud, 1925h, p. 236)

Bion wrote,

> Sooner or later the "wanted" breast is felt as an "idea of a breast missing" and not as a bad breast present. We can see that the bad, that is to say wanted but absent, breast is much more likely to become recognized as an idea than the good breast which is associated to what a

philosopher would call a thing-in-itself or a thing-in-actuality. (Bion, 2014, p. 302)

Green (Donnet & Green, 1973) picks up the thread that joins these two formulations, and in so doing situates the negative at the source of the thinking process. A thought is installed through the experience of loss, which is at the same time the loss of an experience. Thought comes about to make up for this missing experience. What is required for thoughts to develop is the individual's capacity to wait, imposed upon the satisfaction of a need, and then progressively expanded. From the initial tendency to discharge, the search for solutions is introduced and then enlarged, moving from the hallucinatory realisation of the breast (as the first psychic achievement) towards the construction of phantasy as a means to attempt to replicate the missing experience.

This process is taken for granted in Freud: representations, which come from perceptions, will be reinvested by the drive, giving place to a desire. At the same time, the drive will be bound through that process of reinvestment.

In Bion, whose clinical work was centred on psychotic patients, hallucinatory wish-fulfilment is not guaranteed. As illustrated in his discussion of his Grid (Bion, 1977), the most primitive elements that reach the psyche, beta elements, are unthinkable, in part because they relate to a period (*infans*) in which the infant does not have a psychic apparatus with which to think them.

In Bion (2014), beta elements are defined mainly through their negative qualities. They are not fit for thinking; they are sense impressions or undigested emotions, indistinguishable from the things-in-themselves and suitable only for projective identification. If thinking is to become possible, then an object (originally the mother) will be required to intervene in helping to establish a transformative, intersubjective process; a thinker, who, through her reverie and so-called alpha function, contains and transforms this beta element material and returns it to the infant in the form of alpha elements so that they can be introjected.

Bion noted that the mother's reverie incorporates her feelings of love or hate towards her child and its father. "If the feeding mother cannot allow reverie or if the reverie is allowed but is not associated with love for the child or its father, this fact will be communicated to the infant even though incomprehensible to the infant" (Bion, 2014, p. 303). With this statement, Bion introduces triangulation: there is a maternal link with the infant, but also a bond of the mother with the father even when he is not physically present and brings forward the notion of absence, necessary for the creation of thought. Green significantly expands the importance of this last element through his conception of the "generalized triangulation with substitutable third" (Green, 1983b) and later with his notion of thirdness, both in theory and in technique (Green, 2002).

According to Green, Bion's formulations constitute one of the best achieved models of an articulation between the intrapsychic and the intersubjective. It is the combination of the baby's "communicative" projective identification and the mother's reverie (which Bion deduced from his own mental attitude with his psychotic patients) that ultimately will allow the infant not only to reincorporate what he evacuated, but progressively to introject the capacity for alpha function. Once the latter is sufficiently achieved, it will allow for the autonomous development of a capacity to create alpha elements and the development of an apparatus to think thoughts. This is the starting point of autonomous thinking and the capacity for abstraction. It is also provides the basis for learning from experience. Once begun, this process endows the good breast with a psychic quality.

The Bionian model has at its core the theme of transformation of sense impressions into emotional experience. For that to be possible, the infant must be able to tolerate frustration, rather than excessively evacuating primitive material (beta elements), and the object must remain open to absorbing the infant's projections. This model also implies that, from a psychoanalytic point of view, thinking cannot be separated from experiences of pain and pleasure. The mind would then contain elements that cannot be thought of (this is because not all beta elements can be evacuated), thoughts without a thinker, which will be kept excluded; thoughts with a thinker will be added to them. Green points out the proximity between beta elements and the concept of drive, both being primitive and close to the senses or the body. But beta elements can also come from external stimuli, in contrast with the drive, which refers exclusively to the depths of the psyche, in its limits with the soma.

Starting from models coming from different backgrounds (diverse aetiological myths, as expressed by Green (1987)), Freud, Bion, and

Green's theorisations share the fact that in order to acquire the capacity to think, representations, part of the beta elements and alpha elements must be kept in the primary psyche. We must remember that Green brings closer the moment of the emergence of the hallucinatory wish fulfilment with the start of the alpha function.

Green also develops a model that brings together the intrapsychic and the intersubjective thought, his conceptualisation of the drive–object pair, conceived as the fundamental substrate that will give birth to the ego and the other products of psychic structuration, as well as the different statutes of the object. Projective identification supposes a different mechanism to that formulated by Freud for the creation of the pure pleasure ego: ejection. Green proposes the term "excorporation" (Donnet & Green, 1973) for this mechanism, to represent the idea of separating the increased excitation from the body or erotogenic zone. His argument for the use of this term begins with the assertion that projective identification requires awareness of an object into which a projection can be made and postulated in an early stage; it supposes the existence of an object from the beginning. Beyond the external evidence that an object is required to respond to the child's needs, something that Green (1995) will call a "covering object", he insists that the child initially experiences himself as one with the object, and only later is there a sense of separation from the object into a primitive dyad. It is only at this later stage that one can talk of projection. This difference is obviously related with the fact that Kleinian and Bionian theorisation does not include primary narcissism, which has a relevant place in André Green's work, as we shall see later.

From Bion's theorisation, Green also highlights the inclusion of a third factor that establishes a link between the objects, besides love (L) and hate (H): knowledge (K), which is then elevated to an essential emotion, which must be understood as the "desire for knowledge" in order to keep its potential for mental growth without a premature saturation. Postulating K from the start evidences the idea that exclusively from the first two (L and H), or from the good and bad objects, knowledge cannot develop. Green, in his own theorising, maintains that alpha function is not enough for the achievement of K, and proposes the addition of the objectalising function (Green, 1995). This latter concept refers to the unlimited process of substitution and metaphorisation, through which any investment, including investments of psychic processes, can be transformed into a psychic object, as long as it gives significance to the individual. In this way, there is a movement from a conception restricted only to the links between objects (Bion's L, H, and K), to one that proposes the possibility that psychic functions could reach the status of internal objects. This relates to the unlimited creative capacities of human beings.

Bion generally does not speak in terms of representations. In contrast, Green expanded Freud's theory of representation, including body, affect, and thinking, together with Freud's thing-presentation and word-presentation, and added the concept of the "double limit" (Green, 1982). The first limit allows the separation between inside and outside; the second divides the internal space between Ucs, Pcs, and Cs. These should be considered to be transit zones, zones of transformation.

In neurotic structures, in which the pleasure principle has been established, conflict is predominantly intrapsychic, between desire, fixations, and defences. Limits are well achieved; they delimit and yet, at the same time, are permeable. In borderline structures, conflicts situated in the double frontier of the psyche are added to the more familiar neurotic conflicts: the ego is trapped between the drives of the id and the object (which is another subject with its own drives). Anxieties regarding abandonment and intrusion are added to the neurotic anxieties. The importance and the failure of the object are now at the forefront. Green adds to this conceptualisation that of the psychic container (framing structure).

The containment of thoughts, starting from the most elementary and primordial, is essential to avoid either somatisation or expulsion in action, and to initiate the processes of transformation that lead to the different levels of abstraction. Once limits are set up, representations can circulate within the Ucs, going through the Pcs to access consciousness. Tertiary processes (Green, 1975) regulate that circulation. Once thing-presentations and word-presentations are linked together in the Pcs., communication with the outside and with the other is possible through verbalisation.

Regarding this limit, this "between" that separates the subject from the object, it is necessary to remember the importance that Green gives to Winnicott's (1971) concepts of transitional space and transitional zone. In their attempt to define a space that is neither internal nor external (the intermediate space, the potential space of reunion where the separation from the mother was produced), these concepts imply the negative. For Green, the preconscious is also an internal intermediate area. In severe pathology, these spaces are missing, or repeatedly collapse.

In "La double limite" [The double limit], Green (1982) points out his conviction that in psychoanalysis, any theorisations about thinking are obliged to take into account its origins in the absence of the object and its drive-related roots. As Freud (1915c) noted when he defined drive "as a measure of the demand made upon the mind for work in consequence of its connection with the body" (Freud, 1915c, p. 122), the psyche's development is initiated from the hallucinatory wish fulfilment as a first psychic achievement. Since that opening thought, or thought–no-thought, a leap is required for the achievement of thinking proper, which is, according to Green, a construction detached from the pleasure principle, a *theory* of the absence of the breast.

Thinking in itself is not representative, so two negativities must operate in regard to the object: one of its presence, in the negativity of representation (from perception), and one from the representation, which creates real thinking, the secondary one.

Thus, there is not only a transformation of thoughts, but also a creation of new thoughts: thoughts about an object without the object being present. A distance is established from impressions of the senses, with the investment of the links predominating over the investment of objects. In the secondary phase of thinking, thoughts are discontinuous, with bindings produced through links that are not material. Such discontinuity constitutes the normal "blanks" in thinking; its "breathing", which, at the same time, will have an expression in language (Donnet & Green, 1973).

Green uses the concept of negative hallucination as explanation for a significant number of negativisation processes. This is an idea that emerges from a footnote in Freud (1917d, p. 231), who suggests that in order to understand positive hallucination, negative hallucination must be studied. In its structuring aspect, the negative participates in the creation of the framing structure (disinvestment of the perceptual pole), and as we mentioned before, in the passage from one system to another. To represent, and also to create the word able to name it, the thing must be hallucinated negatively. Due to the discontinuity between one psychic system and the other, it is necessary to hallucinate negatively the system that is set aside in order to go on to the next one. Therefore, we must consider that there is no chance of abstraction without the operation of the work of the negative. It must be understood, then, that negative hallucination (together with the work of the negative) is not only or always pathological.

The destructive negative and negative narcissism

Beginning with his paper "Le narcissisme primaire: structure ou état" [Primary narcissism: state or structure] (Green, 1967), André Green considers in his theorisation an identificatory pole, which starts from the primary fusional state with the mother, goes through the framing structure, is followed by the constitution of primary narcissism, and, finally, ends in the establishment of the ego/subject. We are in the hypothetical field of the development of the intrapsychic. This pole allows the unfolding of investments directed towards the object and those directed towards the ego, which must not be considered reductively as mutually exclusive.

In narcissism, the ego finds satisfaction in itself, creating the phantasy of liberation from the feeling of dependence to which it is submitted by the desire, which off-centres it in the search of the object, variable for its inherent otherness. Green links his theory of narcissism with Freud's second drive theory, postulating a dual narcissism. This will be termed "positive" when it is orientated towards the search for a feeling of "subjectal" (subject line) reunification (Green, 1995). In these instances, narcissism acts as a barrier against psychic destruction: when faced with a frustrating experience, investments can be temporarily withdrawn towards the ego. It must be made clear that "positive" in this sense is not equivalent to non-pathological, because this movement will always imply an impoverishment of objectal investments and a withdrawal into the self.

However, when the encounter between the drive and the object has failed beyond the tolerance of the subject, destructivity unfolds and narcissism turns negative; then, the psyche is primarily orientated towards the search for a "zero" state of no tension, of no desire.

For Green, in non-neurotic structures narcissism always comes into play. The variants that it adopts cannot be separated from the response of the object to the drive's demands. When the maternal response is deficient or the waiting for satisfaction turns out to be too long (Winnicott), an unbearable frustration floods the subject, and discomfort and desperation (*Hilflosigkeit*) emerge. Here, the object becomes an object-trauma, turning into a threat to the narcissistic foundations of the subject. It is in these circumstances that, according to Green, drive defusion takes place, activating destructivity. In this case, the work of the negative will lean towards its negativising aspect.

Traces of theorisations about these movements can already be found in Freud (1924b), in his comparative works about neurosis and psychosis. There, he points out that, in the latter, the ego breaks its link with external reality and with the internal reality that surrogates it through a withdrawal of investment. Post-Freudians theorise from there, first concerning clinical work with psychotic patients, and, later, with the study of borderline cases. In these types of structures, diverse phenomena come together, and in variable magnitudes, but what we must always keep in mind is that the core of the psychic activity is, here, attempting to restore the sense of presence of an object from which no adequate separation has been accomplished.. Autonomy, therefore, is always felt to be threatened by the object, while, at the same time, the sought-after object is threatened with destruction by the subject.

In such cases, we also find a faulty development of the framing structure and inadequate processes of representation. The creation of sense and the symbolic organisation of the unconscious might then fail as a consequence of insufficient binding of investments. In negative narcissism, a disobjectalising movement is produced; the object is wilfully denied, getting rid of all dependence from it, because nothing can be expected from it any more. What Green (1993) calls the "logic of hopelessness" is installed (differentiated from the logic of hopefulness founded in the neuroses' unconscious desire). A hateful fixation is produced with the object, from which a structuring separation needed to reach subjectivity has not been achieved. Motivated by this, the attack is not only directed against the relationship with the object, but also against all of its substitutes, and against the subject itself (one's own ego), and, essentially, against one's thinking. The relation with the object is paradoxical; hatred combines with a passionate grasp of it, sustaining an interminable raging demand towards it. Narcissism and masochism establish in this way a tight bond that tends to close the structure: the subject wants to be impermeable to the object. In these patients, the pleasure principle is not able to establish its sovereignty, and the negative character of relationships will take precedence, as Winnicott (1971) suggests. In the same line, Green would say that the subject would negativise its own desire, attacking its links with the objects, until it undermines the libidinal foundations of its own ego. This process is very close to Bion's (2014) conceptualisation of –K, which implies an active disposition against awareness of external and internal reality.

In these non-neurotic patients, repression is not the dominant mechanism. Splitting, disavowal, and foreclosure come into play, negating perception and disrupting the recognition of reality. These mechanisms, linked to destructivity, operate mainly in negative narcissism. In them, unbinding is central, making rebinding difficult or impossible. Thoughts appear divided, with lax or loosened links. Here, the negative cannot be understood as opposite to the positive. There is a constant attempt to expel towards the outside or to split in the inside all that is not tolerable (the object, hate, links, etc.). Given the pressure of the repressed or abolished to return, the process is repeated without ending until a state of nothingness is reached.[1]

Bion (2014) talks in terms of evacuation, which can be intensified to the point of leaving the psyche empty and exhausted, without the material to develop thinking and abstraction. Green (2013), for his part, suggests that the primitive forms of representation (or would it be mnemic traces?) whose character is essentially visual could be erased or destroyed, leaving some sort of painful wound, hole, or blank in the psyche. States of emptiness or futility clinically express these. The mechanism he proposes is that of negative hallucination, which acts not only by cutting contact with whatever induces pain, but also by attacking the thinking process that is an expression of this link. This is a mechanism that refers to perception. It is a process through which the ego can break or interrupt its links with reality, via disinvestment. The rejected perception touches on some aspect linked to the narcissistic integrity of the subject. Green suggests that it could also operate over thinking and representations, suppressing them. Secondarily, unconsciousness of the lack of perception is produced, and forms of hiding or effacing the entire process.

In *The Ego and the Id*, Freud (1923b) expands the field of perception. To that which comes from the exterior and is captured by the sense organs he adds the perceptions that come from the interior, the body in the first place, in the form of sensations and feelings, adding to them the thinking processes, which will be perceptible to the consciousness thanks to word-presentations. They are related to thinking on the one hand and to object-presentations on the other, forming a link between thought, language, and the representation–perception sphere. It is this articulation that allows the understanding of movements between the different components when mechanisms such as those described are in operation.

The negative hallucination is, in these cases, a radical defence that can manifest itself in the impossibility of using words as a tool for thinking. It adds to other procedures used by the ego to avoid psychic pain, but at the cost of an ego impoverishment.

There is a rupture between object and word-presentations at the level of thinking, leading these subjects to the impossibility of formulating and understanding their psychic events to themselves and to the other (the analyst). Sensorial capacities to perceive thoughts or related to external perception will not be lost, but sense and connections will be. We are in the field of the unthinkable.

In the cases in which negative hallucination operates on thinking, the blank, the emptiness, invades the field of representation. This is the pathological blank, connected to the abolition of thought. It is what was originally described in the white psychosis, psychosis without psychosis, or the core of the psychosis (Donnet & Green, 1973), but which can also be found in varying degrees in non-neurotic structures. In certain cases, but not always, positive hallucinations can fill these holes, though, frequently, what happens is that the drive activity constantly invades the ego, producing narcissistic anxieties. Aggression and sexuality are lived as violence coming from the interior, drives that attack thinking, a procedure attributed to an internal bad object.

In some patients, what can be observed is an affective bluntness, which is also a result of the paralysis of thinking. That regime of mental hibernation is the consequence of the persecution of thinking manifested by a constant splitting activity that impedes the establishment of relations between thoughts. A result of this is depression (in the literal sense), a blank, non-affective depression, without psychic pain. It is linked to the fact that the faculty to transform the data that reach the psyche has been lost. It would be more of a loss than a retreat, and explains the feeling of emptiness through which it is manifested.

Clinical material: "James: a case of negative narcissism"

James consults in his forties, having previously made various analytical attempts, which he interrupted after some years without making clear what led him to do so. He has no memories of these processes, and never mentions his previous analysts. He feels depressed, without any motivation, with a meaningless life, feelings he says he has had as long as he can remember. He points out that he does not possess a single pleasant memory. In general, his memories are very few, making it very difficult to have an idea about his story and about the people that surround him. After a long time in analysis, certain significant events of his childhood have emerged, which appear in shreds, and he then takes them back, changing his versions, or temporality, making a reconstruction of his life difficult.

At some point, early in his life, his parents travelled for a period too long for James to tolerate, leaving him and his three brothers in the custody of an uncle on his mother's side, who died some years later after a long illness. During this absence, his isolation seemed to be intensified. He did not establish a significant contact with this uncle, even when the latter made efforts to get closer, which represented a sort of torture for James. His parents then separated and the children stayed with the mother, who was described as very intrusive. James says he thinks that by that time she could have been depressed, or at least that she would not notice his isolation and dissatisfaction. This made him feel very lonely. When he was not at school, he spent most of his time locked in his bedroom, bored. The contact with his father was kept in a constant way, though James would describe it as poor, as father was uncommunicative, "depressive as me". In addition, the bad relationship between the patient and his brothers and his father's second wife emphasised the distance between them.

Before the separation, the patient remembers the fights between his parents, which are doubtlessly what he considers the most important, because of the fear they provoked in him. He describes them as verbally violent, followed by periods in which father would become mute and mother would beg him to tell her what he was feeling or thinking. At those times, James felt extremely lonely and frightened of seeing mother, who was his main support, in such a weak and fragile position in front of his father. In the course of the analysis, I acquired the impression that both his parents' trips and these fights not only made him feel abandoned, but also set in motion intense feelings towards substitutes of the primary scene, with excitation, fear, and rage in the presence of exclusion.

James' life has been affectively very poor. He never established a lasting or intimate relationship outside the family. He does not have any friends, and has not had a couples' relationship that lasted for more than a few weeks. His sex life is very limited. He feels a lack of desire, suffers from impotence, which stirs feelings of deep humiliation, and can spend long periods of time without looking for relationships. Sexual activity is essentially masturbatory, with very limited pleasure.

In contrast, work has been moderately successful, with James occupying middle management positions in companies. This, however, is far from what he expected for himself after finishing his studies. At that stage, he felt intellectually capable and expected to accomplish great things. Despite no objective evidence for the feeling, he fears "being caught" by his superiors, who will see that he actually "does not understand at all what he is doing". However, he rapidly expels this anxiety by declaring that he actually would not care if he lost his job.

James' strongest family relations are with his mother, and loaded with a great ambivalence. He is very dependent on her when making decisions, and her opinions weigh on him as a law, without any questioning on his part. At the same time, and particularly when his mood is worse, or when he has more anxiety, he expresses his resentment towards her for not noticing that he had problems when he was a child.

In analysis, there is evidence of a wish that mother (or both parents) should compensate him for what was lacking in childhood: "I want them to pay". These feelings were intensified when, in the second year of analysis, his mother left to travel alone for long periods of time. Although James and his brothers believed she was isolating herself because she was depressed, her absence actualised the infantile experiences of abandonment, rage, and lack of meaning. As James began to have doubts about the possibility of continuing to depend emotionally upon her, he began to fear that she would die. As his psychic discomfort increased, his only desire was to stay in bed, without thinking. At work, he did not understand what he read or what was talked about in meetings. His thinking was severely affected. Death wishes appeared, even when he used to say that there was not much difference between a real death and the psychic state in which he found himself.

During this period, his dream activity was practically non-existent. But in one session he reported having a dream with sexual content, could give no details, but expressed that in the context of the experience of his "internal death", he felt that this was at least a bit of life.

Following that session, he tried to re-establish contact with his mother through the internet. (He had stopped doing this during her absence because of the frustration resulting from her unavailability.) When that failed, he reported suicidal ideation that resulted in a psychiatric intervention and an increase in his medication. In the first sessions following this episode, James managed to recognise a link between his wish to die and the frustration and rage related to his mother's disconnection. However, this was rapidly erased. It was not just that he did not want to talk about this; what he had previously told me had been completely deleted. There was no memory of having made a reference to this previously; many of the elements that composed the sequence were also suppressed. I believe this is a good example of what Green calls "negative hallucination", which, in this patient, reaches significant magnitudes, affecting his thinking and reducing his possibilities of establishing links that would allow him to give meaning to what happens to him. It was as if he was treating the work of the analysis as Penelope did her weaving, erasing even during the same session something that we had been able to understand, due to the pain it caused to recall it.

During certain periods, but also between one session and the next, important fluctuations in his mood, contact, and thinking could be noticed. At times, he was more communicative, sharing some of his experiences or preoccupations with me, and allowing more of his functioning to be understood. But mostly, for long periods, the sessions are slow, plain, and loaded with a heavy silence. This was more intense during the period I mentioned before, which lasted many months: "What I yearn for is just sleeping, I only want to be at home to be in my bed . . . but when I am there is when I am worse . . . I yearn for a rest, but what I wish is to erase myself from the world . . . with no feelings, feelings are pain, no thinking." This was accompanied by a phantasy of being born again, to a time before everything started, because now there is no chance to recover all the time he has not lived.

Most of my interventions are rejected or questioned; many times he would even say he had not heard them, or would fall asleep for some seconds, losing the thread of what we were talking about. He asks me to repeat what I have said, because he does not hear it or does not understand it. Occasionally, after some time, he might return to these ideas, treating them as if they were productions of his own. On certain occasions, an interpretation of mine that opens something new, not thought of by him before, initially engages his interest. However, anxiety soon emerges, his thinking becomes confused, and he can no longer complete phrases or ideas. A few times when this happens, he asks me to stop the session, frightened by his own mental state.

Beyond the fact that certain external circumstances have undermined James' fragile psychic stability, it seems evident that the analytic situation has reactualised anxieties linked to his primary objects. The transference in this type of patient strains the limits, which are precarious. The search to maintain the autonomy of their thinking takes precedence, creating difficulties in receiving interpretations. What these patients are after is to claim and maintain a feeling of identity, defending the ego's territory in the presence of the object.

The analytic setting encourages the use of language and verbalisation to express psychic manifestations. However, to the extent that the patient feels vulnerable to being overwhelmed by contact, then negative hallucination might be directed towards words, in order to protect against contact with the other, the analyst: language becomes an object of excitement and vigilance. Thus, the patient turns silent, omits. Many other times, James adopted a strong oppositional attitude to my interventions, reacting to my voice as if it was painful for him to listen to, bending double on the couch and covering his eyes. When he does say something, he would then take it back. Avoiding contact for patients like James is avoiding the intrusion of the transferential object, which reactualises the maternal intrusion.

In extreme situations, as when I described his anxiety after an "unexpected" interpretation, when the transferential object is experienced as intrusive and bad, projective activity and, above all, splitting between thoughts is initiated. This is an extreme measure aimed at avoiding psychic pain. While signal anxiety is at work here, it is in the service of helping the patient keep distance from the intrusive object. As in white psychosis (Donnet & Green, 1973), signal anxiety does not lead to a search for solutions through thinking, but a paralysis of thought. In James, a configuration with the parental objects close to that described as bi-triangulation for the white psychosis (Donnet & Green, 1973) can be observed: the parents or their symbolic substitutes constitute a bad intrusive object and an idealised absent object, two sides of the same coin, who are distinguished not by the difference between the sexes, but by the condition of good and bad. Neither one nor the other can produce or sustain the absence needed to structure thought. The bad object is felt to be evil because of its excessive proximity, and the idealised object cannot be used by the subject because of its excessive absence and unavailability. This makes it fall again into the net of the bad object. Green describes a state of "psychic pain produced by a kidnapping of the object (the ego encysts itself with the object in a painful unit where he tries to imprison it)" (Green, 1979, 1980): the narcissistic withdrawal is a corollary of the object disinvestment. But in the return of the investments to the subject, he drags, without being aware of it, the object, but it is an empty object.

Due to the splitting of the object within the subject, there is a split between the bad ego and the good ego, the latter being permanently attacked by the bad one. This can be associated with the paralysis or ejection of thinking that happens in this situation: the attack of destructive drives aims at avoiding consciousness, and, on the other hand, the superego prohibits the expression of the death wish aimed at the omnipotent bad object, and the resentment towards the impotent good object.

Green describes that these patients sometimes do not recognise what has been talked about in analysis, even their own words (Green, 1993). Neither do they understand their meaning. There is a de-subjectivation of thought itself by the subject. This happens frequently in James' analysis, sometimes between one session and the next, sometimes during the same session. A complete sequence of events might be erased, which is what happened initially in regard to the lack of maternal response. The patient himself is significantly disturbed when noticing this. We must understand the cost of these mechanisms, which lead to a loss of understanding of psychic causality. The patient is not able to retain and cannot speculate about his own experiences.

James' functioning corresponds to the description of negative narcissism, but, like white psychosis, it is rarely found in a pure form. Through sustained depressive states, we sense its presence, hidden, in the structure of this patient. Sometimes, as in the described episode, it comes out of its den. Sometimes, because psychic functioning can be completely split, patients in this state will present with an overinvestment of intellectual activity, reaching important achievements.

The evolution of the process in these patients is long and filled with oscillations. In the case of James, I believe that, bit by bit, he has been investing his analysis, being able to use it at times, sharing with me his internal world. At times, he is able to keep, and even retrieve, some of what we have been able to understand together. Despite the apparent difficulties he has in his contact with others, it seems that sometimes he is able to share some pleasure with me, produced by our joint dialogue. This is something that André Green emphasises as a significant step, a sign of renewed investment.

Note

1.   In essence, Green is responding here to a question that Freud raised in "Neurosis and psychosis" (Freud, 1924b, p. 153):

> In conclusion, there remains to be considered the question of what the mechanism, analogous to repression, can be by means of which the ego detaches itself from the external world. This cannot, I think, be answered without fresh investigations; but such a mechanism, it would seem, must, like repression, comprise a withdrawal of the cathexis sent out by the ego.

References

Bion, W. R. (1977). *Two Papers: The Grid and Caesura*. London: Karnac [reprinted, 1989].

Bion, W. R (2014/1962). Learning from experience. In: C. Mawson (Ed.), *The Complete Works of W. R. Bion, Vol. IV* (pp. 259–365). London: Karnac.

Donnet, J.-L. & Green, A. (1973). *L' Enfant de ça. Psychanalyse d'un entretien: La psychose blanche*. Paris: Les éditions de Minuit.

Freud, S. (1915c). Instincts and their vicissitudes. *S. E.*, *14*: 111–140. London: Hogarth.

Freud, S. (1917d). A metapsychological supplement to the theory of dreams. *S. E.*, *14*: 217–235. London: Hogarth.

Freud, S. (1923b). *The Ego and the Id*. *S. E.*, *19*: 3–66. London: Hogarth.

Freud, S. (1924b). Neurosis and psychosis. *S. E.*, *19*: 150–153. London: Hogarth.

Freud, S. (1925h). Negation. *S. E.*, *19*: 233–240. London: Hogarth.

Green, A. (1967). Le narcissisme primaire: structure ou état. *L'inconscient*, *I*: 127–157; 2: 89–116. Reprinted in: *Narcissisme de vie narcissisme de mort*. Paris: Éditions de Minuit, 1983.

Green, A. (1975). The analyst, symbolization and absence in the analytic setting on changes in analytic practice and analytic experience. *International Journal of Psycho-Analysis*, *56*: 1–22.

Green, A. (1982). La double limite. In: *La folie privée: psychanalyse des cas limites* (pp. 293–316). Paris: Gallimard, Folio, 1990.

Green, A. (1983a). La mère morte. In: *Narcissisme de vie narcissisme de mort* (pp. 222–254). Paris: Éditions de Minuit.

Green, A. (1983b). Le langage dans la psychoanalyse. In: *Langages, II Rencontre psychanalytique d'Aix-en-Provence* (pp. 179–206). Paris: Belles Lettres, 1984.

Green, A. (1987). La capacité de rêverie te le mythe étiologique. In: *La folie privée: psychanalyse des cas limites* (pp. 347–368). Paris: Gallimard, Folio, 1990.

Green, A. (1993). *Le travail du négatif*. Paris: Éditions de Minuit.

Green, A. (1995). *Propédeutique: la métapsychologie révisitée*. Seyssel: Champ Vallon.

Green, A. (2002). "De la tiercéité". In: *La Pensée Clinique* (pp. 259–308). Paris: Odile Jacob.

Green, A. (2012). *La Clinique psychanalytique contemporaine*. Paris: Éditions d'Ithaque.

Green, A. (2013). *Penser la psychanalyse: avec Bion, Lacan, Winnicott, Laplanche, Anzieu*, Paris: Les éditions d'Ithaque.

Winnicott, D. W. (1971). *Playing and Reality*. London: Tavistock.

PART V
CLINICAL APPLICATIONS

CHAPTER EIGHT

The work of the negative in action*

Talya S. Candi and Elias M. da Rocha Barros

Introduction

On being invited to contribute to this book, we (the co-authors) decided to try out an experiment. Talya S. Candi (first author) has a solid academic training coming thus from a more scholarly tradition and is a passionate and knowledgeable student of André Green's work. Elias Rocha Barros (second author) comes from a mostly Kleinian–Bionian clinical tradition but is also deeply influenced by other authors such as Thomas Ogden, Nino Ferro, and André Green. He has been mainly a clinician throughout his life, with some theoretical incursions in attempts to elaborate a metapsychology of the symbolic processes. Given these slight but significant differences in our training and intellectual background, and our friendship and deep respect for each other's work, we came up with an idea: Elias Rocha Barros would present a case from his day to day practice and Talya S. Candi would explore this clinical material from the perspective of André Green's concept of the work of the negative. Our common goal would be to try to perceive the work of the negative in action. That is, to see the clinical resonance of a powerful conceptual idea.

---

* The authors would like to thank Alberto Rocha Barros for the editing of the paper.

Peter's story

Dr Elias Rocha Barros reports a clinical case.

Peter was sixty-six years old when he sought me for a new analysis. He tells me he has undergone various analytic experiences, two of them having lasted more than ten years each. The reason for his going back to analysis are two feelings that bother him: (1) a sense of emptiness, of a lack of meaning regarding various aspects of his life, and (2) a permanent feeling of indignation which assumes diverse forms. At times, it is pure irritation over the very presence of other people, who seem always to be doing something inappropriate, and at times a feeling that others demand of him undue and impossible things. He says his decision to make an appointment with me was prompted by a family meeting in which his children and present girlfriend participated and all were telling him that he was unbearable and that if he did not go back to treatment, they would all leave him. Peter refers to his former analyses as mere palliatives. They helped, but deep down did not change anything. He decided to seek me out because friends and his psychiatrist told him that if Dr Elias does not cure you, then there is no hope left. He says this in an ironic and irritated way.

Of his childhood he speaks relatively little. He tells me that his mother spent her life depressed and ended up committing suicide and that his father used to beat up his children and be violent (both verbally and physically) to anyone he despised who crossed his path. Peter was physically abused as a child a lot, "for good and bad reasons", as he puts it. His father also used to beat his mother and their domestics. For these recurrent episodes of violence, the father underwent various legal suits for physical aggression, but, as he was rich and powerful, these lawsuits always ended up going nowhere. After his mother's death, his father left his children; they never got together again until near his death ten years later. The reason for the rupture never became clear to the patient. He says his father claimed above all that his children were a disappointment to him; they never came close to being even the shadow of what he, the father, had dreamed they would be. On dying, his father left half his wealth to his children he had broken relations with and the other half to a learning institution.

Peter has harsh things to say about his siblings. He describes them as "scoundrels", "real idiots", and very superficial people, although they are all successful professionally and he recognises this. Peter was a successful executive, became a wealthy man in his own right, and even doubled the paternal fortune, or better yet, he adds, tripled it. At the moment, he works as a business consultant, having his office in his house. He has three children, all "idiots", as he describes them, although they, too, are persons of recognised professional success with a certain social prominence in their fields of interest. He then tells me that his suicidal mother was also rich and left all her wealth to her grandchildren, excluding and ignoring her children in the inheritance distribution. He says they could have challenged or tried to revoke her will, but he and his siblings decided not to create confusion and, especially, avoid having to explain to the judge that his mother was "a bitch", mentally disturbed, and that she spread a sense of death in her home all her life. And worse, they would have to prove to the judge that they, the children, were worthy of the inheritance.

He emphasises that he came to me without any hope of being able to get better, that he had come because forced to do so by his immediate family and because he wished to preserve what was left of his relationship with his children. He also tells me that, unlike his father, he has already distributed the inheritance in life to his children and that today he lives with not much, just enough to keep him comfortable, but in peace, especially as he still works, and he ends his explanation saying, "When my money runs out, I will kill myself."

Contact with this patient is uncomfortable when not boring. Right up to today, I ask myself what could have led me to accept him as a patient. I think it was a detail in his life that sparked my curiosity. It had to do with his participation in violent gangs during his adolescence and the start of adult life. They were gangs that cultivated violence for violence's sake, at times racists, others ideological, but always dedicated to seeking out a fight. He tells me he has already been prosecuted criminally for aggression more than ten times, including for attacking a judge, but that he always managed to be acquitted or had his charges dropped.

I believe I accepted him in part because I became curious about his involvement with aggressiveness in contrast with his gentlemanly looks and lordly behaviour, and the fact of this patient's always calling to my mind Green's work of the negative. It would be an opportunity for doing some clinical research, I thought. On accepting him for analysis, I had no expectations of being able to transform him. I believe this lack of hope was already part of my countertransference, as was my extreme curiosity over the almost caricature nature of his plight.

I would like to stress that Peter does not immediately strike one as an aggressive person; quite the opposite, he gives the impression of great fragility and his communication is marked by cordialities and a sweet and measured voice. His way of speaking is, most of the time, mild and dispirited, interspersed by moments of extreme aggressiveness in his voice.

Peter: nothing means no-thing

Talya S. Candi now comments on the clinical material.

In 2005, André Green wrote a short text entitled "L'humanité de l'inhumain" [The humanity of the inhuman] as a preface to a book by Claude Balier: *La violence en Abyme: essai de psychocriminologie* [The Abyss of Violence: An Essay on Criminal Psychology). In this work, psychoanalyst Balier presents treatment cases of criminals in prisons in the south of France and confronts us with fundamental clinical and ethical questions on the psychoanalytic treatment of prisoners who have severely infringed human law. In this short preface, Green asks himself (and us) whether there is any possibility for the analyst to bear the wild accounts of horror and violence and control the desire to drastically reject and condemn the authors of these crimes whose stories allow glimpses into a cruel world of violence and sadism. In such cases, says Green, the analyst runs the great risk of becoming himself inhuman, trivialising crime, or internally disengaging himself from the fear and horror.

What, then, would be the analytic attitude with which to approach these criminals? Green says,

> The analyst cannot turn from a fundamental psychoanalytical attitude: to listen, be receptive to one's own affects, control one's own rejection, understand (intuiting an unconscious meaning in the life drive of the Id), interpret (more for oneself actually than for the patient) and finally, not let oneself be taken over by the negation, the repetition and the acted out violence. (2005, p. xi, translated for this edition)

For Green (1983, 1990c, 2007) this acted out violence, non-psychic, throws the subject into a turmoil of actions, not represented, not thought, unimaginable by any human mind, ruled by the crazed pleasure of pure excitation and its discharge. These non-mentalized impulses produce an undifferentiated mental emptiness: emptiness of the very subject, emptiness of the external object, which is not structured because of the lack of distinction between an "I" and the external world. The destructiveness short-circuits and eludes any contact and recognition of the other. It is to deny at all costs the psychic reality and to safeguard from pain, relying on non-recognition, non-representation, and non-existence. In the psyche of such criminals, a process takes over, leading to the repeated erasure of any and all traces of affective and emotional experience with a caring external object, resulting in a sense of non-existence of both the self and the other.

In this context, the destructive acting out arises as the fastest means to relieve the subject of intense, unbearable excitation in its pure state, a brutal excitation with no representation or object (internal or external) through which it can be contained. This excitation presses towards discharge and ends up striking indiscriminately both the subject itself and the external world. In 1967, André Green postulated the existence of a negative narcissistic structure characterised by the valorisation of a state of non-being. The inhuman is this perverse capacity to nullify any feeling, transforming the other and the very "I" into "nothing", into "no one", as though any attempt at giving a name and meaning to the world were violently exterminated. "Evil is without cause," Green tells us, "its raison d'être is to proclaim that all that exists has no meaning, obeys no order and pursues no aim. Evil depends solely on the power it can exert to impose its will on the objects of its appetite . . ." (Green, 1990c, p. 400, translated for this edition).

I would like here to turn to commenting on the material *per se* of Peter's sessions and to show how André Green's ideas bear upon this clinical case.

Peter goes on a new search for analysis after two failed attempts at analysis. At sixty-six, he presents symptoms that provoke rejection from his closest objects. Even so, pressured by a wish to improve his relation with his children and threatened by being left by his girl-friend, he ventures on a new analytic relation which should, this time, in principle make the difference, though he enters it without any hopes. Peter complains of the emptiness and the lack of meaning in life and of a constant irritation with others who never seem to be in the right place and who arouse in him criminal wishes. I believe that what drove Peter to look for a new analysis was that his death anxieties (of dying as well as of killing someone) had become overwhelmingly threatening and unbearable

Peter's story related by the analyst is not, however, an empty story. It allows us glimpses of powerful characters who confront us with feelings of terror, cynicism, trivialisation of evil, sadism, destruction, and impotence. The beings in his surroundings seem like characters out of a Dostoevsky novel.

Green, as well as Balier, endorses the possibility of therapeutic action for convicted prisoners via the intersubjective aspects of the analytic relation. Could contact with another human, a *nebenmensch* [fellow being], as Freud indicated in 1895 in the *Project*, produce any therapeutic effect?[1] They recognise, however, the dual effect of the resonance which takes over the session. The inhuman, the evil, the nothingness, the "no one" and their traumatic correlates resound in the psyche of the analyst activating powerful defences that can annihilate any compassion, but also, and concomitantly, the traumatisms of the patient and the analyst come into resonance, reaching the psychical resources of the analyst that are necessary to listen and comprehend. This double attack makes the analyst's attendance extremely difficult and painful.

The analyst is engaged by the provocative plea: would he actually have the capacity to make a difference, to help Peter live a better life? Could this analysis finally help Peter recover some pleasure (be it the slightest) in feeling alive and foster a reconciliation with his affective relations, past, present, and, possibly, future?

On transforming the acted out violence and the emptiness of meaning of Peter's life into a project, a Greenian dream, the analyst fights against the resonating effects of Peter's traumas and stands for Eros and life in the working through of the negativity. The non-representation of life, the anguishes of death, the nothingness and the "no one" of Peter's way of being are opposed internally to a representation that might allow the analyst to recover the patient's link with humanness, something that will afford him self-recognition and an existence, a story: "I am not like Peter, I am not a nothing and a no one", the analyst seems to scream complementarily, in my view. In this context, André Green would be a live container, a hope that could give meaning to Peter's non-meaning, as well as sustenance to the analyst's faith (Bion, 1970) in the existence of an inner affective psychic reality. I think that the work of the negative notion evoked by the analyst is a way of trying to connect to some good, perhaps idealised, object, which could create a sufficiently strong affective link to instil psychological sense in Peter's empty life.

How can we psychoanalytically understand Peter's persistent irritation and destructiveness? How could we explain that, even after three failed analytic experiences, Peter still seems to listen to his psychiatrist and continues in his search for an analyst who could perhaps help him in his desperate quest for atonement, for possibly legating an *affective* (and not merely a monetary) inheritance to his children?

Balier's patients, as well as Elias da Rocha Barros' Peter, are exemplary of what Green (1983) would term the borderline patient, the patient at the limits of analysability, patients who bring to analysis the non-neurotic or psychotic parts of the mind. It was these patients and this type of situation that led André Green to revisit Freudian metapsychology and introduce new concepts such as the work of the negative, death narcissism, the dead mother, the framing structure, the chain of Eros, and so many others.

It is these patients who require from the psychoanalyst that he rethink the work from an intersubjective model that takes into account the structuring role of the human subjectivity of the analyst, the role of *nebenmensch*. These patients do not seem to have mnemic traces and memories of experiences of satisfaction that could link the brutal force of the drive to representations that give an internal sense of coherence and stability to their subjectivity. It can, however, be asked, who is or what is this experience of satisfaction of which the non-neurotic patient seems not to have strong enough internal memory traces?

The work of the negative

In 1980, in the paper "Passions et destins de passions, sur les rapports entre folie et psychose" André Green (1990a) describes a myth of origin that allows us to understand and situate the structuring role of the external object for good psychic and emotional development of the child.

The drive in its essence, says Green, is an excessive, mad force and when it does not have an external object that will organise this force in a network of meaning, it manifests itself as a demonic blind force that wants to impose its will on the objects of its appetite. Madness is a constituent part of human nature and is linked to the vicissitudes of the excesses of primordial Eros, the indomitable forces that are transformed into impetuous amorous passions that wish to take possession of the objects of satisfaction.

The binding process of the drive is always made in a relation with another human being, a *nebenmensch* who binds the force to a meaning and inserts life and a story. When the self of the child is able to establish an egoic organisation, a regimen of stable investment, and a constant level of excitation in a trusting ambience, he will still have the task of fighting with the potentially maddening internal bodily excitations. The child can then develop defence mechanisms to elaborate the drive through phantasy.

But why mechanisms of defence? Why would the subject, on being born, need to defend himself from making way for what was called psychism? The drive, which is aroused in the first encounters of the child with its objects of need and care, produces an intense impact in their presence and, concomitantly, a profound helplessness in their absence. Thus, then, the quality of the first encounters is crucial, for both the presence and absence potentially hold the capacity to madden the subject in coming to be. It is this drive (excess of/in the presence as well as of/in the absence), this blind and silent passion, without limits of time and space, which obliges the child to defend himself using precarious instruments, defence mechanisms that allow him to free himself of the excesses of excitation. How to see what blinds us? How to narrate, to speak of the instant and place from which words derive? The psyche needs to eliminate part of itself to be able to survive.

Humanity arises from a "No!", the negativising of the drive, which demands an interminable work of disengagement and reintegration, in such a way that all and any drive associated movement needs to be re-presented to be able to be appropriated by the self and become an active part of the subjectivity. From this perspective, the subject is the agency of an endless work of the negative, a work of death that serves to preserve life. It is this arduous work which presupposes a gradual establishing of defences, more or less rigid and pathological, that is going to institute limits (a psychic topography) regulating the level of

excitation and distress, and activating the back and forth that characterises the process of symbolisation. The notion of the work of the
negative allows us visualise the paradoxical functioning of the psychic
apparatus as it places side by side the concepts of psychic working
through and the defences, and, concomitantly, emphasises not the
annihilation of the conflict, but, rather, the hiatus (time and space)
which will install itself between the working through and resistance.
The psychic movement (the substitution of the object and displacement of the affective investment) necessary for the process of symbolisation of the emotional experience will arise in the breathing space of
the conflict, on the borders of the self.

From the metapsychological point of view, the concept of the work
of the negative emphasises the dialectic logic of forces which propels
the psychic conflicts not only on the intersubjective level, but also the
intrapsychic level. Green's idea is to point to the existence (or non-
existence) of a breathing space of the forces involved in the conflicts.
As such, André Green reorganises psychoanalytic theory, installing at
the centre of metapsychology conceptual dyads that work dialectally
in interaction, each in conjunction with the other, each in opposition
to the other: unconscious–conscious, drive–object, infantile–adult,
transference–countertransference, binding–unbinding.

The role of the good enough external object is dual. On the one
hand, it is the object of identification and, on the other, it supplies the
necessary care for the development of the child. The mother should
effect three basic functions to waken the force of the drive and create
meaning: containment (Bion), which regulates the amount of anxiety,
setting off the circulation of distress via transformative working
through processes, equivalent to the digestive/metabolic process;
holding (Winnicott), which accords temporal support to the gesture of
the child, sustaining the hope of the drive, in time, to find the object;
finally, reverie (Bion's concept highlighted by Green) as the element
which introduces the link of mother and father. Asking himself what
the mother dreams of, Green points to the father, as third, other, who
is in the mother's mind. "To dream of the father is to dream of the link
existing between the parents and between the child" (Green, 1990b,
p. 352). Reverie brings together what the maternal care accorded by
the mother or her substitute tends inevitably to separate. Reverie
installs the primitive triangulation and enables an opening to alterity.
It is useful to recall that the confrontation with "alterity" is always

threatening, irritating, and disappointing. Reverie might, therefore, be a disrupting element because it is in some way a representation of the link between the parents which excludes the child.

In the light of this, the mother will only accomplish these tasks if she is able to live with her own drives and passions, if she herself has a stable and consistent emotional organisation, to thus *waken* the child to instinctual life and be able to receive without fear of being submerged by the imperious demands of the child. As such, she serves as a container to bind this force in a way that renders it acceptable and digestible. The care of a mother is paradoxical: on the one hand, aiming to incite and foster the wakening of the drive which is life itself, and, on the other, make tolerable the unbridled passion (love, jealousy, envy) and also the very force of bodily impulses she arouses in the child. Potentially, the mother oscillates between excess of gratification and excess of frustration. If the psyche of the subject is invaded by intolerable anger or a sense of impingement, the object will give rise to withdrawal, because narcissism will always do its best to ensure that disengagement remains possible; this is what Green (1993, p. 155) calls "subjectal disengagement", which he links to death narcissism (1967).

In this model proposed by the myth of origin, the determining factor is the substantial investment of the mother which Green links to ordinary maternal madness, an exacerbation of sensitivity ensuing from the primary maternal preoccupation (Winnicott, 1966/2006). The maternal libidinal investment must hold an intensity that gives an affective consistency to the mother–child bond. This affective consistency sustains, in the moments of absence, the hope of her return and triggers the hallucinatory wish fulfilment which will enable the child to hallucinate the shared moments of mutual pleasure. When the child feels well enough accompanied by these moments of shared affective experiences, he can forget the mother and venture to discover and invest in new objects. The maternal libidinal investment and her care can be negativised and transformed, then, in a blank canvas, in a primary narcissistic framing structure (Green, 1967), a colourless canvas (Levine, 2012) which should be thought of as a maternal container, a carnal container, as a mirror, a mirror that does not only attract images, but which is the matrix of all reflexivity essential for symbolisation processes. When the primordial object is unable to perform the constitutive functions and serve as support to structure the child's psyche, the ego will not only have to struggle internally against instinctive impulse and bodily excitations, bearing ever the germ of madness, but will also have to cope externally with the disorganisation of the unbound impulses of the object. It is the struggle against these external agents that should be allies and have become enemies which will be responsible for the radicalisation of the split and exacerbation of the force of the drive that will become destructive, a consequence of a double attack on the ego from the external environment and the internal demand.

Starting with the conflating of different Freudian, Winnicottian, and Bionian concepts that indicates that both playing and thinking emerge from phenomena associated with absence and loss, André Green (1974/1975, 2000a, 2007a) proposes what he called "the work of the negative". This work shows itself in different forms and oscillates between two extremes. At one extreme, we have what could be considered to be a successful work of the negative, when the process that it involves allows the emergence of a representation of an absence that is a potential presence. This potential presence is the *primordio* of the internal space for phantasy and dreaming and is essential for developing the capacity for thinking. At the other extreme, we have what we could call an unsuccessful, failed, or even lost, work of the negative. In this case, the representation of the absence is lost and the process of psychic organisation that allows for effective thought is blocked.

A failed work of the negative results in a destruction of the internal space, which produces a "black hole", a deadly excess of absence or a destructive, unrepresented presence that annihilates all the potentialities to be, to think, and to differentiate past, present, and future. Thus, we see that the work of the negative can assume pathological or structuring features depending on the degree of discontinuity that negativity brings about, resulting either in the establishment of healthy psychic limits (firm and flexible) that can alternate binding, unbinding, and promote rebinding of the force of the drive to a representation or a process of anti-thought and psychic unravelling and destruction.

We should always remember that interruptions, shutdowns, and breaks are necessary for a structuring psychic function, because they install distance and difference between the self and the object. When the frustration of the breaks can be tolerated, the void will be internalised in such a way as to result in the creation and reinforcing of an "open" internal space, in which the subject can arise through representations, unconscious fantasies, and thinking. Green (2000a) called the creation of this space *encadrement*.

Thus, the result of the work of the negative depends basically on the nature and success of the individual's defensive activity. In the primary defences of which repression is the prototype, the polarity binding–unbinding is accompanied by a rebinding in the unconscious. The further one is from repression, the more one notices in the other primary defences (splitting, foreclosure) that unbinding tends to predominate, limiting or preventing rebinding. We should consider that some radical defences, such as projective identification, reinforce the "disavowal of splitting" which encourages disobjectalisation and blocks a rebinding process (Reed, 2002).

Building upon Winnicott's elaborations, Begoin (1989) defines trauma as the situation that deprives the subject of the external environment conditions necessary for good psychic functioning. The trauma emerges in this sense from repeated failed encounters between the drive impulse and an external object that could awaken, sustain, contain, reflect, and dream (reverie), and attaches structuring meaning to the life drive of the child. We should not however always refer the traumas to failures of the external objects; a child can also reject the place or time that the external object can accord it and insist on perpetuating failed encounters. There are, nevertheless, many different ways of making the situation of non-satisfaction less painful and traumatic, including desire, memory traces, and repression (through hallucinatory wish fulfilment and fantasies). They are all intended to avoid the appearance of an excessive quantum of anxiety and despair with the potential for the mutilation of psychic life itself.

Major mechanisms characteristic of the life and death drives are binding and unbinding. The life drive might include within itself both binding and unbinding, whereas the death drive involves only unbinding. The life drive is directed towards "objectilisation", to significant affective investment. The aim of the death drive is, through unbinding, to perform a "disobjectilising", decathecting function, and this leads to the concept of negative narcissism as aspiration to the zero level, the expression of the maximum possible degree of "disobjectilisation", as observed in autism. The aim of the life drive is the process of symbolisation. It is the hope and anticipation of meeting with an object that can bind the force and provide a meaningful meeting that sets in motion the displacement of the force of the libido and promotes the infinite substitutions characterising symbolisation. Finally, it is worth noting that the force of the objectilising function will always need to overcome a force opposing it, which André Green called the disobjectilising function. The latter seeks to inhibit the drive force, minimise the movements, and disinvest the objects. Disobjectilising proceeds to an action that makes it so that the drive evolution loses that which is in it and is apt to deal with the object's more singularising properties (Green, 2007b). Disobjectilising works in the service of the death drive so that the objects are transformed into "nothing" and "no one", but also into "anyone".

Summarising the process of psychic links, the objectilisings underpinning what we usually call object relations, André Green introduces the concept of the "chains of Eros" (1997). This chain structures itself upon the links of psychic work (drive–object) organised in a spiral movement. It starts off from the impulse of the drive and its dynamic force pressing for immediate discharge. This link, when worked through, transforms itself into the affective states, upon the introduction of pleasure and its correlate, unpleasure. The affective states will, in their turn, be able to organise the experiences of desire that express themselves in the search for objects (external and internal). It is the hopeful expectation of finding and meeting the object of desire that allows for the emergence of the kernels of unconscious fantasies that organise the scenes of hallucinatory wish fulfilment. These scenes, when worked through, allow space finally for the language of passions involving love and hate, with all the richness pertaining to affective and erotic life.

What is at stake, then, is to follow in the patient's material the dynamics of the movements of the binding processes and their transformations, knowing that these binding processes are inseparable from their antagonist, the unbinding processes, not only the aggressive or sadistic, but also the destructive processes of disinvesting and disobjectilising (1997, pp. 278–279).

How could we save Peter from the wolves?

Let us return to Peter's sessions related by Dr Rocha Barros.

As early as in the first session, he tells me that he had three recurrent dreams which repeated themselves in versions always round the same theme.

The dreams were:

1. He was walled up alive and in possession of all his faculties in the wall of his home when adolescent, and in this state observed his parents and siblings, to whom he was invisible.

2. He was constantly provoked by a crazy neighbour, who spent her day throwing objects in his direction. He always reacted with indignation.

3. This dream was repeated the day before the start of his analysis. He dreamed that he was being chased by an enormous, very ferocious dog like a St Bernard (the type that rescues people in Switzerland after avalanches) from which he ran away without stopping. He tells me that this dog appears many times with names suggestive of his father's name.

These dreams are told after about fifteen minutes of silence.

I tell him that I consider that these three dreams mentioned and related in this first session announced the themes of his analysis: his feeling of being condemned to observe his family life crowded by the violence of his father and the depression of his mother without his being able to do anything about it, and I add that life for him seemed to be a thing which passed before his eyes without his being able to do anything, overcome by a sense of being walled up, a sense of condemnation.

After a while, he says, "You were going to comment on the other dreams."

I tell him that while the second dream is like a remembrance, it refers to how he lived his mother's depression, or, better, her as a crazy woman always aggressive towards him, with her grievances thrown on him, resulting in his feeling of indignation.

He murmurs, "Bravo!"

I add that the third dream perhaps referred to his attitude before this new analysis that today was beginning. I suggest that he fears my being a persecutor, like his father, who will get upset over his immobility, his inertia, but who yet curiously bears a hope in the form of a barrel like that carried by a Swiss St Bernard, coming to the rescue of someone who was buried under cold feelings. Swiss because he was afraid I was as distant as he—a feeling he feared, given the lack of love, but which also carried some hope that I might be neutral and capable of defending myself from his aggression.

After ten minutes of silence, he comments ironically, "Daddy, Mummy, and I and you insisting on saving me. It is useless but I recognise that your last comment about the Swiss nationality is intelligent and something different from the incompetents who analysed me before!"

I comment that it would probably be pointless my saying that he had just finished burying my comment, covering it with his coldness and effacing any possibility of hope.

To which he says, "Voi que entrate lasce ogni esperanza" referring to the inscription on the gates of hell. (Abandon hope, all ye who enter here!)

Comments by Talya S. Candi

Peter tells his analyst about three old repetitive dreams, which became more present on the eve of his beginning analysis as though they have forever been awaiting being able to be told. The dreams have a hallucinatory character; they are pictures[2] of the terrifying internal world in which Peter lives.

In this way, the analysis starts, through an invitation by the patient for the analyst to feel submerged by these scenes/hallucinations. Peter does not dream (Ogden, 2004) in my view (although Dr Rocha Barros thinks he does and interprets his dreams), does not fantasise, does not associate (Green, 2000b); he throws these pictures towards the analyst in the hope that they will be gathered. There is the sensation of a self submerged in debris that does not even let him sleep in order to, at some point, awaken, and that wants to be freed of these bizarre images that fill his mind, persecuting him, and in which he feels imprisoned. These images poured out in the session testify to Peter's fragile capacity for introspection and psychic working through. The references to the terror and catastrophe seem to correspond with the patient's experience and attest to the existence of memory traces of diurnal terrors deeply buried, but, however, still active (Green, 2000).

The images, as I see it, are bombs Peter throws to test the vitality of the analyst, his capacity to resist the violence of the crazy family, the neighbour who attacks, the mad dog that pursues him.

In this surprising scenario, the analyst does not become paralysed by, or afraid of, the bombs; he is interested in the pictures Peter throws, gathers them in, discovers sense, makes connections, links past, present, and future, contextualises these pictured scenes, inserting personages and affection, trying to set in motion the psychic working through. The analyst transforms the bombs into stories and, therefore, deactivates them.

From the perspective of Green's Eros chain, I believe that with Peter we are working the first link in the chain, which is to attribute a psychic quality to the drive force, install the primordials of what was called experience of satisfaction, contain what would be pure evacuative discharge, understand that these objects carry a scream, a plea, and install and differentiate the registers internal–external, pleasure–unpleasure, Peter–analyst.

In my view, the analyst is not frightened, he does not let himself be intimidated by the violence and terror, he deactivates the bomb and gives it back in the form of a ball and, thus, transforms Peter's throwing of objects into a ball game: there, where at first we see only evacuative discharge of the drive's forces transformed into scenes of terror, the analyst inserts psychic work; he transforms the bombs into scenes with stories, feelings, and personages. This game indicates a shared work experience that provides surprise and pleasure.

On asking the analyst to comment on the second dream, I believe that Peter seems to be saying he likes the game. Thus, the game continues, with the analyst deactivating the second bomb and transforming it into a ball. This second experience of satisfaction leaves Peter happy and excited. The "bravo" is an expression of surprise and of his excitation on having found a companion to play ball/bomb with him.

In this first encounter with Elias, we can point to two dynamic axes of working through defences (work of the negative) in which the intersubjective game can happen.

One is a reflexive axis: seeing the other is opposed to being seen/admired. When Peter is seen he exists, if he is not seen, he is invisible and disappears. The pair see–be seen and its underlying basis, voyeurism–exhibitionism, are at the heart of this analytic process. It is worth emphasising here the importance of "seeing and being seen" and of the mirror role of the mother as a first form of recognition (Lacan, 1998; Steiner, 2011; Winncott, 1971).

This first axis of the work is revealed already in the first dream. In his invisibility, Peter is not seen, but sees all. This scene takes us to a phenomenon that Green calls the self-disappearance of the "I" (moi), which refers to the disengagement of the self (Green, 1993, p. 207). We are speaking here of a phenomenon called "subjectal disengagement" (Green, 1993) where *seeing* and *being seen* do not engage the self, do not possess subjective implications, do not engender association, thought, or conflicts. The pictures poured out by Peter point to this type of paradoxical functioning by which he sees all but knows nothing. Only when the analyst describes what he sees in the images and relates the images to Peter's story does the patient begin to know something about the images that crowd his mind. In this sense, the analyst's interpretations truly grant existence to Peter.

On the other hand, I suggest that this very primitive defence, this self-disappearance of the "I" (*moi*) works on a hallucinatory axis that does not discriminate between a showing of self, being seen, and seeing the others. The "bravo" that Peter shouts out, surprised and excited, to the analyst is a "bravo" which he hallucinatorily receives.

The second axis of the work of the negative is of omnipotence in which having all and being all that characterises self-sufficiency and arrogance are opposed to destruction, annihilation, and nothingness.

The analyst's third intervention seems to have been triggered from this axis, which I believe arises from what we call *resonance to the trauma*. Peter's screamed "bravo", the absence of affection and psychic conflict, Peter's coldness, produce in the analyst a sense of asphyxiation, of death in life. It seems to me that at this moment the analyst convokes an internal working through in search of hope and a neutral territory safe from violence. On suggesting that the patient feared that the analyst would be a persecutor, just like his father, and mentioning the need to defend himself from the coldness and aggressivity, the analyst shows that the ball is, in truth, a bomb that could explode at any moment. The analyst gives concreteness to the bombs and transforms the analytic field into a battlefield. I think this interpretation frightens the patient, interrupts the game brutally, and ends Peter's excitation.

I believe the patient felt the interpretation as if the analyst had said something like this: "Things are not well; let's stop exciting ourselves over a game and start working", or, maybe, "Who do you think you are? You think you are big enough to seduce and play with my wife?"

I believe that Peter responds ironically ("Daddy, Mummy, and I and you insisting on saving me. It is useless," says Peter) to the analyst to protect himself from the attack and coldness of the analyst himself who, on making this interpretation, very quickly transforms himself into an insensitive father who does not understand and respect the unique moment of self-discovery, pleasure, and excitation that he was finally able to find.

Peter's destructiveness, clearly present at the end of the session, does not indicate here the sadistic pleasure which characterises the sadomasochist. Here, the narcissistic dimension prevails. Peter does not know what to say, do, to relate with another human being, a *neben-mensch*; he cannot imagine what would be a relation with a caring object. He throws the nightmares/bombs at the analyst because it is the way he knows how to relate with others. He is afraid of being attacked by bombs and tries to control the analyst, who escapes from his control and transforms himself into a very dangerous enemy. The analyst surprises him by not retaliating with bombs and this surprise transforms itself into excitation/exaltation, in the form of "bravo".

In this session, the analyst oscillates, to my mind, as seen by Peter between being, on the one hand, the ideal mother who receives him and admires him and whose presence becomes indispensable to the feeling of existing and, on the other, a dangerous and intrusive enemy whose penetration and aggressiveness needs at all costs to be controlled and neutralised.

I believe that this oscillation between ideal mother and enemy reflects Peter's internal splitting caused by the lack of internal object links. On the one hand, there is the identification with a maternal object, who accepts playing but leaves off the game when it heats up dangerously, and, on the other, a paternal identification with an invasive, authoritarian father who gives substance to his violence.

Let us return to the session reported by Dr Elias Rocha Barros.

> He misses the next session and, in the third session of the week, tells me that he had another dream. In this one there was a firefighter with a fire extinguisher putting out little fire outbreaks. The scene was intriguing and, at the same time, like a caricature. The firefighter was American. He knew this by the richness of the equipment, but that, at the same time, it was ridiculous to carry all that sophisticated equipment to put out "little spots of fire". It looks like—and at this moment he finds this quite funny—a little boy putting out a fire by pissing on it.
>
> I say nothing and wait. The patient remains totally motionless until he says that when he was a child he wanted to be a firefighter, a bit before wanting to be a vigilante or, who knows, a serial killer, but then decided to follow a career associated with law. He comments that he had the

luck or the misfortune of being very intelligent, and despite never having studied much he had always been a good student and had always featured in the top marks on examinations. I ask him if he recalled how we/he had ended the last session.

He says yes and comments that "I quoted Dante at the gates of hell."

Talya S. Candi comments

As I see it, Peter misses the next session having left his game partner alone, without hope, at the gates of hell. I suggest thinking that he did not come to the session because he became irritated at the analyst's interpretation and because he does not want to be bothered with things that leave him irritated. Perhaps Peter does not want to be saved by the analyst, much less by his Daddy and Mummy. But the analysis game awakened his curiosity and his power of seduction and, thus, he returns wanting to test the toy once more. I think that he returns because of the "bravo", the admiration he feels for his own intelligence and that of the analyst.

Reflecting on the why of the transgression, Balier suggests that the violent transgressive action of prisoners emerges from an effort, each time greater, to be seen and admired by a mother whose attraction and fascination they were unable to overcome and separate themselves from (Balier, 2005, p. 24).

It is the fascination for a mother to whom they always remain invisible which obliges them to effect a transgressive act. The violent transgression becomes a spectacular way to demonstrate, as much to themselves as to an other, that they exist.

Working from this hypothesis, I think that, on an unconscious level, Peter returns because he has found an ideal mother object he wishes to enchant and seduce, a mother that has very sophisticated equipment, who knows how to deactivate the bombs. A mother who could admire and find him very funny when he plays at putting out the fire spots by pissing on them.

The term "ideal mother" deserves some clarification. As said before, I believe that Peter comes to analysis because his death anxiety has become unbearable. I now further suggest that the pressure provoked by his death anxieties manifests itself in the search for an object who will condone his cynicism and his perverted actions. On an unconscious level, I believe that Peter wants to establish a "perverse pact" (Nos,

2014) with the analyst, a pact that will protect him from the reality of his destructivity. The ideal mother that I am alluding to here is a representation of this perverse pact, by which the analyst could become an accomplice in his disavowal of his terror of death and in his avoidance of separation. Nevertheless, I think that the movement towards the search for this "ideal mother" (the drive cathexis) carries also the potential for transformation of his death anxiety.

The analyst in this second session does not seem to want to embody this mother who is enchanted by the transgressive pranks of the son, the mother who knows how to deactivate bombs, who lets herself be seduced by the son, and looks on him with admiration when he plays at being a serial killer.

Peter left the analyst without hope, I believe, at the gates of hell in the previous session and disappeared. On remembering and talking about the last session, the analyst reinstalls the inferno and the bombs into the analytic scene and the conversation happens along the destroy/be destroyed, all/nothing axis.

Let us return to the account of the session.

Dr Elias Rocha Barros

I tell him that maybe the dream is reflecting his feelings on leaving my consulting room and ask him what this idea seems to him.

He says it seems like nothing, and nothing means no thing except in the heads of analysts, that is why analyses do not work, are innocuous.

I suggest I was under the impression that his comment showed his battle against having any sort of hope and that perhaps the fire of the firefighter he saw as ridiculous was a reference to what he needed to do, put out the small flames of human warmth that yet remained in him, his wish to be saved from the flames of his hate/indignation, and that, in return, he preserved his vocation for the hatred of a serial killer, of a killer.

He says "Bravo!" and I add that he transforms my interventions into a spectacle of self-promotion and him into the mere spectator of this theatre.

He leaves, saying, "Sorry if I disappoint you."

I recall his father, who breaks up with his children saying that all were a disappointment to him.

Talya S. Candi comments

I will say that on mentioning the end of the last session, the analyst disrupts the climate of mutual enchantment and fascination that Peter comes in search of in the session.

I think that the patient feels the interpretation as though the analyst had said something like this: "There is nothing funny in wanting to be a serial killer; it is a thing of a spoiled brat who wants to impress his mother and finds himself big and strong and attacks the serious work of his father." The voice of the analyst here is significant.

I think the interpretation reveals that the analyst is committed to the work, that he cares, and that Peter's destructiveness did not damage his sophisticated "American" firefighting euqipment.

In this session, the analyst becomes a container for Peter's unbound drive's force. He holds the inferno and bears staying with it without disengaging from the emotional experience during Peter's absence.

Here, we see a binding process taking shape. The investment of the analyst opposes Peter's disinvestment (marked by his missing a session); the analyst inserts, in the context of a meaningful relationship, live emotional experience into Peter's disengaged, unbound instinctual drive. On according meaning and sense to the evacuative drive, the analyst inserts humanity into Peter's "nothing is anything" nothingness: "I suggest I was under the impression that his comment showed his battle against having any sort of hope and that perhaps the fire of the firefighter he saw as ridiculous was a reference to what he needed to do, put out the small flames of human warmth that yet remained in him, his wish to be saved from the flames of his hate/indignation, and that, in return, he preserved his vocation for the hatred of a serial killer, of a killer." The analyst suggests here the existence of an internal conflict, a struggle between having and not having hope, and, by doing so, accords meaning to Peter's empty acting out; in this way, he inserts representation, story, and affect that oppose the meaninglessness, the nothingness, the no one of disobjectilising and disengagement that characterise the inhuman.

I believe the "bravo" of this second session is a new attempt of Peter's to seduce the analyst, to speak of his need to be seen and admired. The asking forgiveness that closes the session is a plea, by which the patient says something along these lines: "Do not give up on me. I know I disappointed you but since I don't have a mother, I need a father that can stand my destructiveness." Different from the first "bravo", where no discrimination was discerned between the self of the analyst and Peter's, the "bravo" and the asking forgiveness are directed at the analyst who now embodies fully the powerful, violent, and admired father who abandoned his children. At this moment, the analyst recalls the rupture of the father with the son and, for a second, perceives the helplessness of his patient.

Let us return to the session.

Dr Elias Rocha Barros

In a following session, he dreamed he was at the Einstein Hospital emergency department and that there was a group of doctors round him trying to discover what was wrong with him as he did not present any external, internal, or laboratorial signs to indicate a pathology. But he screamed and fought, saying that he was very hurt, gravely wounded, but did not know where or how he had been hurt.

The single association presented was: this is how I feel, and he spent most of the rest of the session in silence after my having said to him that the dream indicated that he felt very hurt but, just as in the dream, he had no image or sign that allowed him point out to me anything that would allow me to treat him, and that in this state he remained self-enclosed, crying out "I am hurt."

Talya S. Candi comments

I believe the work of the analyst in the previous sessions allowed Peter to have a relation with an object capable of holding, containing, and giving meaning to some aspects of his emotional experiences. Peter can finally suffer the pain of feeling alive and speak of his desire to seek external objects that can provide help. This picture contains once again a calling, a plea; Peter calls on the mother of fascination that he found in the first session, a mother who is enchanted, interested, takes in the inexplicable pain, the fear of death, who knows how to deactivate the bombs and transform the fear and the scream into words, into song, into stories.

Here, the analyst appears as a representation of the invasive object who seems to be saying, "It's no use crying and calling for your mother. She will not come, and if you do not collaborate, your father is going to give up caring for you."

Final considerations

We know there are various models to explain the origin of non-neurotic pathologies. *Grosso modo*, we can point to two: (1) the "psychic conflict" model that goes back to the theorisations of Klein and Kernberg, emphasising the role of aggression, innate envy, and psychic conflict (between the part of the personality dominated by the paranoid–schizoid position that does not recognise the alterity of the other and the depressive position which accepts alterity/otherness), and (2) the deficit model which, based on Kohut and Winnicott, highlights the lack of attunement of the environment to the infant's primary needs. The latter model underlines the difficulties of the subject in self-regulation and achieving a stable, consistent enough level of internal organisation when not provided with a reliable external container or holding environment. Across the years, these models have led to diverging points of view in therapeutic action. According to Ruggiero (2012), the conflict model, which seems the one used by Dr Elias da Rocha Barros, places emphasis on the stability of the setting (which assures that the analysis can survive the patient's destructiveness) and on the interpretation of the psychic conflict, thus enabling confronting the patient with his own aggressiveness. The deficit model, in its turn, underlines the need of providing containment and holding to allow the areas that remained unavailable for representation to be consolidated and integrated. This part of the work consists in creating the backdrop of a blank canvas (Levine, 2012) that will serve as a framing structure (Green) on which the patient's story can be drawn and inscribed. Peter's analysis is characterised by rapid, sudden oscillations and alternations between idealisation and persecution: we have, on the one hand, a desperate quest for fusion (and confusion) with an object that seems to have been lacking in his primary object relation, and, on the other, moments of persecution before an object that deflagrates his destructiveness and his attempts of seduction.

Among the manifold difficulties the analyst must deal with to carry to the end this arduous task, we point out the intense quota of destructiveness that non-neurotic patients bring and activate in the relation with the analyst. Whether it is determined by an innate envy or a failure of primary objects, the containing of destructiveness constitutes an inevitable technical knot and hard test. I believe that, in a case such as Peter's, it is necessary to accord to the patient the possibility of experiencing the analytic setting as an authentically trustworthy, safe, and true container, which can take some time, before interpreting the conflict and destructiveness that, as I see it, arise from frayed, destructured, non-psychical areas that are not ready for representation or available for thought. Finally, I would like to say that the concept of the patient at the limits of analysability introduced by André Green (1974/1975) is very welcome for thinking about Peter's case, as it refers exactly to those patients who test the humanity, the perseverance, and the mental functioning of the analyst to the limits of the tolerable.

Notes

1. It is in 1895, in *A Project for a Scientific Psychology*, that Freud introduces the notion of *Nebenmensch* as one of the absolutely necessary elements for the achievement of the specific action that characterises the experience of satisfaction.
    Freud says in the *Project*:

    > At early stages the human organism is incapable of achieving this specific action. It is brought about by extraneous (*Nebenmensch*) help, when the attention of an experienced person has been drawn to the infantile condition by a discharge taking place along the path of internal change. (Freud, 1895a, p. 336)

    That is, the presence of this *Nebenmensch* ("fellow being/neighbour") is an integral part of the specific action and the starting point of a series of processes that unfold thereon, as Freud makes clear:

    > When the extraneous helper has carried out the specific action in the external world on behalf of the helpless subject, the latter is in a position, by means of reflex contrivances, immediately to perform what is necessary in the interior of his body in order to remove endogenous stimulus. This total event then constitutes an "experience of satisfaction", which has the most momentous consequences in the functional development of the individual. (Freud, 1895a, p. 336)

2. We can recall the conversation between Gustav Janouch and Kafka: "The necessary condition for an image is sight", Gustav claims to have said to Kafka. Kafka supposedly smiled and replied, "We photograph things in order to drive them out of our minds. My stories are a way of shutting my eyes" (Peucker, 2007, p. 104).

References

Balier, C. (2005). De la transgression au déni de l'humain. *Champ psychosomatique*, 2(38): 22–37.

Begoin, J. (1989). La violence du désespoir, ou le contre sens d'une "pulsion de mort" en psychanalyse. *Revue française de psychoanalyse, 2*: 619–641.

Bion, W. R. (1970). *Attention and Interpretation*. London: Tavistock Publications [reprinted London: Karnac, 1984].

Freud, S. (1895a). *A Project for a Scientific Psychology. S. E., 1*: 283–397. London: Hogarth.

Freud, S. (1915c). Instincts and their vicissitudes. *S. E., 14*: 111–140. London: Hogarth.

Green, A. (1967). Le narcisisme primaire structure ou état? Le narcisisme primaire. In: *Narcissisme de vie narcissisme de mort*. Paris: Minuit, 1983.

Green, A. (1974/1975). L'analyste, la symbolisation et l'absence dans le cadre analytique. In: *La folie privée: psychoanalyse des cas limites* (pp. 63–102). Paris: Gallimard.

Green, A. (1983). *Narcissisme de vie narcissisme de mort*. Paris: Minuit.

Green, A. (1990a). Passions et destins de passions, sur les rapports entre folie et psychose. In: *La folie privée: Psychanalyse des cas-limites* (pp. 141–193). Paris: Gallimard.

Green, A. (1990b). La capacité de rêverie et le mythe étiologique. In: *La folie privée: Psychanalyse des cas-limites* (pp. 347–368). Paris: Gallimard, 1990.

Green, A. (1990c). Pourquoi le mal? In: *La folie privée: Psychanalyse des cas-limites* (pp. 369–401). Paris: Gallimard.

Green, A. (1993). Le clivage: du désaveu au désengagement. In: *Le travail du négatif* (pp. 157–215). Paris: Minuit, Paris.

Green, A. (1997). *Les chaines d'Eros: Actualité du Sexuel*. Paris: Odile Jacob.

Green, A. (2000a) Le cadre psychanalytique; son interiorisation chez l'analyste et son application dans la pratique. In: A. Green et al., *l'avenir d'une disillusion* (pp. 11–45). Paris: PUF.

Green, A. (2000b). La position phobique centrale avec un modele de l'association libre. In: *La Pensée Clinique* (pp. 149–186). Paris: Odile Jacob.

Green, A. (2005). L'humanité de l'inhumain. In: Balier, C. *La violence en Abyme* (pp. xi–xvi). Paris: PUF.

Green, A. (2007a). Le sens, entre Eros et pulsions destructrices. In: *Pulsions Représentations Langage* (pp. 235–246). Paris: Delachaux et Niestle.

Green, A. (2007b). Pulsions de destruction et maladies somatiques. *Revue française de psychanalyse*, 2(32): 45–70.

Lacan, J. (1998/1949). O estádio do espelho como formador da função do eu. In: *Escritos*. Rio de Janeiro: Jorge Zahar.

Levine, H. B. (2012). The colorless canvas: representation, therapeutic action and the creation of mind. *International Journal of Psychoanalysis*, 93: 607–629.

Nos, J. P. (2014). Collusive induction in perverse relating: perverse enactments and bastions as a camouflage for death anxiety. *International Journal of Psychoanalysis*, 95: 291–311.

Ogden, T. (2004). This art of psychoanalysis: dreaming undreamt dreams and interrupted cries. *International Journal of Psychoanalysis*, 85: 857–877.

Peucker, B. (2007). *The Material Image*. Stanford, CA: University of Stanford Press.

Reed, G. S. (2002). Review of the work of the negative. *Journal of the American Psychoanalytical Association*, 50(1): 343–347.

Ruggiero, I. (2012). The unreachable object? Difficulties and paradoxes in the analytic relationship with borderline patients. *International Journal of Psychoanalysis*, 93: 585–606.

Steiner, J. (2011). *Seeing and Being Seen: Emerging from a Psychic Retreat*. London: Routledge.

Winnicott, D. W. (1966/2006). A mãe dedicada comum. In: D. W. Winnicott, *Os bebês e suas mães* (pp. 1–11). Rio de Janeiro: Imago.

Winnicott, D. W. (1971). Mirror-role of mother and family in child development. In: *Playing and Reality* (pp. 111–118). London: Tavistock.

CHAPTER NINE

Repetition, transformations, and *après-coup**

Rosine Jozef Perelberg

André Green's psychoanalytic understanding of time

G reen suggested that two temporal axes permeate Freud's work: the genetic, that articulates development with the biological dimension of the individual's life, on the one hand, and the structural, present in Freud's various models of the mind, on the other. They are associated with spatial configurations—unconscious, preconscious, and conscious in the topographical model of the mind, and the id, ego, and superego, in the structural model (2002).

In his books that specifically deal with temporality, Green traced the development of Freud's ideas that led him to discover a model of time that is truly psychoanalytical, in contrast to a linear and conventional, chronological sequence (2002). In the French preface to the translation of the *Controversial Discussions* (1996), Green challenged the common use in the Anglo-Saxon world of the term "early" to indicate the most primitive and, at times, what is "deeper". He says the term is untranslatable in French since neither "*précoces*" nor "*primitive*" account adequately for that which would need to be designated each

---

* The clinical example developed in this paper has been more fully published in 2015 (Perelberg, 2015).

time as *"survenant très tôt dans la vie"* [literally, "occurring early in life"] (2002, p. 164). This latter phrase denotes a confusion between topographical regression (from conscious to unconscious) and a temporal regression (from the present to the past). The Anglo-Saxon world, according to Green, influenced by Melanie Klein, has emphasised a genetic perspective, whereas Freud's notions of time have more complexity and include multiple dimensions. Green attributes to Lacan the shift in French psychoanalysis away from any sort of geneticism to an emphasis on *Nachträglichkeit*. In the essay that follows, I use Green's work as a lens through which to revisit that of Freud and develop some further ideas about time, transformation, repetition and *après-coup*.

As early as his *Studies in Hysteria* (1895b), Freud introduced the idea of "strangulated affect", implying a time that has stopped, blocked by fixation—a movement frozen in time. It was also in the *Project* (1895a) that Freud's ideas on *Nachträglichkeit* are presented for the first time. In *Studies*, the account of Emma's case establishes a link between temporality and trauma. A symptom is formed by a constellation of characteristics. Some are connected to the memory of a scene that is most recent and accessible to consciousness (Scene I). Subsequently, through a chain of associations evoked by the analytic treatment, Scene I is associated with Scene II. This latter occurred earlier in time and was not accessible to consciousness at the time of Scene I. Scene II is pre-pubertal whereas Scene I is post-pubertal. Scene II was accompanied by a sensation of sexual pleasure. In Scene I, there was a sexual release of the post-pubertal kind, different in nature from the pre-pubertal sexual pleasure of Scene II.

It is only in the analysis of the Wolf Man (Freud, 1918b) that the notion of *Nachtraglichkeit* takes on a metapsychological status, establishing a link between trauma, temporality, and unconscious phantasy. The primal scene leaves its mark on the child who witnesses it, yet he cannot know the effect it will have on him. For this, the individual will have to wait for the effects of post-pubertal sexuality that will then, retrospectively, reinterpret that earlier scene.

In *The Interpretation of Dreams* (1900a), Freud put forward the conception of the bi-directional nature of psychical processes, progressive and regressive (Green, 2002, p. 11). The hypothesis of the timelessness of the unconscious is described. The rules that govern dreams are that of the *primary* processes. Dreams refer back to an infantile scene, which is modified by the present. Images are contrasted with language (topographical regression). In their own way, images "think". Dreams "neither think nor calculate" says Freud, but there is a work of transformation that takes place.

"A dream might be described as a substitute for an infantile scene modified by being transferred onto a recent experience. The infantile scene is unable to bring about its own revival and has to be content with returning as a dream" (1990a, p. 546).

The *Three Essays on the Theory of Sexuality* (1905d) laid the foundations for the aspect of temporality that follows the curve of the life-cycle: birth, childhood, puberty and adolescence, adulthood, old age, and death (Green, 2002, p. 13). Dreams had enabled Freud to identify a dismembered temporality, of non-unified time. The sexual theory returned to a time ordered traditionally in terms of development. The notion of sexual diphasism is introduced, the effect of the combination of maturation and repression that grounds sexuality in two stages, separated by a period of latency. Latency is the period when infantile sexuality is put to rest. The infant's body is not ready to confront sexuality, particularly with its incestuous objects. A time of waiting is necessary.

In the analysis of Little Hans' phobia (1909d), Freud takes a step forward theoretically as he discovers the *infantile sexual theories.* Sexuality not only integrates the data coming from the body (that is, biologically determined) but also the parental discourse. The child's sexuality is penetrated by the imaginary history of the parents' sexuality; bodily experiences and projection have an important role.

In "Remembering, repeating and working-through" (1914g), Freud suggests that some patients repeat *instead of* remembering; repetition is a substitute for memory. The pendulum had now swung back to the structural pole establishing a new relation of correspondence between memory and action.

With "Mourning and melancholia" (1917e), the loss of the object in mourning forces the psychical apparatus to sacrifice a part of the ego in order to make up for the void left by the loss; it also refers back to an initial fixation, to the "oral–cannibalistic" phase of development.

Freud oscillates between a diachronic perspective grounded in childhood in which sexuality, unconscious desire, and now the loss of the object are at stake, and "a structural perspective opposing psychical systems that are organised differently. In fact the two axes, historical and structural, are complementary" (Green, 2002, p. 19).

The notion of *Nachträglichkeit* is central in the analysis of the Wolf Man. Freud is almost obsessionally trying to identify the dates at which each event took place. The notion of *l'aprés-coup* (*Nachträglichkeit*) raises the question of knowing what the earlier anticipatory event, "*l'avant-coup*", as Green suggests, might have been. Freud raises questions about the status of the unconscious phantasies and how they are transmitted. How do the cultural and the individual relate to each other? This specific question will permeate all his sociological books. An answer will have to await one of his final books, *Moses and Monotheism* (1939a) (Perelberg, 2009).

Freud became concerned with the individual's prehistory, with the beliefs that the child has elaborated as answers to the mysteries of his own and his parents' sexuality, which are related to the question of his own origins. *Totem and Taboo* (1912–1913) anticipates the concept of the superego that would be identified ten years later. It introduces a second pole of memory, collective rather than individual, anthropological and socio-historical rather than bio-psychological, hereditary rather than acquired. This thread in Freudian theory surfaced again in 1921 with *Group Psychology and the Analysis of the Ego* (1921c); then in 1927 and 1930 in *The Future of an Illusion* (1927c) and *Civilization and its Discontents* (1930a), finding its fullest expression in *Moses and Monotheism* (1939a).

Beyond the Pleasure Principle (1920g) establishes the compulsion to repeat as a mode of drive functioning—of all drive functioning—owing to the eminently conservative function of the drive.

Thus, Freud's ideas on temporality are not linked to individual experience alone; they combine the effects of nature and culture. "Here the exactness of Freud's ideas is less important than identifying the main lines of his thought and the problematic issues to which they attempt to provide an answer" (Green, 2002, p. 24).

According to Green, the superego is the main innovation of the second topography, the presence of the past and the guidance towards the future. In the structural model of the mind, there is an opposition between the time of the subject and the time of the other, subsuming under this term the two factors external to the ego: the deepest level inside, that is, of the psyche reaching right down into the body and the soma, and that which is most remote on the outside, that is to say, the world and culture in which human relations play their part, working towards the discovery of otherness proper (2002).

André Green has suggested that what characterises the analytic situation is the phenomenon of irradiation, the interplay between retroactive reverberation and anticipatory annunciation that finds its meaning in the process of analytic listening (Green, 2000; Perelberg, 2017). In an analysis, all these different temporalities come together in what, Green suggests, is *"le temps eclaté"* (shattered time).

Descriptive and dynamic après-coup

Over the years, I have developed the idea that the psychoanalytic work takes place in the *après-coup*; its force is derived from the link between the here and now, and there and then, the scene of the unconscious (Perelberg, 2006, 2009). One of Freud's major discoveries, in the analysis of Emma and also of the Wolf Man, was that trauma is constructed in two times, and neither is meaningful on its own. In the subsequent scenes of both these analyses, the invisible links with the infantile were delineated. Freud did not fully recognise in his conceptualisation that these earlier scenes acquire the element of thirdness in the here and now of his interpretations. In addition to the scene of seduction witnessed by the Wolf Man aged eighteen months and its transformation and elaboration in the dream of the wolves, aged four, it is as a young adult, in the here and now of his analysis with Freud, that the two previous scenes acquired meaning. I am not referring to the chronological sequence so intensely sought by Freud in this analysis, but to the crucial relevance of the psychoanalytic model that he then inaugurates. It is in the *après-coup* that a radical, psychoanalytic understanding of time is initiated (Perelberg, 2013).

I have previously suggested that the concept of *après-coup* is what gives meaning "in the final analysis" to every other concept in Freud's work. The concept of *après-coup* is related to a theory of the mind that includes multiple temporalities. There are, at least, seven dimensions: development, regression, fixation, repetition compulsion, the return of the repressed, the timelessness of the unconscious, and *après-coup*— like a heptagon, I suggest. These different dimensions of time constitute a dominant structure (Althusser, 1970), and this dominance resides in the *après-coup* (Perelberg 2006, 2008).

I now give an illustration as to how this can be understood in clinical practice.

Clinical example

Boris's words flowed uninterruptedly throughout his sessions, with no resonance or affect. He brought me dreams, associations, and interpretations himself. He induced in me a state that was slightly detached and also somewhat immobilised. I was, at the same time, also aware of having, from the outset, thoughts about a traumatic experience that could not be fully put into words. Boris used to go to the toilet before and after each session, and this gave me a sense of something that was not being contained in the sessions themselves. His mode of communication had a mechanical quality. For instance, in the first few months he sometimes spent part of the session describing his long journey from home to my consulting room and his need to get to the toilet in time. He would mostly describe streets, buildings, buses, and trains. Any description of meeting people early in the mornings as he came to his sessions contained some menacing quality, such as the fact that he would find himself walking behind a woman in the alleyway that connected his street to the railway station. Would she be frightened of him, or was he of her? The links between these scenes and the experience of himself in the consulting room were spelled out, but did not seem to reverberate with actual, live meaning. For quite some time, he told me about his encopresis as a child, in bed at night, as well as several accidents at school. Sometimes, he would soil his pants on the way home and simply wait until his mother came to find and clean him.

It was quite some time into his analysis, however, before Boris told me that after each session he would go to a café nearby to write notes about the session. These notes also contained his thoughts about the session; he would then search the psychoanalytic literature in order to look up references that felt relevant to his thoughts. He was his own analyst, and his analysis was to be conducted by himself, away from the consulting room. I was excluded from this process.

I had a double experience of him: on the one hand, the flooding of words, the excess that had to be evacuated into the toilet, or to be expressed before and after the session, and, on the other hand, the distance he kept, a sense of unreachability and closure in this process whereby he was his own analyst. Thoughts about danger, threat, and trauma were somewhat present in my mind. I thought that these were the various ways in which he tried to find containment for himself and to feel safe.

Boris was married and had a child, but he and his wife had not had any sexual relationship for quite a few years. This lack of intercourse outside the sessions was expressed in the sessions through my very experience of him. No live, meaningful exchange was taking place.

Of his early life, Boris told me that his mother had been seriously ill when he was born, with some unspecified illness. He told me that his father had taken him home and looked after him. He thought that it had taken two weeks for his mother to come back from hospital. There was, thus, a reference to an early traumatic beginning, marked by his mother's absence and the threat to her life that his birth had inflicted on her.

A couple of years into analysis, Boris had a dream in which he was surrounded by glass and could not reach the people around him. This captured my experience of being with him in the room. As he told me the dream, I had a visual image that I communicated to him: "This makes me think of a baby in a glass cot/incubator." (The image I had in mind had been very precise: it referred to a *blue* glass cot/incubator.)

Boris was very struck by this. A profound silence invaded the session after my comment.

At the following session, Boris said that he had spoken to his mother and found out that actually his father had not taken him home with him when she was ill in hospital. He had stayed in hospital with her for the three weeks, but she was so ill that she had not been able to pick him up. He had, in fact, spent some time in an incubator.

This was a striking new piece of information that brought a different narrative to the beginnings of his life. It was something that he had not known about. It gave an uncanny new meaning to my experience of him in the analysis. A past that had not been registered at the representational level at the time it had occurred had been repeated in the relationship with me in the analysis: the whole experience of having to provide containment for himself, to be his own analyst, as there was no mother available to carry him in her arms or attend to his needs. The narrative of the dream, together with my own experience of him in the consulting room, had led to a visual image in my mind; when I put it into words, this led to some new information about his life. We were in the domain of the unthought known (Bollas).

A few weeks before the session I shall describe in a moment, a traumatic and shocking event had taken place in his son's school: a five-year-old boy had been sexually assaulted by three eight-year-old children, who had put soap in his anus. His son, who was also five at the time, had run to call a teacher who came to the toilet and stopped what was going on. Since then, his son had been bullied by the other children. Two days had passed before Boris spoke about it to me, and only then could he take the decision to go to the school himself to speak to the teachers about what had taken place. His initial reaction had been one of utter passivity and detachment. The transferential aspect of him experiencing himself as the five-year-old who was being sodomised in the sessions by my simply speaking to him did not escape us, and I interpreted this to him. This activated him to go to the school and eventually he and his wife decided to remove their child from this school. Boris was, however, extremely upset about his lack of immediate action and utter passivity, although he also turned this into masochistic self-blaming. This event also evoked for him episodes of being bullied at school as a child himself, and feeling unable to tell people.

The following session took place a few weeks later, the first session after a half-term break of a week. He missed the Monday session, as he was away, and came back on Tuesday.

> *Patient*: I had a dream last night. In the first part I was going to leak some documents to the *Guardian*. They contained embarrassing information and they were going to force the resignation of the Chancellor of the Exchequer. I was running through some suburban streets . . . I was being chased by a black car, the police. I had the feeling that I was not going to get the document out to the journalist. It was something to do with my son's school, about child abuse. I knew I was going to be arrested, so I started shouting loudly in the street so that the information would be imparted . . .
>
> Then I was arrested and handcuffed with my hands behind my back; the cuffs were brown and red and this meant that I was going to serve a life sentence. I was protesting, but my protests were falling on deaf ears. I was taken to a mental hospital. There was a journalist around who was sympathetic to what was happening to me, but was unable to stop anything. I was secured to a chair; a woman, who was a long-term resident, half crazy, and a kind of matron, arrived and was inflicting a punishment on me. She shaved my hair with a razor. It reminds me of pubic hair being shaved before some operation. She started at the top of my head and was very rough, uncaring. While she was doing this, there was a screen, so that I was separated from the others by glass. The journalist was there but

could not stop what was going on. But he could ensure that this glass door was somewhat ajar, and not completely closed, so I was not isolated with her.

[He pauses.] [I am thinking that he sounds detached from the dream, but not as detached as he usually is. The glass door is perhaps a bit ajar . . . I had also paid attention to the word "leak" (the documents).]

He continues.

Patient: I can only presume that this dream was about a deeper fear of returning to the analysis. Although you had suggested before my sense of fear, I don't have access to these feelings . . .

I was struck by the image of the glass cubicle. It resonates with the session before the break, your thoughts about my experience of being separated at birth by glass from my mother . . . She told me now that I was in hospital with her for three weeks after I was born . . . She could not pick me up and I had to spend a lot of time in an incubator . . .

. . . I thought on my way here that perhaps it was hopeful that my feelings about you were distributed between the journalist, the matron, and the police officer . . . I woke up when I was being shaved . . . *It was not as if the emotion was absent, but it was muted, low level* . . . I am thinking about the glass cubicle and the door being left ajar . . . I was being handcuffed with brown and red handcuffs that meant a life sentence, twenty-five years. The colours were somehow organic, brown and red.

Analyst: Blood and faeces . . . [I had in mind all the sessions with the material about toilets and soiling himself as a child, the consequences for him now, a life sentence.]

Patient: Yes! I had this same thought on my way here. It was something about the helplessness of the situation in which I found myself on that chair. It could have been the couch. I also think that it relates to everything that happened with Tony [his son].

[I had the thought that the one helpless on the chair is also me, the way I can feel handcuffed with very little freedom of movement during my sessions with him. I note, of course, that he responds to my interpretations by saying he had thought about that himself.]

Analyst: You feel helpless and have to do it all by yourself. You want to pass on the information that child abuse has taken place . . . but the tyrannical Chancellor of the Exchequer in yourself as well as myself does not want to know . . .

He seems thoughtful about all this.

Patient: I did feel more in touch in this session.

[Silence]

Analyst: It is time.

Discussion

There is something of a paradox in Boris's analysis in the way in which words and thoughts can be denuded of meaning and depth because of the lack of accompanying affect, of libidinal investment. As he relates the dream, he is aware of various potential layers of meaning contained in the manifest content of the dream. However, he conveys his states of mind to me through interplay between "leaking" and withholding, the excess that floods outside the consulting room through his actions, on the one hand, and the flowing of words without libidinal investment, in the consulting room, on the other. To fully know what he lets me know is to take away the powers of a tyrannical part of him. He comes to his sessions with his guardian/analyst, but he also runs away from the sessions as a fugitive from the police. He wishes to tell someone that sexual abuse is taking place, but he is confused as to who is abusing whom.

Boris's masochism registers my interpretations as abusive and as sodomising him. I am also a castrator, in the way that I shave his hair and leave him feeling exposed. He is, at the same time, unaware of the way he leaves me paralysed, on the other side of the glass. The journalist can do nothing but watch or report. What strikes me most strongly about this session is not the content of his narrative, but the impact that he has on me. It is from my own experience of feeling handcuffed by his blood and faeces, his bodily excesses, that the meaning of a traumatic event that involves abuse and persecution is reached. This session feels like a transformation of the scene of sexual abuse between the children in the school toilet. Boris had felt totally paralysed in relation to that scene. It also has links with the glass incubator that I had visualised a few weeks earlier, the experience of total abandonment, helplessness, and confusion.

Different time dimensions are present. The experience I have of being with him over the years of his analysis reach representation in his dream of being surrounded by glass. This dream, that achieved figurability in my mind though an image and transformed my interpretation, led to the reappropriation of an infantile experience at birth; the scene between the five-year-old children in the bathroom indicated the eroticisation, *après-coup*, of the earlier experience of helplessness. Now all this gains further representation in the narrative of the dream in *this* session that also elaborates and anticipates that which takes place in the session itself.

The session has a different feel from a few years before. Boris himself refers to "muted" feelings or a glass door that is half open. He is not totally alone with a half-crazy woman, a depressed mother in the hospital, any more. There is a man, an observer part of himself, who can register and witness his traumatic experiences.

Temporality in the analytic encounter

Boris's analysis evokes fundamental questions about the way in which one can understand temporality in the analytic encounter.

In 1920, Freud discovered a drive that does not correspond to any representation but expresses itself in the repetition compulsion. This formulation is at the basis of Green's formulations on the negative, of mental structures where representations have disappeared from theoretical descriptions (Levine et al., 2013). Green is here inspired by the works of Bion (his notion of the beta elements as the domain of thoughts that do not have a thinker, for example) (Bion, 1967, 1970) and Winnicott (1971) Green, 1997, 1998, 1999). There are implications for a theory of technique: the role of the analyst is not that of interpreting what "is already there" in the mind of the patient, but, rather, that of inaugurating the symbolic domain and the world of representation and introducing the patient to a new temporal dimension. In Viderman's (1970) words, any interpretation does not (only) say what it is, but gives origin to what is being said. This becomes especially relevant when dealing with a new population of patients who come for analysis, who tend to live in an ever present, frozen temporality.

In my presentation of the clinical material, I have indicated how all these ideas come together in clinical practice. The image of the baby in the incubator emerged in my mind in the course of Boris's analysis because of my experience of being with him in the room over a long period of time. The dream of the room surrounded by glass evoked an image in my mind; glass became a signifier that Freud identifies with *Knotenpunkten* (1900a), nodal points that establish a link between the network of associations in the present, traumatic but conscious, here and now situation, and another that is unconscious and that belongs to the infantile, there and then, the scene of the unconscious. Several time dimensions are also present: the here and now of his analysis, and himself at the hospital at birth. The narrative of the scene between the five- and eight-year-old boys in the bathroom captures an experience that Boris himself had had as a child and indicates the eroticisation of the experience of helplessness. All these different temporalities come together in what Green has designated as "shattered time".

Conclusions

One cannot but wonder how it is that the experiences that cannot be contained in the field of representation and symbolisation can be transformed through analytic work. The process of elaboration and working through takes place through a complex bringing together of affect, representation, sensorial and somatic experiences, dreams, associations, and enactments as they are gathered and found meaning *après-coup* through analytic work (Perelberg, 2016).

In our practice as analysts, we know that it is always the next moment of a session, the next day, or the next year that might clarify something that took place before. In any given session in time, one may reach a retrospective meaning of what has taken place and an anticipation of what will happen in future—the two aspects of *après-coup*. Something, nevertheless, is always being left out, the model being the navel of the dream, the contact with the unknown. There is a kind of reassurance in the process: by definition, one does not fully know the meaning of what is happening at any moment in time. In Levinas's (2010) terms, "time means that the other is forever beyond me, irreducible to the synchrony of the same".

An analogy with music comes to mind. Elgar (2014), in connection with his *Enigma Variations*, Opus 36, makes reference to the theme that is not played:

> The Enigma I will not explain – its "dark saying" must be left unguessed, and I warn you that the apparent connection between the variations and the theme is often of the slightest texture; further, though and over the whole set another and larger theme "goes", but it is not played.

In the example I offered, the fragmentation of the experiences, in the process of being gathered in the analysis, are *variations* and transformations of the original traumatic infantile experiences. It is the repetition of the trauma in the analytic process and its elaboration through the analytic listening that transforms a sequence of *coups* into *après-coup*, inaugurating a psychoanalytic temporality.

References

Althusser, L. (1970). Marx's immense theoretical revolution. In: L. Althusser & E. Balibar (Eds.), *Reading Capital* (pp. 182–193). London: Verso.

Bion, W. R. (1967). A theory of thinking. In: *Second Thoughts* (pp. 110–119). London: Heinemann. [First published in 1962 as: The psycho-analytic study of thinking. *International Journal of Psychoanalysis, 43*: 306–310.]

Bion, W. R. (1970). *Attention and Interpretation*. London: Tavistock.

Elgar, E. (2014). Cadogan Hall Programme. Summer Music Festival with Pinchas Zukerman. *Enigma Variations*, Opus 36.

Freud, S. (1895a). *Project for a Scientific Psychology. S. E., 1*: 281–391. London: Hogarth.

Freud, S. (1895b). *Studies on Hysteria. S. E., 2*. London: Hogarth.

Freud, S. (1900a). *The Interpretation of Dreams. S. E., 4–5*. London: Hogarth.

Freud, S. (1905d). *Three Essays on the Theory of Sexuality. S. E., 7*: 123–245. London: Hogarth.

Freud, S. (1909d). *Notes Upon a Case of Obsessional Neurosis. S. E., 10*: 153–320. London: Hogarth.

Freud, S. (1912–1913). *Totem and Taboo. S. E., 13*: 1–162. London: Hogarth.

Freud, S. (1914g). Remembering, repeating and working-through. *S. E., 12*: 145–156. London: Hogarth.

Freud, S. (1917e). Mourning and melancholia. *S. E., 14*: 237–260. London: Hogarth.

Freud, S. (1918b). *From the History of an Infantile Neurosis. S. E., 17*: 3–123. London: Hogarth.

Freud, S. (1920g). *Beyond the Pleasure Principle. S. E., 18*: 7–64. London: Hogarth.

Freud, S. (1921c). *Group Psychology and the Analysis of the Ego. S. E., 18*: 65–143. London: Hogarth.

Freud, S. (1927c). *The Future of an Illusion. S. E., 21*: 1–56. London: Hogarth.

Freud, S. (1930a). *Civilization and Its Discontents. S. E., 21*: 59–145. London: Hogarth.

Freud, S. (1939a). *Moses and Monotheism. S. E., 23*: 1–137. London: Hogarth.

Green, A. (1996). Preface à l'edition française par André Green. In: P. King & R. Steiner, *Les Controverses Anna Freud Melanie Klein* (pp. xi–xiii). Paris: Presses Universitaires de France.

Green, A. (1997). The intuition of the negative in 'Playing and Reality'. *International Journal of Psychoanalysis*, *78*(6): 1071–1084.

Green, A. (1998). The primordial mind and the work of the negative. *International Journal of Psychoanalysis*, *79*: 649–665.

Green, A. (1999). *The Work of the Negative*. London: Free Association Books.

Green, A. (2000). The central phobic position. *International Journal of Psychoanalysis*, *81*: 429–451.

Green, A. (2002). *Time in Psychoanalysis*. London: Free Association Books.

Levinas, E. (2010). *En découvrant l'existence avec Husserl and Heidegger* Paris: Vrin.

Levine, H. B., Reed, G. S., & Scarfone, D. (Eds.) (2013). *Unrepresented States and the Construction of Meaning*. London: Karnac.

Perelberg, R. J. (2006). Controversial discussions and après-coup. *International Journal of Psychoanalysis*, *87*: 1199–1220 [reprinted in *Time, Space and Phantasy* (pp. 106–130). London: Routledge, 2008].

Perelberg, R. J. (2008). *Time, Space and Phantasy*. London: Routledge.

Perelberg, R. J. (2009). Après-coup dynamique: implications pour une Théorie de la Clinique. *Revue Française de Psychanalyse*, *73*: 1583–1589.

Perelberg, R. J. (2013). Paternal function and thirdness in psychoanalysis and legend: has the future been foretold? *Psychoanalytic Quarterly*, July.

Perelberg, R. J. (2015). On excess, trauma and helplessness: repetitions and transformations. *International Journal of Psycho-Analysis*, *96*(6): 1453–1476.

Perelberg, R. J. (2016). Negative hallucinations, dreams and hallucinations: the framing structure and its representation in the analytic setting. *International Journal of Psychoanalysis*, *97*(6): 1575–1590. [Also in Perelberg, R. J., & Kohon, G. (Eds) (2017). *The Greening of Psychoanalyisis: André Green New Paradigm in Contemporary Theory and Practice*. London: Karnac.]

Perelberg, R. J. (2017). Introduction: André Green: the arborescence of a conceptual paradigm. In: R. J. Perelberg & G. Kohon (Eds.), *The Greening of Psychoanalysis* (pp. 1–44). London: Karnac.

Viderman, S. (1970). *La Construction de l'espace analytique*. Paris: Denoel.

Winnicott, D. W. (1971). *Playing and Reality*. London: Tavistock.

CHAPTER TEN

A universal psychotic core: some clinical consequences of André Green's contributions

Francis D. Baudry

I n this chapter, I first summarize some key concepts proposed by André Green that profoundly altered both the prevailing theory of neurosis and its clinical management. I then outline some of the earlier literature that preceded some of his ideas, and present a number of clinical vignettes of my work. Some, early in my career, antedate Green's contributions. showing how I missed an opportunity to intervene effectively, and others show a change influenced by Green's new conceptions.

Green (1975) starts out by indicating that the changes in his overall approach were necessitated by difficulties and failures in the treatment of non-neurotic or borderline patients who did not respond well to the classical technique of searching for meaning and interpretation of underlying unconscious fantasies. Perhaps the most significant departure he suggests lies in revising the model of neurosis and suggesting a new implicit model for borderline states that might even be applicable to neurotic conditions. Green reminds us, following Freud, that the initial implied model of neurosis was based on perversions (neurosis as negative of perversion) but that nowadays most psychoanalysts would agree that the appropriate model is that of psychosis. This means that earlier stages of life are best understood by making an analogy between primitive mechanisms of defence and undifferentiated ego states and the various vicissitudes of psychotic mechanisms. This model is already hinted at in Freud's later papers.

This change in model also alters the nature of anxieties confronted by the self. For neurosis, the core anxiety is castration anxiety, whereas

> The implicit model of these borderline states leads us back to the contradiction formed by the duality of separation anxiety/intrusion anxiety. Furthermore the difference of the sexes which separates two objects may be mistaken for the splitting of a single object whether good or bad. The patient suffers from the combined effect of a perse-cutory intrusive object and of depression consequent on loss of the object. (Green, 1975, p. 6)

The second addition to our theory pursues further the conse-quences of impoverishment of the mental apparatus, whether primary or, later, after establishment of object relations. This is spelled out in Green's (1980) paper on the dead mother (Green, 2001). In his concept of the negative, which includes blank psychosis, Green emphasises the role of de-cathexis, the defensive abandonment of the object lead-ing to a void and absence in the mental apparatus. His emphasis on this term, used only infrequently before in the analytic literature (in contrast with anti-cathexis), is derived from Green's conviction that the death drive is a useful concept, de-cathexis being clinical evidence for its relevance.

Following Bion, Green distinguishes between "nothing" (an absence which eventually could be replaced by a presence) and a no-thing, a void that cannot be filled. In the latter, because the object is never absent it cannot be thought. Conversely, the inaccessible object can never be brought into the personal space or, at least, never in a sufficiently durable way. Thus, it cannot be represented by the model of an imaginary or metaphorical presence. As a result, wish and wish fulfilment in terms of pleasure and gratification are no longer central and could become secondary to the exigencies of the survival of the self. While action and emotion can be present, the thought behind the wish—that is, the concept of unconscious fantasy—might not be. The consequence of this situation in the cases with which we are dealing is not manifest psychosis, where mechanisms of projection operate in a wide area, or open depression, where the work of mourning could take place. The final result is paralysis of thought which can be expressed in negative hypochondriasis, particularly with regard to the head: for example, a feeling of empty-headedness or a hole in mental activity, associated with an inability to concentrate. My third vignette illustrates the consequences of this aspect of pathology.

Green goes on to state that we are attuned nowadays to listen to psychotic defence mechanisms. He goes further, implying that no analysis is complete until the psychotic level is reached. Sometimes, this psychotic level is subtle but present all the time. At other times, it can be covered over by what appears to be almost impenetrable, rigid character defences. My first vignette illustrates this latter point.

From an ego psychological point of view, this so-called psychotic core or level could be thought of as an early pre-oedipal core, thus freeing it from what sounds like a purely pathological formation. Whether it should be thought of as pathological depends on complex factors to be elucidated further. From a technical point of view, these remains of early mental functioning generally do not enter the process of symbolisation and are only partially amenable to a search for meaning. For the purpose of this discussion, I am describing extreme positions. In actual clinical practice, there are many gradations where symbolisation and representation function in some sectors and to a varying degree, as my second vignette illustrates. It is never an all-or-nothing situation.

Early theoretical formulations: Freud, Glover, Winnicott, and Bion

The idea that we all, more or less, have a potential for emergence of primitive manifestations is not a new one. This idea was already present in the early 1930s. Glover (1932), in his book *On the Early Development of the Mind*, wrote that any classification of the psychoses must relate them to normal development, "but to do this we must realize how psychotic normal development is" (p. 165). Freud, in some of his early papers, refers to passive or active primary repression. By this he means the fate of early traumatic states that occur before early structure formation and, thus, do not achieve the level of representation allowing for developmental transformation (Frank, 1969). Relevant here is one other, somewhat ambiguous, Freudian concept, "Repetition compulsion", which has an uneasy place in our theory, sometimes referring to the push of drives for actualisation but sometimes referring to a pressure to repeat early traumata, either to evacuate them or to master them in the hope of creating a different ending. In Freud's theorising, repetition compulsion seems to be an autonomous factor not reducible to conflict. This might be why it is accorded a separate place in Waelder's "Principle of multiple function" paper (2007).

In one of his last papers, "Analysis terminable and interminable", Freud (1937c) wrote as follows:

> Every normal person, in fact, is only normal on the average. His ego approximates to that of the psychotic in some part or other and to a greater or lesser extent; and the degree of its remoteness from one end of the series and of its proximity to the other will furnish us with a provisional measure of what we have so indefinitely termed an "alteration of the ego". (p. 235)

In a slightly later paragraph Freud adds that these alterations of the ego can either be innate or acquired as a result of development. He is suggesting that someone with a primarily neurotic organisation might have hidden psychotic kernels.

Both Winnicott (1974) and Bion (1957) have contributed to our understanding of this pathology, which often includes states that have been experienced but not integrated, as is typical of responses to severe or protracted trauma. In his article "Fear of breakdown", Winnicott (1974) points out that, in those patients who have this fear, the breakdown has, in fact, occurred in the past but has not been "experienced" or "lived" by the individual in question at the time of its occurrence. This non-experience and its primitive inscription is what causes the fear. These patients suffer from what Winnicott calls primitive agonies, to distinguish this affect from the more benign term of anxiety. He refers, among others, to fears of dissolution or a return to an unintegrated state, or a loss of capacity to relate to objects, or a fear of falling. Winnicott also points out that the psychotic phase also serves defensive purposes, avoiding some of these unbearable agonies. Some of the best description of the early phases are in his 1945 paper, "Primitive emotional development". Bion (1957) also describes the co-existence of psychotic and non-psychotic elements, even in the more disturbed schizophrenics.

As Green puts it, our greatest failure is our inability to put the patient in touch with his internal world. There is a gap between what the patient communicates and the analyst's ability to understand it and utilise it. In the more neurotic patient, the analyst may rely on the patient's ability to associate and understand the complex transformations that the early conflicts, largely centring on the oedipal phase, have undergone. This is not possible when we deal with the psychotic core, mostly based on either early traumata or states that could not, for one reason or another, be capable of symbolisation, or only partially so. Bion has coined the term "inaccessible unconscious" to describe this situation.

My clinical experience

In reviewing my analytic experiences, both past and present, I found that a number of patients who seemed eminently suitable for analysis, functioning at a high level consistent with a basically neurotic structure, exhibited a more or less hidden evidence of a more primitive level of function. Sometimes, the lying-down position seems to promote the irruption of a psychotic core. At other times, the analyst's silence, or his temporary unavailability, might bring it to the surface. Other patients, as my first vignette shows, have a slightly different version of this clinical picture. The psychotic core is hidden behind an impenetrable, rigid character fortress that no amount of "analysis" (as I practised it early in my career) can budge.

In all my patients with a discernible psychotic core, I have found a history of chronic childhood trauma that, on the surface, did not seem to lead to either overt borderline or psychotic symptomatology. This should not be taken to mean that everybody (since we all have a primitive core) suffers from childhood trauma. It is the degree of its intrusion in the functioning of the personality that determines the presence of what we would consider pathology.

I believe that either my missing the presence of this psychotic core and/or my lacking the tools to deal with it was responsible for a number of limitations, or even failures, in treatment early in my career, which I shall now turn to. The following three vignettes illustrate the various ways the psychotic core can show up. In the first, the core, mostly hidden and inferred, led to an impenetrable fortress of defences and unusual character rigidity behind what looked like an amiable, friendly façade. In the second, the psychotic part lives alongside a more structured part but interferes with overall adjustment. In the third case, the more primitive part is subtly present at all times, manifested by a fear of inner chaos and turmoil, and sometimes erupts in dissociated rage attacks directed mostly towards a spouse.

Vignette 1

McDougall (1972) has, in one of her papers, coined the term "anti-analysand" to describe a situation in which she was unable to mobilise deeper layers in a patient with an extreme rigidity of character defences. Although she does not mention it, I believe her patient had a psychotic core. One of my early patients in whom I failed to recognise this primitive structure fitted into this same grouping. This case illustrates very well Green's idea that

> The limits of analyzability can only be those of the analyst, the patient's alter ego . . . the real problem . . . is the gap between his (the analyst's) capacity for understanding and the material provided by a given patient as well as gauging the possible effect across this gap, of what he in turn can communicate to the patient. (Green, 1975, p. 9)

My case fits in very well with Green's mention of patients "who cannot use the setting as a facilitating environment. It is not that they fail to make use of it, it is as if somewhere inside them they leave it intact in the non use they make of it" (p. 9).

Very early in my career, I was consulted by an extremely well-meaning, kind, gentle, intelligent professional with a superficially very friendly and smiling demeanour. He sought help because he felt stuck in his emotional life. He cared in a very empathic manner for his patients and was especially alert to the difficulties of old age. My patient's personality structure was quite rigid, with a mixture of some obsessional qualities and affective limitation. He felt more and more emotionally cut off from his wife, who was an active, assertive professional. In his marriage, he seemed completely blind to the ways in which, while being well meaning and apparently respectful towards his wife, he could alienate her. For example, he repeatedly put on a cologne she disliked before going to bed in the evening. He seemed to forget that she had asked him not to do this, in spite of her growing irritation at his persistence. This behaviour seemed rooted in a lack of empathy with his wife's feelings, as though he were dissociated from parts of himself. The patient was completely unaware of his considerable aggression towards his mate. Initially, he seemed well suited to undertake an analysis, which I thought could help him. Eventually, his wife decided to leave him.

My patient's early years had been very traumatic. His parents divorced when he was seven months old and his father moved to a far-away country. The mother remarried some years later and the stepfather adopted him. In order to maintain their small store, on which their livelihood depended, his mother and stepfather had decided to send him alone from age five every Sunday on the train to a kindly woman who would pick him up at a station some twenty miles away and care for him, along with half a dozen other children she managed during the week, as a foster mother. He got very little personal attention, as the foster parent was too busy managing the physical situation. His parents never called during the week but dutifully picked him up on Fridays at the station. The boy's mother was completely insensitive to the repeated trauma the little boy suffered every week.

In order to cope with this trauma, the patient developed states of withdrawal and self-sufficiency behind an outward friendly demeanour.He would rely on no one and put up a brave front of independence. In the treatment, he appeared to co-operate but his associations remained intellectualised. He was not able to recognise his difficulty. His relation to me was cordial and distant, superficially friendly and co-operative, but very constricted. No amount of interpretative work seemed to make an emotional impact, even though he understood intellectually that he was repeating some earlier adaptive mechanisms. He built an emotional fortress around himself that no amount of analysis or understanding could penetrate.

What Kohut might have described as a "self-state dream" occurred in the third year of treatment. My patient dreamt of a double-decker English bus that was trying to get through a tollgate. In the middle, the bus got hopelessly stuck and could go neither forward nor backward. We were both stuck. The tollgate represented the analysis. The patient was not able to vent his frustration at the lack of progress. He remained the child at the mercy of abandoning adults. At the time, I did not have the tools to deal with this stalemate. By this, I mean I lacked the understanding to enable the treatment to attain the delicate entry into what I suspected later was a terrifying internal word of psychotic proportions. This immobilisation probably encapsulated early traumata of major proportions, which could not be identified through a search for meaning or asking for associations. Instead, as Green indicates, what is demanded of the analyst "is more than his affective capacity and empathy. It is his mental functions which are demanded for the patient's structures of meaning have been put out of action" (1975, p. 6).

To reach my patient emotionally would have required a closer monitoring of my countertransference (discouragement, feeling stuck, withdrawal and anger combined with frustration) and a greater reliance on intuitive images and feelings. I also failed to appreciate that his state of withdrawal, leaving me impotent, was repeating the early relation with the abandoning parents. He was the parent enacting the abandonment. He was also putting me in the position of the abandoning parent. I failed to understand the nature of my countertransference. Thus, a key object relation scenario of a traumatic nature was being enacted right in front of my eyes but, at the time, I did not recognise the possibility of using this element to reach my patient emotionally. What this case also illustrates is that the analyst must be on the lookout for the way that pathological early states emerge in the transference only via early object relations scenarios. Finally, I assumed, incorrectly, that the point of entry into his inner world would be afforded by an understanding of his free associations. However, these could not encompass the pre-symbolic, not yet represented, proto-mental states.

Cases such as these, unless understood in this fashion, can lead to interminable analysis. It might be no accident that one of this man's children developed ulcerative colitis as an adolescent.

In contrast to this vignette, in which the psychotic core was present but mostly silent, the next vignette demonstrates the opposite: its noisy, continual intrusion, mostly limited to the analytic hour. Again, neither I nor my supervisor had the awareness that this symptom was a manifestation of a psychotic core and I certainly did not have the tools to deal with it. Although the case seemed to go well, I was quite surprised when, during a pre-graduation treatment centre presentation, my supervisor casually mentioned that he thought this patient had borderline features. This had never come up during our supervision. The case material shows the complex admixture of co-existing primitive aspects of functioning alongside a neurotic superstructure. Only the latter could be analysed in the usual fashion, including the search for meaning and use of classical interpretations.

Vignette 2

The patient was a very aggressive and anxious man with multiple manifestations of impaired functioning. He was prone to impulsive acts and judgements that interfered with his work. He exploded with bouts of anger, and was very demanding of his subordinates. Yet, he clearly had a neurotic superstructure: his reality testing seemed, for the most part, intact. Also on the positive side, the patient had an unusual capacity to associate in a productive fashion. He could observe himself and he also had a well developed sense of humour. His awareness that he desperately needed help, in both his career and his personal life, allowed him, in some obscure fashion, to trust me in a way he had never trusted anyone else in his life. The analysis lasted three years and led to dramatic improvement in many areas of functioning both professionally (eventually leading to important promotions) and in his relation to his wife, whom he began to love deeply, overcoming severe ambivalence.

One of his earliest behaviours was what he termed, later, "carrying on". He would shout violently on the couch, screaming at the top of his voice, leaving me in a state of terror and helplessness. My supervisor urged me to try to "understand" the meaning of this behaviour, telling me the patient had me "on the ropes". (That did not help me. On the contrary, it increased my sense of shame and helplessness.) Neither of us realised at the time that any attempt to get the patient to associate to this behaviour would lead nowhere. There was no "meaning" behind this behaviour or unconscious fantasy which could be elicited.

Although the patient indicated that his father would often be accused of carrying on, this insight did little to alter this behaviour, which seemed quite ego syntonic to him. Violent altercations between his parents were recalled, as well as his father's booming voice. We later reconstructed early exposure to the primal scene as a component, but this clearly did not exhaust the implications of this behaviour.

In telling me his story, the patient could identify clearly the presence of a number of severe early experiences, including, first, brutalisation by an older sibling, second, the violent death of another sibling when he was six years old. The earliest event concerned the sudden disappearance and institutionalisation of another impaired female sibling who had attacked him as an infant. This event was constructed, but not part of his conscious memory, as it took place when the patient was only eleven months old. For a long time, the patient, when lying on the couch, protected the back of his head with his hand. This was eventually related to a need to protect himself against the fear of my attacking him physically.

One day, during one of my patient's shouting episodes, a colleague called me on the phone, advising me that the noise from my office was interfering with his work next door. To my amazement, when I informed the patient about this, he immediately stopped this behaviour. I had never assumed it could be so easily turned on and off like a tap. This seemed to contradict what I believed at the time. When I later questioned him about this capacity, he stated that somewhere within him he had the fear I would send him to the institution where the defective sibling had been living for many years. This confirmed the presence of a primitive identification with the defective sibling, plus the presence of a *quasi* delusion

Towards the end of treatment, there remained a few troubling persistent beliefs or preconscious fantasies, such as "they" were coming to get him and also that if he stopped being active and vigilant, he would run the risk of becoming a passive, helpless blob, similar to the way he saw his father. These remaining issues had not changed as a result of our work in the analysis, which, at that time, consisted of standard analytic techniques dealing primarily with oedipal issues and neurotic defence mechanisms against dangerous sexual and aggressive conflicts and including the examination of complex compromise formations. The intensity of these beliefs suggested some break in reality testing in a limited sector of functioning, That is to say, these beliefs bordered on what we would call an unconscious fantasy and a *quasi* delusion. This fear, I later realised, was evidence of what Green described as the effect of the "persecutory intrusive object" (1975, p. 6). I was not able to identify to my satisfaction a clearly oedipal relation to the mother, who was seen instead as a dangerous, intrusive person.

I was somewhat hesitant to terminate the analysis, but, following my experienced supervisor's opinion, I went along with the patient's desire to end treatment. The patient felt he did not need any further help at this time and could point out the many areas of improvement in his life.

The patient later consulted me again and, during a second period, had persistent psychosomatic intestinal ailments that responded to analysis and concerned the attempt of his body to get rid of noxious internal presences. This patient has occasionally returned for brief periods of psychotherapy and has managed, for the most part, to function quite well except for occasional bouts of anxiety and inner turmoil, particularly at night. He feels that one of the aspects of continuing treatment which seems helpful is this "carrying on", a modified, limited form of letting loose with his thoughts (he does not scream any more), using my office as a toilet, as it were. This behaviour is exactly what Green has described in non-neurotic patients as one of the means of evacuation of affective states which fail to achieve the level of representation.

By chance, some forty years later, the patient returned for weekly sessions, complaining again of severe distress of near panic proportions. While on the couch, he lay sideways with one foot on the floor and the other foot poised as if getting ready to flee. He did not know why he was doing this. He then let out a blood-curdling scream and said, "This is what I heard as a baby when my defective sister screamed at the top of her lungs, terrifying me." The intensity of the scream jolted me. I realised quickly that the patient was re-enacting in front of me the terrifying scenario. He was identifying with the defective sibling and I was him. As part of his character, a looseness of boundaries was evident, so that transitory identifications with his siblings was an important factor in his makeup. I realised then that although the affect of screaming and rage was always in his preconscious, it had never been connected in a visceral way with the disturbed sibling's behaviour. It seemed as if a sensory outburst or perception was necessary to make the connection.

I would have to include other possibilities in my reconstruction. Was the mother herself also frightened for him and communicated this to him early in life? Did she tell him stories about this event later on in his childhood, thus giving a structure to his experience. It is hard to ascertain how much an eleven-month-old child could register without the capacity to understand or mentalize. Was this experience connected with other, later, events, including brutalisation by an older half-brother? The combination of these traumas then permeated his character structure. The patient confided one day that when working quietly at home, writing, he would occasionally let out a scream that would make him feel better.

In summary, this case illustrates early, unrepresented, preverbal trauma that is repeated in action in the analytic situation and elsewhere and seeks containment and articulation via a construction that makes sense out of the behaviour for and with the patient in the light of the patient's early history. Again, this is not a repressed memory awaiting emergence via analysis, but something unrepresented awaiting a construction to make sense and coherence of it in the context of the patient's known life history

Vignette 3

Using the concept of de-cathexis and psychic holes, Green explains that some patients become attached to the setting rather than to the analyst. The setting becomes a substitute object. That is, treatment is continued endlessly not only because of unresolved higher-level issues (although the patient easily justifies the need for more treatment by bringing up new "problems"), but, rather, because the setting and the relationship affords him a much needed structure to fill an empty space. This helps to repair a damaged primitive organisation that cannot manage properly processes of identification and of internalisation and is easily overwhelmed by negative affects. In the case presented, the patient had a chronically depressed and, at times, psychotic mother. Rather than hate her, my patient achieved a distance from her mistreatment of him, but paid the price by having so-called psychological holes in his psyche.

One of my long-term patients, well past retirement age, had been in continual "analysis" since his early thirties, entailing considerable financial sacrifices. I was the fourth analyst he consulted. He had stayed with the two previous therapists until their death even though they clearly showed evidence of poor judgement. He presented himself as a well-functioning, respected professional who taught in a local university, where he was universally liked by his students for his lively lectures and engaging manner. He wanted help for some continued anxieties, depression, and feelings of loneliness he was experiencing.

From a lower middle-class origin in a neighbouring state, his family was saddled with multiple tragedies. Death haunted him his entire life. Some cousins the same age as my patient were sent to live with the family after losing a parent. At age six, a year after the birth of a younger brother, my patient lost his father under particularly traumatic circumstances. The father came home one evening suffering from acute abdominal pain. He had been sent home by a doctor he consulted. He then took Epsom salts and had to be rushed to the hospital in the middle of the night, screaming in pain. The patient visited him just once in the hospital, seeing him in bed connected to many tubes and moaning. The father never returned home, dying a week later from a burst appendix. His death was never discussed or alluded to. My patient was not taken to the funeral. Desperate for the attention he needed, he described episodes in which he scribbled on the wall with a crayon. Yet, the distraught family even disregarded this blatant plea for attention. Some time later, he would spend hours lying on the sofa in an altered state, throwing spitballs at the ceiling, perhaps hoping to reach his father in heaven. Six months later, according to a story that was never disputed, the father's mother banged her head on a wall out of despair and died shortly thereafter. The patient later hallucinated seeing her severed head at night.

As a result of an inability to pay the mortgage, the family's house was repossessed by the bank and they had to move several times to smaller and more uncomfortable quarters. During early adolescence, the patient had to share for several years a small bed with his mother and brother. He both craved closeness to her and feared the accompanying sexual excitement. The mother, who was chronically depressed, at least since the death of her husband, could never mourn her loss. Periodically and unexpectedly, she developed psychotic-like symptoms during the night, getting up running in the small apartment, screaming and groaning, rubbing herself and gesticulating, terrifying everybody. The patient's grandmother, who lived with the family, would simply ignore these terrifying outbursts, saying they would stop eventually, which they always did.

When the mother returned from work, she would often take to her bed. The only relief came on Sunday, when she would pull herself together sufficiently to bake a cake. At other times, when the mother could not manage my patient's childhood pranks, she would take a butcher's knife and threaten him by saying she would plunge it in her chest. Alternatively, she would lock herself in the bathroom, saying she would take iodine, leaving my patient frantically banging on the door pleading with her to come out. My patient developed in adult life a passion for cooking and a phobic fear of being made sick by bad food. This fear was further "confirmed" when the mother died of aspiration pneumonia after profuse vomiting following an episode of food poisoning when my patient was in his early thirties.

Relying on his unusual capacity to use words, the patient would create for me beautiful narratives about his traumatic, Dickens-like early life. These narratives seemed rich, full of affect, and induced in me a sense of great sympathy for him and pity for the isolation of his childhood. The patient seemed attentive, well related, and very psychologically minded, associating easily with well connected thoughts. This could look like fruitful associations, but it eventually emerged that the patient left out subtle affective elements and fears of inner chaos. As a result, very little in his life changed. He was always very courteous, leaving at the end of sessions without protest, though occasionally, as he reached my door, he would groan, saying, "Ahh ahh" with outstretched arms, often adding a short phrase, such as, "This is dire", seemingly unconnected with the content of the hour. At other times, he wanted to lie on the floor and hammer on it, saying words could not express what he had inside. Among other meanings, the floor represented a safe grounding. Also, during treatment, he often experienced episodes of whimpering or soft crying with no content. When I tried to put into words thoughts or fantasies he might be having, he retorted that I did not understand. Finally, one day I said, "You just feel chaos and dread." He then beamed at me said, "You finally understand."

Eventually, it became apparent that he skilfully avoided certain parts of reality, "living elsewhere", as it were, in a dissociated state. After a number of years on the couch, which fostered these silent, dissociative states, generally hidden from me, I suggested to my patient that he use the chair instead. This led to improved contact with himself and with me.

During his current marriage, my patient began to describe episodes of blind rage triggered by his wife's sloppy eating habits or poor kitchen management, such as her carelessly leaving a raw chicken on the counter or a failure to properly clean the sink, leaving crumbs behind. His greatest conscious fear was that her sloppy kitchen habits would contaminate food. At those times, she often seemed to him to be in another world. His requests for her to be more careful with food were often ignored. After these outbursts, he felt exhausted and needed to go to another room. He said that sometimes he felt the experience was in part like a sexual release. He would then have to lie in bed, often in a foetal position, wishing he were dead, thinking he might jump out of a window but being quite sure he would never do it. After a fitful night, things returned to normal the next day. For quite some time these episodes were never discussed by the couple.

It took a great deal of work to realise that my patient was also relying on massive projective identification, using his wife (and, rarely, me) as a receptacle for disavowed parts of himself. His choice of a particularly non-motherly woman as a mate was no accident. He needed to repeat the early traumatic states that allowed him to vent otherwise unmanageable rage states that threatened to destabilise him. It was very difficult to convince him that some of these rage states were a displacement from the rage he might have felt as a child towards his mother and also towards the father who had left him alone to cope When I would suggest this to him, he would generally reply that she was the only parent who offered him a modicum of stability and that he could not afford to lose her.

We discovered that behind the rage at his wife for her absent states lay a severe anxiety. My patient had an overwhelming need for his wife to be present and stable to assist his own sense of fragility, always threatened with some disruption. During some of these *quasi* dissociated rage attacks, there seemed to be an identification with the psychotic part of the mother and we were able to construct the despair of his childhood and the traumatic effect of his surroundings. He had developed an outer façade of seeming in control in order to cover up a chaotic inner world that rarely emerged. He was terrified that he might go crazy in my presence and who knows what could happen then? Going crazy meant losing control of his inner world, with total disruption and disintegration following shortly thereafter.

The "crazy" part of his functioning was also associated with a feared feminine component. His own masculine identification was, in fact, quite fragile. In general, his dissociated rage states did not invade the transference except in one instance I could never forget. One day, during a session on the couch, as I was silently drinking some tea to soothe a cough, he erupted in a frightening rage attack. The intensity of this rage was temporarily destabilising for me as it was so unexpected. I became the abandoning unavailable mother threatening the position he needed for me to be in: a *quasi* fusional, omnipresent, loving object. It became crucial for me to evaluate my countertransference so as to try to disentangle my own personal conflicts and vulnerabilities (unfortunately, as a child, I had a very angry and controlling mother) from the crucial non-verbal communication of important internal states.

A reaction to the absent mother was to become the premature adult, treating the mother as the child who desperately needed to be brought out of her absence. My patient recalls childhood games where he would plan a fashion show, dressing himself and his brother in mother's clothing and parading in front of her. Or he might organise little plays for her, enacting a courtroom scenario searching for the criminal.

Along the same lines, the patient himself became a very motherly, kind man towards needy children of some of his women friends who were not particularly caring for their offspring. The young children climbed on his lap and caressed his cheeks as he recounted marvellous stories he skilfully invented for them, to their endless delight. He lived out the fantasy of treating them the way he would have liked to be treated. This unusual capacity, often commented on by his friends, could be seen as the development of a compensatory hypersensitivity to the needs of young children. The irony is that he could only very rarely allow himself to be nurtured in spite of his desperate need. In line with Green's concept of the dead mother, one could say that he replaced the absent mother with a premature reversal of roles. He became the mother instead. Yet, the mother imago was very complex, since it included, besides a depressed mother, also a mother who could have psychotic episodes and who clung to him in a desperate way, as he did to her, two unhappy souls sharing unmentionable losses.

It should come as no surprise that this patient was also particularly sensitive to absence and separation. But his concept of separation was not the more advanced one of missing the real object. He had no problem during vacation breaks. It was, rather, his missing the anticipation of a return he knew would be disappointing. As a child he would often stand by the window, saying to himself, "When mother comes home she will make things better." Of course, this never happened.

The same scenario repeated itself with me. On a Friday, he would say to himself, "Well, I can wait until Monday and the session will bring me relief and cure." It never could satisfy all his needs for integration and he would leave disappointed.

Part of this bizarre universe was the guarantee that any satisfaction was unattainable and that the search is bound to be futile—a trip to nowhere which cannot be given up even though it is guaranteed to be unfulfilling. This was lived out in the transference, in which I became the distant, unavailable audience unable to bring relief. I was seen at those times as disconnected from his suffering, unable to appreciate his intense pain that could never be put into words.

It took quite some time to realise that, in the transference, often I was not a real object in the classical sense, or a representation of earlier parental figures. Sometimes, I was an absent, wished for father. At other times, he needed some sort of fusional mirroring to maintain his sense of self—a narcissistic structure. Still later, I was a silent depersonalised witness to his suffering. Late in the treatment, he confessed he lived in a dream that he and I had a special closeness that had to remain hidden so as not to disturb it. This is in line with Green's concept of de-cathexis and search for the unattainable, distant good object as an alternative to the paranoid, intrusive object.

The dream of an idealised loving analyst remained a secret. It spared him from facing disappointment in the "real" analyst. In my patient's case, the mourning for the lost (idealised) father he had hardly known could never be completed. Being in treatment kept the quartet alive (himself, the father, the abandoning mother, and the analyst). Although the major trauma occurred after the death of the father, I suspected that his mother had always been deficient in offering him needed structure and bonding during his first five years. The mother was seen almost like a vampire clinging to the child out of desperate neediness to be made whole.

It was no accident that my patient was very taken by the universe so well described by Kafka: a place of aloneness alienation with latent threat of an impersonal judge accusing him of being guilty for an uncertain crime (occasionally parricide, or even a retaliatory suicide). Yet, Kafka is also very sympathetic to the suffering of those stranded in space like the trapeze artist.

Technical consequences

Three technical departures from the usual modes of listening, as taught in ego psychology, follow: one is the careful attention to subtle enactments of primitive object relations scenarios in the analytic space, as was the case with my first vignette; the second is the especially close monitoring of the analyst's countertransference, as this is the recipient of massive projective identifications which are characteristic of the psychotic functioning (this is well described by the Kleinians). A third factor in these patients is the preponderance of action and sensory perception rather than words as the carrier of unconscious primitive registration. This was already evident to Proust, who was able to recapture hidden experiences of a distant past through accidental perceptual experiences, such as the taste of the madeleine. I have suggested to one patient that he might act some of the traumatic scenes in front of me, as just talking about them was of limited value for him. The patient in my second vignette spontaneously resorted to this mode when recapturing the primitive early brutalisation by an impaired sibling.

Dealing with the above issues implies giving a renewed importance to the relationship with the therapist. Although the idea of the importance of rapport was always acknowledged, in the early days of analysis, even as late as into the 1960s, it was seen more as a necessary backdrop to create a positive working alliance or a therapeutic alliance. In more recent writings, it becomes the stage that allows the replaying of early scenes. Greater attention is paid to communication outside the level of conscious awareness, including the data offered by the analyst's dream-like states, as conceptualised by Bion and Ogden. The difference, thus, is one of emphasis where the interactional dimension replaces the near total concentration on the intrapsychic. This mirrors the developmental approach that conceptualises the intrapsychic as largely born in the mother–child interaction.

Our theory sensitises us to look for data that, in earlier times, might have been overlooked or, at least, not accorded the significance it has. It also means being wary of using words that mask the underlying affects. The patient in my third vignette would experience terrifying episodes of what he called darkness in the middle of the night. He would come to the office in his more usual state and could talk about these episodes, but, as he was not in them at the time, the exchanges we could have would not touch the intense terror he really felt in the middle of the night, which would lead to suicidal thoughts. When the patient is living out his terrifying fears, he is in no position to observe himself or control himself. It was a relief to my patient when I found myself suggesting to him that, if we were lucky, maybe we could experience these states together and see what happened.

The job of the therapist, as Bion has stressed, is to help the patient create a mind capable of containing often violent affects and to infer their role in the psychic economy. The development of new techniques by authors such as Bion (1957), Ferro (2002), Civitarese (2010), Levine and colleagues (2013), and others, opens up new vistas in treating patients who, until recently, were not amenable to traditional psychoanalytic exploration. As with any new theory, it cannot be evaluated by its truth value, but only by its usefulness either in organising data and giving them a certain coherence or by suggesting more effective ways of dealing with states which, until then, would not respond to traditional techniques.

Discussion

Although the concept of psychotic core incorporates some of the findings of borderline phenomena, it is clearly differentiated from them by its more transitory nature and its co-existence with other, better integrated levels of functioning. There are some important theoretical divergences from traditional ego psychology that need to be underlined and have crucial technical implications. Green (1975) has alluded to them in his paper on symbolisation and absence in the analytic setting. First, according to the view I am proposing, the differences in functioning between the neurotic and the psychotic level are not simply quantitative, they are qualitative. The damage responsible for it is of a structural nature, often occurring very early in the development of the person. The key question is to understand how very early trauma, or even major trauma during the middle childhood, is inscribed and the nature of its representations in the mental apparatus. In contrast with neurotic structures, the ego in these patients is much more fragile and frequently threatened with disintegration, as is the sense of self, often fragmented or split in different parts.

The concept of transference in this group of patients also has to be broadened beyond the classical view of actualising prior repressed unconscious fantasies in the relation to the therapist. It should also include the construction of a meaning from raw emotional experiences generated in the bi-personal field or their opposite, the absence of emotions and a dead space lived out continually in the analytic setting. Finally, the transference is often characterised by subtly hidden nests of mistrust, often difficult to confront.

Although classical ego psychological analysis has certainly been aware of the contribution of the pre-oedipal period to pathology, it has not really developed the overarching theoretical and clinical model adapted to dealing with this pathology and its primitive anxieties. Some of these issues have been developed in Europe by the Kleinians and Bion, and in France by Green. What is required is a different type of listening, tuning in, as it were, to a different wavelength, picking up data consistent with the early level of anxieties encountered as well as the specific mechanisms used by patients with early pathology. For example, it is important to be on the lookout for fears of chaos, of falling apart, and disintegration,. Such states can be associated with dissociation and splitting. The patient in my third vignette often seemed to dwell elsewhere, even during treatment hours. Initially, when put on the couch, this mode of defence made treatment almost impossible and I asked the patient to sit up after realising the couch allowed subtle dissociation to exist unbidden and silent

Had I been aware of these methods of treatment earlier in my career, it would also have allowed me, in the case of some of my patients with a mixed clinical picture, to reach some of the more primitive levels of functioning and, one hopes, to reduce mental suffering.

Before ending, I need to address a possible misconception. Reading my chapter, one could conclude that the manifestations of the early pre-oedipal core are most often a sign of pathology. Nothing could be further from the truth. The creative artist, whether a novelist, a poet, a painter, or a composer, must be able to access this aspect of his mind in order to succeed in his work. The early core will influence the form rather than the content of his creations. Transformation and sublimation are required to tame the early material.

References

Bion, W. R. (1957). Differentiating the psychotic from the nonpsychotic personalities. *International Journal of Psychoanalysis, 38*: 266–275.

Civitarese, G. (2010). *The Intimate Room: Theory and Technique of the Analytic Field*. London: Routledge.

Ferro, A. (2002). *In the Analyst's Consulting Room*. London: Routledge.

Frank, A. (1969). The unrememberable and the unforgettable – passive primal repression. *Psychoanalytic Study of the Child, 24*: 48–77.

Freud, S. (1937c). Analysis terminable and interminable. *S. E., 23*: 211–253. London: Hogarth.

Glover, E. (1932). *On the Early Development of the Mind*. New York: International Universities Press.

Green, A. (1975). The analyst, symbolization and absence in the analytic setting. *International Journal of Psychoanalysis, 56*: 1–22.

Green, A. (2001). The dead mother, K. Aubertin (Trans.). In: *Life Narcissism, Death Narcissism*, A. Weller (Trans.) (pp. 170–200). New York: Free Association Books.

Levine, H. B., Reed, G. S., & Scarfone, D. (Eds.) (2013). *Unrepresented States and the Construction of Meaning*. London: Karnac.

McDougall, J. (1972). The anti-analysand in analysis. *Revue française de Psychanalyse, 36*: 167–184.

Waelder, R. (2007). The principle of multiple function: observations on over-determinism. *Psychoanalytic Quarterly, 76*(1): 75–92.

Winnicott, D. W. (1945). Primitive emotional development. *International Journal of Psychoanalysis, 26*: 103–107.

Winnicott, D. W. (1974). Fear of breakdown. *International Review of Psychoanalysis, 1*: 103–107.

INDEX

Abraham, K., 32, 34, 40
affect(ive), xvii, xx, 5–6, 19, 25, 35, 38,
    48, 71–72, 79–80, 84, 87, 105, 120,
    127, 138–139, 141, 144, 155, 166,
    170, 178, 188 *see also*: depression
  attention, 41
  attunement, 33
  barring of, 26
  blank, 40
  bonds, 99
  capacity, 182
  colour, 25
  consistency, 144
  of emptiness, 40
  flooding, xxii–xxiii
  investment, 143, 146
  -less, 50
  limitation, 180
  link, 141
  loss, 40
  mobilisation, 98
  negative, 186
  opposition, 84

  peremptory, xxiii
  psychic reality, 141
  relations, 140
  representation, 5, 91
  states, 147, 185
  strangulated, 162
  system, 88
  tone, 36
  unconscious, 71
  violent, 193
  withdrawal, 36
aggression, 30, 34, 36, 39, 42, 54, 83,
    89, 91, 95–98, 102–103, 136–138,
    147–148, 151–152, 157, 181,
    183–184
Althusser, L., 165
anxiety, 33, 35, 42, 74–75, 102, 120,
    127, 129, 143, 146, 176, 178, 183,
    185–186, 194
  castration, 73, 103, 176
  contradictory, 98
  death, 140, 153–154
  extreme, 98

Made in United States
North Haven, CT
27 December 2022